Human Resource Management in Europe

Text and cases

Edited by

Sarah Vickerstaff

CHAPMAN & HALL
University and Professional Division
London · Glasgow · New York · Tokyo · Melbourne · Madras

Published by Chapman & Hall, 2-6 Boundary Row, London SE1 8HN

Chapman & Hall, 2-6 Boundary Row, London SE1 8HN, UK

Blackie Academic & Professional, Wester Cleddens Road,
Bishopbriggs, Glasgow G64 2NZ, UK

Chapman & Hall, 29 West 35th Street, New York NY10001, USA

Chapman & Hall Japan, Thomson Publishing Japan, Hirakawacho
Nemoto Building, 6F, 1-7-11 Hirakawa-cho, Chiyoda-ku, Tokyo 102,
Japan

Chapman & Hall Australia, Thomas Nelson Australia, 102 Dodds
Street, South Melbourne, Victoria 3205, Australia

Chapman & Hall India, R. Seshadri, 32 Second Main Road, CIT East,
Madras 600 035, India

First edition 1992
Reprinted 1993

© 1992 Sarah Vickerstaff

Typeset in 10.5/12 Bembo by Best-set Typesetter Ltd, Hong Kong
Printed in Great Britain by Richard Clay Ltd., St Ives plc.

ISBN 0 412 45380 0

A catalogue record for this book is available from the British Library
Library of Congress Cataloging-in-Publication Data available

Human Resource Management in Europe

Contents

Contributors

Dimitrina Dimitrova, Research Associate, Trade Union and Social Affairs Research Institute, Sofia. Sociologist and chief researcher on the fieldwork at the Metals and Materials enterprises discussed in Case 8. She is currently studying for a doctorate in the Department of Sociology at the University of Toronto. Address for correspondence: c/o John Thirkell, Keynes College, University of Kent, Canterbury CT2 7NP Kent, UK.

Professor Michel Feron, Head of the Human Resource Management faculty area, lecturer in Business and Labour Law, Reims Business School (Groupe ESC Reims, 59 rue Pierre Taittinger, BP 302, 51061 Reims, France). He is currently Programme Director of the CEFA Postgraduate Diploma in Business and the Masters in European and International Business at ESC Reims. He is also in charge of executive development programmes organized in Reims for Russian managers. Co-author of a book on employment legislation in France, his current research interests include comparative human resource management and management development in Eastern and Central Europe. Address for correspondence: see above.

Dr Henk van den Hondel is an independent organization and training consultant. In former years he was employed as an internal consultant for Philips, as a Lecturer in personnel management, and as a senior consultant for a consultancy agency he specialized in organizational change. His main interests and specialism involve consulting on, and training and facilitating in, organizational change in industry and in the service and health sectors. His most recent publication is 'De manager als veranderaar' (The manager as change-agent), *Personeelbeleid NVP*, 28 nr. 2, NVP Utrecht (1992). Address for correspondence: van den Hondel Consult bv., Elsakkerpad 14, 4861 TA Chaam, 01619-2539. The Netherlands.

Linda Keen, Research Associate, Canterbury Business School. After many years teaching public sector management on DMS programmes and short courses, she took an MBA specializing in Human Resource Management. She has done consultancy work for a number of public sector organizations and is now researching for her PhD on 'The changes in management practice in local government'. Address for correspondence: Canterbury Business School, University of Kent, Canterbury CT2 7PD Kent, UK.

Gloria Moss, Training Manager (UK) for Eurotunnel is currently responsible for the Language and Management Training at Eurotunnel. She has been a Training Manager at Courtaulds and has also taught Personnel Management and issues at the Open University and City Polytechnic. She has been a judge on the National Training Award Scheme and has run her own consultancy providing French courses for business, as well as courses on recruitment and graphology. She is currently completing a book 'Graphology and Business'. Address for correspondence: 13 Gayton Road, London NW3 1TX.

Thomas V. Murphy, Lecturer in Human Resource Management, University College Dublin. On leaving school he spent eight years with Ireland's national airline Aer Lingus, during which time he trained in all aspects of personnel management and industrial engineering and reached middle management rank. He worked for a period as Personnel Officer with Ireland's Agricultural Research Institute. He served on the Board of Ireland's Employment Equality Agency from 1982–87. He was one of the founders in 1979 of *Industrial Relations News*, a weekly news publication serving practitioners. He is currently completing his PhD on 'Women in Trade Unions'. Address for correspondence: University College Dublin, Department of Industrial Relations, Faculty of Commerce, University College, Belfield, Dublin 4, Ireland.

Dr Andrew Pendleton, Lecturer in Industrial Relations at the University of Bradford Management Centre. He has also taught at the Universities of Kent and Bath. He has conducted research into British Rail's industrial relations over a number of years and has published articles in the *British Journal of Industrial Relations*, *Industrial Relations Journal* and *Work, Employment and Society*. He is also currently involved in a comparative European study of profit sharing and employee share ownership. Address for correspondence: University of Bradford Management Centre, Emm Lane, Bradford, West Yorkshire BD9 4JL, UK.

Dr David Perkins works for the South East Thames Regional Health Authority as Joint Director of their MBA in Strategic Health Services Management, based at Canterbury Business School. Formerly head of management development for the Health Region, he is involved in management education and development in the UK and abroad. He has a particular interest in the use of new forms of management education and development of practising managers in the public and private sectors. Address for correspondence: Canterbury Business School, University of Kent, Canterbury, Kent CT2 7NP, UK.

Dr Bill Roche, Acting Head of the Department of Industrial Relations and Senior Lecturer in Industrial Relations and Human Resource Management, University College Dublin. He is also Director of the Master of

Business Studies Programme at UCD's Michael Smurfit Graduate School of Business and developed the School's new core courses in Human Resource Management on the MBA programme. He has published extensively on issues in industrial relations and human resource management. In 1991 he co-edited *Working Time in Transition: The Political Economy of Working Hours in Industrial Nations*, Temple University Press, Philadelphia. He is also author of a forthcoming book, *Social Integration and Strategic Power*. Address for correspondence: University College Dublin, Department of Industrial relations, Faculty of Commerce, University College, Belfield. Dublin 4, Ireland.

Professor Jose Maria Rodriguez, Professor of Organizational Behaviour, IESE, the Business School of the University of Navarra, member of the International Association of Applied Psychology. He has wide consulting experience, especially in the areas of team development, process consultation with management groups, in-company leadership training and implementation of participation programmes. He is author of the book *El factor humano en la empresa*, Ediciones Deusto, Bilbao, 1989, and co-author of three reports about Personnel Policies and Practices in Spanish Business Firms, 1981, 1985 and 1989. Address for correspondence: IESE, Universidad de Navarra, Avenida Pearson 21, 08034 Barcelona (Pedrales), Spain.

Professor Richard Scase, Professor of Organizational Behaviour at the University of Kent at Canterbury. He has written several books within the general area of management, including (with R. Goffee) *The Real World of the Small Business Owner* (1987), and *Reluctant Managers: Their Work and Life Styles* (1989). He has also published widely in academic journals as well as in less specialist magazines and newspapers such as *The Guardian*, *The Times* and *The Financial Times*. He is currently researching into the management of creativity in large organizations and preparing an introductory textbook on organizational behaviour. Address for correspondence: Rutherford College, University of Kent, Canterbury Kent CT2 7NX, UK.

Dr Heribert Schmidt-Dorrenbach, Senior Consultant in Human Resources with the Deutsche Gesellschaft für Personalführung mbH, and Chairperson of the Manpower and Social Affairs Committee, OECD, Paris. He studied Law and Economics at the Universities of Freiburg and Marburg and took a Doctorate in Law from the University of Cologne. He has over 25 years of HRM experience, before taking up his present posts he was Personnel Director at Henkel KGaA in Düsseldorf for a number of years. Address for correspondence: DGFP mbH, Niederkasseler Loweg 16, 4000 Düsseldorf 11, Germany.

Dr Sandra Schruijer, Lecturer in Organizational Sociology at Tilburg University. She graduated in Organizational Psychology at Tilburg University and obtained her PhD from the same University in 1990. During 1990 and 1991 she was Lecturer in Human Resource Management at the Canterbury Business School. She currently teaches organizational change, organizational analysis, communication skills and organizational sociology. Her research concerns intergroup relations, organizational culture and international human resource management. One of her recent publications is a book entitled *Norm violation, attribution and attitudes in intergroup relations*, Tilburg University Press, 1990. Address for correspondence: Tilburg University, Faculty of Social Sciences, P.O. Box 90153, 5000 LE Tilburg, The Netherlands.

Dr John Sheldrake, Senior Lecturer in the Department of Politics and Government at the City of London Polytechnic. His main interests are in the areas of labour relations, local government and organizational behaviour. He is author of several books the most recent being *Industrial Relations and Politics in Britain 1880–1989*. Address for correspondence: City of London Polytechnic, Calcutta House, Old Castle Street, London E1 7NT, UK.

Dr Tony Snapes is a Chartered Occupational Psychologist who lectures in Human Resource Development at the London Management Centre. He consults to a wide range of organizations from banks to the NHS, at the moment specializing in the assessment and development of managers, including career planning processes. He has a special interest in 'spotting' and 'developing' under-utilized talent in organizations. He holds degrees from the universities of London and Leicester. Address for correspondence: 55, Clarence Gate Gardens, Glentworth Street, Marylebone, London NW1 6QS, UK.

Dr Tharsi Taillieu, Associate Professor of Organizational Psychology and staff member of the Tilburg Institute of Academic Studies where he teaches organizational design and organizational development. He is a graduate of the University of Leuven, Belgium, and received his PhD from GSIA Carnegie-Mellon University. Currently his research concerns the change of management roles associated with utilization of information technology and the formation of international networks of organizations. Recent publications include: *Managing Human Resources in Transnational Assignments*. Address for correspondence: Faculty of Social Sciences, Tilburg University, P.O. Box 90153, 5000 LE Tilburg, The Netherlands.

Professor James Tedeschi, Professor of Social Psychology, State University of New York at Albany where he has taught for the past 22 years. His research interests include self-presentation, power and influence, social conflict and human aggression. He has published over 150 journal articles, written numerous chapters in edited books, authored 3 books and edited 4 books. He is a Fellow in Divisions 7 and 8 of the American Psychological Association, and an Affiliate Member of the European Association of Experimental Social Psychology. Among his most recent publications are Tedeschi J. T., and Nesler, M. (1992) 'Grievances: Development and Reactions', in *Aggression and Violence: a social interactionist approach*, (eds R. Felson and J. T. Tedeschi) Washington

D.C. American Psychological Association. Address for correspondence: Department of Psychology, University at Albany, State University of New York, 1400 Washington Avenue, Albany, New York 12222, USA.

John Thirkell, Senior Lecturer in Industrial Relations, and Director, Centre for Russian and East European Management and Labour Relations, Canterbury Business School. His principal research interest is in labour relations in Eastern Europe currently pursued through an ESRC-funded project on 'Labour Relations in Transition-restructuring and Privatization' based on case studies in Bulgaria, Czechoslovakia, Hungary, Poland and Russia (Novosibirsk region). Publications include: *Labour Relations in Eastern Europe: Organisational Design and Dynamics*, Routledge 1991 (with K. Petkov); *Strategies, Issues and Events in Industrial Relations: Disclosure of Information in Context*, RKP, 1987 (with J. Jackson-Cox and J. McQueeney). Address for correspondence: Keynes College, University of Kent, Canterbury, Kent CT2 7NP, UK.

Dr Sarah Vickerstaff, Senior Lecturer in Public Relations (Human Resource Management), Canterbury Business School. Currently Director of the full-time MBA programme, her main research interests have been in training policy and practice. She has recently written on the training problems of smaller firms. She is co-author with J. Sheldrake of *The History of Industrial Training in Britain*, Gower, 1987. Present research activities centre around an international collaborative project on eastern European industrial relations: 'Labour Relations in Transition-restructuring and Privatization' funded by the ESRC. Address for correspondence: Canterbury Business School, University of Kent, Canterbury, Kent CT2 7PD, UK.

Translator for Case 17: Marie-Claire Delprat, graduate student in Management, University of Kent.

Preface

The advent of 1992 has forced practitioners, teachers and students to broaden their perspectives on human resource management. It has become increasingly important to extend the curriculum to include a wide range of European cases and texts. Events in eastern and central Europe have inspired a re-evaluation of methods and techniques as western European academics are called upon to give 'expert' advice to the ailing economies of the old Eastern bloc. In this context there is a renewed interest in how companies and organizations in different countries deal with the familliar problems of personnel management: recruitment, selection, training, reward, industrial relations and participation. Business schools are internationalizing their faculty and extending their links with partner institutions outside their own country in an effort to reflect these changes.

This volume seeks to respond to some of these developments in a text that offers a wide range of real cases and exercises from around Europe and across the broad spectrum of human resource management issues. The cases, which have arisen from primary research, consultancy activities and the professional personnel practice of the authors, offer readers an insight into the theory and practice of human resource management in real life situations, in a wide variety of cultural contexts.

This book is necessarily only a beginning. It does not claim to explain the different cultural and economic bases for the variety of human resource management practices that we can identify throughout Europe. The cases and texts are not intended to be representative of particular trends or practices in different European countries. Instead this book offers the reader the opportunity to reflect upon the nature and significance of similarities and differences in practice and, hopefully, to appreciate the diversity of human resource management techniques and policies.

Human resource management has to a large extent been an American import, both in the form of articles and books written by American management theorists and in the practice of American multinational firms operating in Europe. This has made some wary of the notion of human resource management, fearing it is possibly just a new fad, or more seriously that it represents a set of responses to specifically American economic, political and cultural conditions.

The success of the Japanese export industries and the increasing penetration of Japanese companies into Europe has also led to an examination and appraisal of techniques of human resource management in these firms; raising anew questions of the transferability of management practices from one culture to another. Typically management texts continue to offer universalistic panaceas that can be pressed into service in any, or all, cultural and economic contexts. Some commentators, notably Thurley and Wirdenius, have argued for the need to develop a specifically European approach to management. The Social Charter of the European Community seeks in some measure to harmonize the conditions of employment throughout the member states and create a floor of basic employment rights; implying the desirability of a common approach to employee relations issues.

Research, especially in organizational psychology, however, has pointed to the enduring uniqueness of the different national cultures that make up Europe (e.g. Hofstede), putting question marks over the 'European project' and cautioning against the hegemony of American management theories and approaches. What is clear is the extent to which no European country can act in isolation and without scrutiny from its neighbours. What is interesting is to gain more knowledge and understanding of how personnel management practices vary and compare in an age when labour is expected to be more mobile throughout Europe, and when companies are looking to extend their markets and perhaps their organizations into new countries.

The book is divided into six parts, which cover the main areas of human resource management activity broadly defined. Each of these sections will begin with an editorial introduction setting out the key issues in current practice and theory. The cases and texts have been designed to provide classroom teaching material, either in the form of traditional case studies and role plays, or as topics for workshop discussion. The cases have been framed so that they can be reasonably accomplished in a one-hour or two-hour session with students. Each text provides a guide to key readings relevant to the topic.

The book can be treated as a textbook which covers the standard areas of human resource management policy, working systematically through the sections: the role and significance of the human resource management function; the nature of people management, issues of motivation, control, work organization and design; employee resourcing; human resource development; reward management; and industrial relations. Alternatively, individual sections can be dipped into for specific cases or texts. The text assumes that these different areas of human resource management policy and practice are necessarily interdependent and, therefore, each case or text has implications beyond the section division in which it is contained.

The value of using case material and discussion texts in the teaching context is to give students the opportunity to criticize and apply and assess standard techniques against the rigours of a real example. The working through of case examples in the classroom provides students with the means to develop and extend important skills such as: comprehension, analysis, problem solving and solution evaluation and justification. By working in groups on cases, students are also encouraged to enhance their communications skills, the ability to present ideas, listen to others, summarize points, negotiate and persuade. Using cases from different cultural, economic and political contexts should give students the means to begin to assess their own assumptions and cultural heritage.

PART ONE

The Human Resource Management Function

In recent years the title human resource management (HRM) has taken over from personnel management in many organizations and has become a staple element of many MBA programmes. To a large extent the term HRM is an American import; there is a continuing debate as to whether it constitutes a fundamentally different approach to the management of people than the more traditional personnel management.

Leaving aside for a moment the question of possible differences between HRM and personnel management, the whole issue has resulted in a renewed interest in the question of how the personnel function should be organized and who should be responsible for the operation of personnel policies: line managers or specialist personnel staff. All organizations have personnel functions in that they all select, appraise, develop, reward and discipline their staff, but how these policies are determined and managed varies considerably from company to company and from country to country. Not all companies have a dedicated personnel department: in small companies in particular, the managing director and line managers may deal with employee relations issues as they arise.

The development of specialized personnel or human resource departments is one way in which management in the organization tries to co-ordinate and stabilize responses towards employees. Pressures external and internal to the organization encourage the development of specialized human resource functions. The pressures leading to specialization have been identified as follows in Fig 1.

Product or labour market pressures may push the organization to try and increase predictability and control of its human resources in order, for example, to reduce costs, improve effort and productivity, ensure labour supply or pursue a quality strategy. The extent to which managerial responses to these pressures are constrained is in part conditioned by the trade union context. The development of industrial relations systems has been another very significant factor in the growth of personnel management. The need to create strategies for the containment of, or accomodation towards, trade unions has helped to shape the specialist personnel activity.

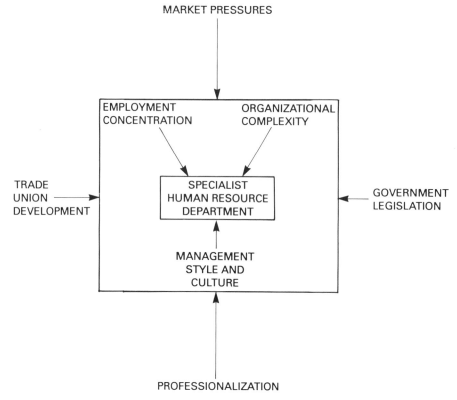

MARKET PRESSURES

EMPLOYMENT
CONCENTRATION

ORGANIZATIONAL
COMPLEXITY

TRADE
UNION
DEVELOPMENT

SPECIALIST
HUMAN RESOURCE
DEPARTMENT

GOVERNMENT
LEGISLATION

MANAGEMENT
STYLE AND
CULTURE

PROFESSIONALIZATION

Fig. P1.1 Pressures leading to the development of specialised personnel management.

The growth of state intervention in individual and collective labour issues in most European countries has led many organizations to develop specialist functions to deal with the administration of employment related law and regulations. Governments may also encourage certain patterns of human resource management by practice in public sector employment. There may also be pressures from what Watson (1986) has called 'career-ist' factors, namely a growth in the number of managers interested in pursuing specialist human resource careers. This may be reflected, as in the British case, by the growth of a professional association defining and representing the specialist role.

In organizations, the pressures that lead to a more general division of labour within management are also significant in the development of personnel management; namely growth in size and complexity. These factors create pressure for the greater coordination and control of an increasingly large and differentiated workforce and will be mediated by the organization's prevailing management styles and culture. The development of the personnel function will reflect managerial responses to these dynamics.

This brief discussion of the development of specialist personnel management begins to indicate why the actual organization of personnel policies may vary considerably from case to case. Within Europe it is clear that the traditions and practice of personnel management vary widely. The legal context of employment relations as it differs from country to country sets the tone for the skills required and roles expected of human resource specialists. Thus, personnel managers in Germany and Italy are far more likely to have a degree in law than their counterparts in Britain. The different industrial relations systems with their particular patterns of trade union organization and collective bargaining will condition the kinds of skills which a company needs at individual plant level. In countries where wage negotiations are dominated by national or sector agreements, personnel managers at the enterprise level will have less of a role in wage issues, as for example in Italy.

In other countries where the economy has been historically dominated by small and medium sized enterprises, as in Denmark, personnel policies may have traditionally been the prerogative of line managers rather than specialists; as organizations grow in size this tradition is maintained, with personnel managers playing an advisory and service role to line managers who have the main responsibility for delivery of personnel policies. In

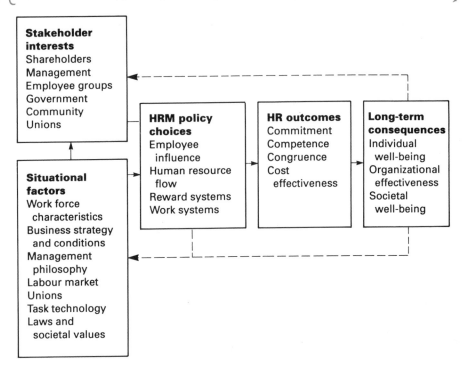

Fig. P1.2 Map of the HRM territory (from Beer *et al.*, 1984, p. 16). Reprinted with the permission of The Free Press, a Division of Macmillan, Inc., from MANAGING HUMAN ASSETS by Michael Beer, Bert Spector, Paul R. Lawrence, D. Quinn Mills, Richard E. Walton. © 1984 by The Free Press.

this situation the process of professionalization may be less significant and distinctions in the educational and training background of personnel managers in contrast to other managers may be less marked (Arkin, 1992).

Companies in eastern Europe which are looking for possible models of personnel management, now that basic people management policies are no longer the preserve of the communist party structure within the organization, face a myriad of possible alternatives in personnel practice in western Europe.

These examples remind us of the need to locate human resource policies in their wider organizational and environmental contexts, what Beer *et al.* (1984) have called the HRM territory (see Fig.2).

This map both situates human resource management activities in terms of economic, political, social and industrial contexts and suggests the links between human resource policy outcomes and organizational effectiveness. The model is prescriptive, arguing that human resource management should be a planned and coordinated activity, not simply a set of discrete relatively independent functions.

In the past it was typical to list the job of the personnel department as a series of different policy areas, for example: personnel records; recruitment and selection; training and development; wage and salary administration; industrial relations; health and safety; welfare etc. The approach suggested in HRM Map above is to define the personnel management job as a package of necessarily interrelated policy areas as indicated in Figure 3.

In the last ten years it has been increasingly argued that human resource management – people management – is a critical management function.

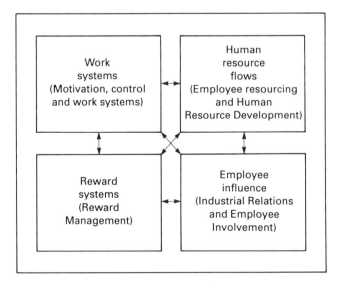

Fig. P1.3

In contrast, in the past personnel management has often been seen as a largely administrative and service function; a collection of *ad hoc* tasks. There is now a renewed focus on the impact of human resource policies on organizational effectiveness. The normative model offered by Beer *et al.* (1984) suggests that human resource policies must be planned and coordinated with corporate strategy or, put another way, that human resource management should be strategic. A number of writers have explored the issue of what constitutes a strategic approach to human resource issues.

Guest (1991) has identified at least four different senses of strategy within the literature. These are: seeing employees as a strategic resource for gaining competitive advantage; developing human resource policies that are long term, planned and proactive; the integration and coordination of human resource policies in different areas to ensure a consistent approach; and finally, matching human resource policies to business strategies. The linkage between human resource policies and organizational effectiveness is often asserted, the literature on 'successful' companies prescribed a strategic approach to people management issues along the lines mentioned above (for example, Peters and Waterman, 1982). However, in practice the assumption that human resource policies should flow from corporate strategies is not unproblematic: it implies that it is possible to simply 'read off' the appropriate HRM strategy from the business strategy. In reality the process of strategy formulation and implementation is a far more complex and multi-layered process (see for example, Hendry and Pettigrew, 1990) In practice, the delivery of human resource policies ('HRM Policy Choices' in the Beer *et al.*, model) will be a set of responses to perceived contingencies. Personnel policy will be delivered by line managers and general managers who may or may not understand the theory, the assumptions, or the legal requirement behind a particular way of doing things. The espoused policy or mission is retranslated, modified and adapted by different departments, groups and individuals within the organization, so that the operational effect may bear little resemblance to the paper policy.

The power of the human resource specialist, if such exists in an organization, will vary enormously from case to case. As one indicator of this we can see that the likelihood of human resource specialists being on the main Board of Directors of large companies varies considerably from country to country. In Sweden and France there is a high probability, in large UK firms the likelihood is a little under 50:50; in Italy very few personnel specialists are directly represented at board level. (Price Waterhouse/Cranfield Project, 1991) This may indicate the different significances attached to the personnel function. Much of the work of personnel managers is routine administration and advice; the vision of a powerful, strategic role suggested by many of the HRM textbooks may be restricted to a relatively few large and successful companies.

The delivery of human resource policies is a complex organizational process in which managers at different levels respond and adapt to the pressures they perceive and face. The 'Map of the HRM Territory' taken from Beer *et al.* reminds us that management operates within the context of different and often competing stakeholder interests.

HRM textbooks typically present a view or a picture of what people management *should* look like, they are deliberately normative and prescriptive. This has led many to criticize the HRM literature, especially of American origin, as managerialist in the sense of focusing upon what organizations would like to have happen rather than what they actually do (for example, Beaumont, 1992). The objectives for human resource management activity indicated in Figure 2 are commitment, competence congruence and cost effectiveness: simply put this means that policies are aimed at providing a well trained, effective and motivated workforce at a price the organization is willing to pay. This reminds us that personnel policies are about control and coordination of employee behaviour in pursuit of organizational goals. This has led Watson (1986) to cynically suggest that personnel management should be defined as follows:

> Personnel management is concerned with assisting those who run work organizations to meet their purpose through the obtaining of the work efforts of human beings, the exploitation of these efforts and the dispensing with of those efforts when they are no longer required. Concern may be shown with human welfare, justice or satisfactions but only insofar as this is necessary for controlling interests to be met and, then, always at least cost. (p. 176)

The debate about human resource management and its vaunted differences from personnel management will continue and is increasingly being informed by research into what organizations are actually doing rather than what they should do (Storey, 1992). That the management of people is undergoing constant shifts and changes should hardly be surprising; that companies and countries differ in their approach to personnel issues is to be expected. The nature of human resource management is necessarily a political and ideological question, the exercise of managerial power will always be subject to possible challenge from other managers, from trade unions, from individual employees, from pressure groups and governments. This is arguably what makes the subject interesting; it is never a purely technical question of picking the 'right' policy.

To some extent this book is prescriptive, from section to section it offers an introduction to ideas of good practice. However, perhaps more interestingly, through the case studies it offers readers the chance to see how considerably more complex, and more interesting, the reality of human resource management is.

The contributions in this section include a programme for European personnel management as set out by the European Association for Personnel Management (EAPM). In the context of the common market, and the progressive reintegration of eastern and central Europe into that economic market, it becomes more pressing that personnel specialists and other managers learn from each other and define common standards for their activies. (Thurley, 1990) In the second text we have a view of the implications of the single European market for managing human resources.

The first case is based on recent research in two borough councils in England and explores the real and imagined differences between an HRM as opposed to a personnel management approach to the management of people. It reminds us of the need to look at actions as well as paper policies. This case gives us the opportunity to assess how two different organizations responded to the challenges of operating in the same newly competitive environment.

SUGGESTED READING FOR PART ONE

Arkin, A. (1992) Personnel management in Germany. At work in the power-house of Europe, *Personnel Management*, (February), 32–5.

Arkin, A. (1992) Personnel management in Denmark. The land of social welfare, *Personnel Management*, (March), 32–5.

Beer, M., Spector, B., Lawrence, P. R., *et al.* (1984) *Managing Human Assets*, The Free Press, New York.

Beaumont, P. B. (1992) The US human resource management literature: a review, in *Human Resource Strategies* (ed. G. Salaman), Sage, London, pp. 20–37.

Brewster, C. and Tyson, S. (1991) *International Comparisons in Human Resource Management*, Pitman, London.

Caplan, J. (1992) Personnel management in Italy. It's the climate that counts, *Personnel Management*, (April), 32–5.

Guest, D. (1991) Personnel management: The end of orthodoxy?, *British Journal of Industrial Relations*, **29**, (2), 149–76.

Hendry, C. and Pettigrew, A. (1990) Human resource management: an agenda for the 1990s, *International Journal of Human Resource Management*, **1**, (1), 17–43.

Kochan, T. A. and Capelli, P. (1984) The transformation of the industrial relations and personnel function, in *Internal Labor Markets* (ed. P. Osterman), MIT Press, Cambridge, Mass. pp. 133–61.

Miller, P. (1991) Strategic human resource management, *Human Resource Management Journal*, **1**, (4), pp. 23–39.

Peters, T. and Waterman, R. (1982) *In Search of Excellence*, Random House, New York.

Pinder, M. (1990) *Personnel Management for the Single European Market*, Pitman, London.

Storey, J. (1992) *Developments in the management of human resources: an analytical review*, Basil Blackwell, Oxford.

Thurley, K. and Wirdenius, H. (1989) *Towards European Management*, Pitman, London.

Thurley, K. (1990) Towards a European approach to personnel management, *Personnel Management*, (September).

Watson, T. (1986) *Management Organization and Employment Strategy*, Routledge and Kegan Paul, London.

TEXT 1

The European Association of Personnel Management

Below is a statement of aims from the EAPM. It indicates both the extent of international networking and some of the personnel issues which are seen to be of major significance in Europe at the present time: international work mobility; the impact of an ageing workforce and the effects of changes in eastern and central Europe.

EUROPEAN ASSOCIATION OF PERSONNEL MANAGEMENT

The EAPM was founded in 1962 and has 17 member associations covering 18 countries in Europe. These are Austria, Belgium, Denmark, Finland, France, Germany, Greece, Hungary, Italy, Netherlands, Norway, Portugal, Spain, Sweden, Switzerland, Turkey, UK and The Republic of Ireland (IPM). Two representatives from each national association are elected to the Delegates' Assembly which meets once a year. Normally the representatives are the head of the national association together with the person in charge of international affairs.

The current President is Aydin Akbiyik of the Turkish association, Peryon, who in June this year hosted the 15th EAPM Congress in Istanbul. The Secretariat of the EAPM is run from the headquarters of the Institute of Personnel Management in London.

The EAPM, which is an independent and non political organization, has the following aims:

1. To provide an association of professional standing for its members through which the widest possible exchange of views can take place.
2. To disseminate information and develop a continuously evolving professional body of knowledge to assist members to do their jobs more effectively in response to changing demands and conditions.
3. To provide opportunities to develop and maintain professional standards of competence.
4. To encourage and undertake investigation and research in the field of personnel management and subjects related to it.
5. To develop and present a European viewpoint on personnel management and to establish and develop links with other bodies, both European and international, concerned with personnel.

The EAPM organises the European Congress once every two years which brings together speakers and representatives from all of the 18 EAPM countries.

The EAPM is also a member of the World Federation of Personnel Management Associations (WFPMA) which is a federation of regional personnel management associations consisting of the Society of Human Resource Management (SHRM) covering the United States and possibly in the near future Canada; the European Association for Personnel Management (EAPM), the Inter American Federation for Personnel Administration (FIDAP) covering most of Central and Southern America and the Asian Pacific Federation of Personnel Administration (APFPA) covering the Asian Pacific region. The World Federation, its regional associations and individual National Associations are constantly developing to form a more established and effective support for personnel management worldwide.

The networking opportunities for individual National Associations are great and ever improving. The WFPMA also organise a Congress once every 2 years. The next congress will be held in Madrid in the first week of June 1992 and will be hosted by a European regional (EAPM) member in association with the Spanish Association (AEDIPE). The theme of the congress is: The Human Dimension for Tomorrow's Business.

Over the past two years the EAPM has committed itself to upgrading its activities and profile. This has resulted in the setting up of 3 separate working parties comprising of different EAPM member associations.

Group 1: Belgium, France, Greece, Italy, Switzerland and Turkey completed their survey on Obstacles to Mobility in Europe in June this year.

Group 2: Denmark, Finland, Norway, Sweden, UK and Republic of Ireland will publish their report on Motivating the Older Worker at the World Federation Congress in Madrid at the beginning of June 1992.

Group 3: Austria, Germany, Hungary, Netherlands, Portugal and Spain are currently looking at the impact of change in central and eastern Europe on European Personnel Management and hope to be producing a report at the same time as Group 2.

The EAPM has also undertaken a major research project with the leading Swiss Management Institute (IMD) on the emerging role of the human resource manager. This project involves all EAPM national associations and will endeavour to find some answers to how the future human resource manager may successfully accommodate shifts in value, the changing nature of work and so on.

Finally, the European Commission approached the EAPM to participate in a quarterly newsletter on European employment and social affairs. This newsletter is now off the ground and is a practical medium for communicating the relevant EC Social Policy information on a regular basis to the EAPM members, whilst at the same time providing a forum for EAPM national associations to put forward an independent practitioner's viewpoint.

This newsletter is an addition to an internal EAPM newsletter which facilitates greater networking and co-operation between the individual members.

The EAPM is currently being approached by other European national associations with regard to membership and hopes in the long term to incorporate all the countries in greater Europe with similar objectives in the field of personnel management.

DISCUSSION QUESTIONS

1. Is it possible to define personnel management as a profession in the sense that we recognize lawyers, doctors or architects as professionals?

2. Is it desirable or necessary to have common standards of qualification for personnel managers throughout the European Community?
3. What are likely to be the main barriers to the transfer of personnel specialists from one national context to another?

SUGGESTED READING

Tyson, S. and Fell, A. (1986) *Evaluating the Personnel Function*, Hutchinson, London, Chapter 4, pp. 51–70.

Lawrence, P. (1991) The personnel function: an Anglo-German comparison, in *International Comparisons in Human Resource Management* (ed. C. Brewster and S. Tyson) pp. 131–44.

Papalexandris, N. (1991) A comparative study of human resource management in selected Greek and foreign-owned subsidiaries in Greece, in *International Comparisons in Human Resource Management* (ed. C. Brewster and S. Tyson) pp. 145–58.

Managing human resources in the Single European Market from a German point of view

Heribert Schmidt-Dorrenbach

I. It is generally accepted that human resources management means having the right number of properly qualified workers and managers at the right time and at the right place, and motivating them to maximum performance with the right material and immaterial instruments. Responsible for finding optimum solutions to human resource problems within a company are its management, the supervisors and, above all, the staff of the personnel department. And these people are basically of the opinion that their duties will not significantly change with the completion of the Single European Market as of January 1, 1993, and the dismantling of barriers within Europe which until now have impeded the free movement of capital, goods, services and persons.

This view continues by considering that if until now and despite existing business barriers, multinational operations in Europe have successfully delegated personnel to other European countries and have had employees transferred from abroad into the home country, how much easier will all this be in future with the abandonment of economic constraints and regulation.

And if until now those in charge of personnel at multinational companies have regularly exchanged views and consulted with the personnel officers at the subsidiaries and affiliates in other European countries on how best to cope with personnel problems in the individual countries, then it can safely be assumed that this form of cooperation will continue all the more intensely in future.

Yet such an all too simplistic analysis fails to do justice to the consequences resulting in the wake of the Single European Market. We must realize that Europe as it has existed up to now with its individual consumer and labour markets sealed off from each other will as of January 1, 1993, no longer exist. Europe on the road to political union, and shortly reaching a milestone in the form of the Single European Market, will henceforth no longer have any autonomous economic markets. For the population of all the member countries there will then only exist the 'European domestic market'

- within which the products and services of companies operating in Europe can be offered and marketed directly and without any obstacles;
- and from where products and services can be exported into other economic areas such as North America, South-East Asia, Japan or into which products and services from these regions can be imported.

The consequences of this are twofold insofar as they affect personnel policies, personnel management and personnel leadership: the product groups and services of a company, irrespective of where they are controlled or coordinated, will reach out as far as the borders of Europe. And for these product groups and services, companies will require management and specialists able to take direct action at local level throughout the Single Market. In view of the anticipated competitive pressure, such direct action will have to be taken more and more frequently and more and more quickly. Managers will have to concern itself directly with all the production locations and branches belonging to its field of responsibility; management will have to concern itself directly with European customers in their entirety, customers that, nonetheless, still differ in terms of individual cultures and languages.

With the dismantling of economic and other barriers existing to date, there will inevitably be a rapid and intense flow of information between those employed within this 'European domestic market'. And this applies not only to management and specialists recruited from the various cultural and linguistic regions, but also to those employed within a company who, as a consequence of their profession, until now have tended to remain and work at one location. As they can now move freely within Europe, can set up business and work wherever they want, they, too, will be more interested in what the economic regions within Europe have to offer, the special interests of the employees, their specific economic and labour conditions, their social systems, the possibilities of management-labour consultation in factories and plants.

In order to arive at a better appreciation of various types of behaviour and institutions inside Europe, people will enquire into the respective socio-cultural and economic backgrounds. For instance, an EC member country with a codified set of labour laws will tend to appreciate the attitude of the British[1], who are critical of codified labour laws, if this

---

[1] Maastricht Summit of December 9/10.12.91

   Social Policy Reforms

   Only 11 of the member countries intend to proceed along the path of the Social Charter 1989. Britain to opt out.

   All 12 members countries including Britain agree on a Protocol on Social Policy. The 11 member states are authorized to adopt and apply the necessary resolutions in the field of social affairs.

criticism counteracts the efforts of the EC commission to regulate centrally from Brussels on the subject of labour law. Also, the EC countries will more readily appreciate the codetermination and works constitution rights that are traditional in Germany and which in the past have largely accounted for peaceful industrial relations.

II. The foreseeable trends within the Single Market represent a particular challenge to personnel officers in multinational companies operating within Europe:

First, they must orientate their human resources towards Europe. To begin with, this applies to management development. It means continuing tried-and-tested systems and procedures.

- for pinpointing management requirements in terms of quantity and quality;
- for comparing requirement profiles with the performance and potentials of junior managers and experts, both in terms of the present and the future;
- for evaluating potential through assessment centres or through interviews, etc.;
- identifying the expectations and needs of tomorrow's managers;
- developing and implementing induction programmes; into the job, on the job and off the job;
- career planning, and planning who will succeed to which positions within the hierarchy.

It is essential that all the employees at the subsidiaries, affiliates and branches within Europe are integrated into such programmes (fig. 1). All of the employees must be accorded equal opportunities within the company, irrespective of their nationality. Eventually we must arrive at a

Under the protocol, the 11 countries that signed will 'have recourse to the institutions, procedures and mechanisms of the European community' in adopting measures to implement a common social policy. The Social Community of the 11 agree separately and additionally to relax the voting procedures for social initiatives of the EC Commission in the following respects:

[++] Qualified majority of the 'Social Community of the 11' on subjects such as

- labour conditions
- advising and consulting with employees
- equal opportunities for men and women
- integrating into the labour market individuals excluded from it

[++] Unanimity on subjects such as

- Social security and social protection
- Dismissal protection
- Collective representation of employee interests (incl. codetermination)
- Conditions of work for citizens from third countries

[++] The following areas continue to fall within the national competence of the 11 nations

- Rates of pay
- Rights to enter coalitions
- Rights to strike/lock out

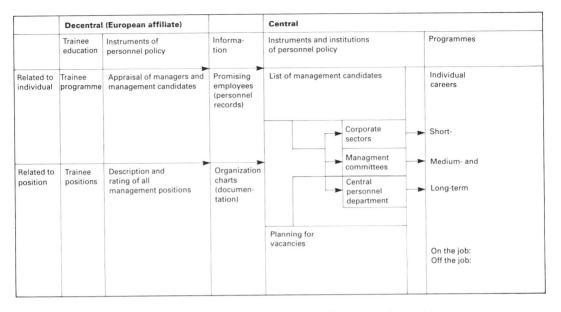

Figure T.2.1 System of European management planning (schematic).

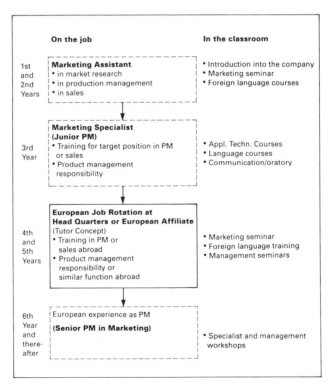

Figure T.2.2 European training programme for management candidates in marketing.

situation in which employees from the various European countries are working within the various units of an organization (figs. 2 and 3). This means intensifying language courses and intercultural training. Companies will only succeed if their employees become familiar with local cultures, if they learn to interact with people of other countries, if they acquire a knowledge of the language of the market where the company's products are being sold.

In this context I also would refer to the need for personnel marketing efforts aimed at Europe's universities and polytechnics, the sources of tomorrow's business talent. In the wake of demographic trends in all the European countries, the number of qualified applicants will steadily drop. Competition to recruit qualified and motivated staff from the labour markets of Europe will tighten. And so, particularly in the early years of the Single Market, staff recruitment will become one of the most important strategic tasks of a company.

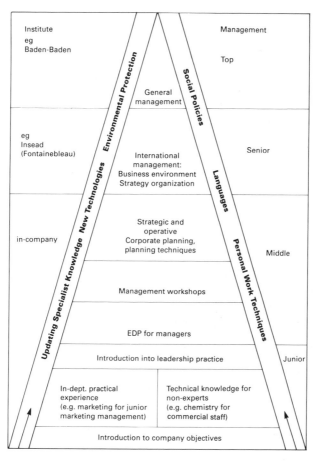

Figure T.2.3 Advanced training for managers.

Finding qualified staff will be one of the key problems facing pan-European enterprises. A company's success will largely depend on whether it succeeds in recruiting the right numbers and the right quality of management and specialist staff. In order to meet this challenge, companies will have to revert to proven instruments and methods of personnel marketing, but this time tailored to the larger European market. Companies will have to find answers to the following questions:

- What are the needs of company; how many and what kinds of managers and specialists will it need now and in future?
- What are the expectations of managers and specialists employed now and in future in the individual European regions of a company; what is their perception of the company in its entirely and in its individual aspects; what do they regard as the strong and the weak points?
- What potential attraction has the company in the various regions of Europe and what specific steps should the company undertake in order to recruit staff from the labour markets of Europe and, especially, from its universities and polytechnics?

Such questions can only be answered on the basis of comprehensive information. That is why pan-European personnel planning and research constitute the information base of tomorrow's personnel marketing efforts.

Personnel marketing efforts targeted at Europe's universities and polytechnics for the purpose of attracting qualified 'Europeans' encompass trainee courses, sandwich courses, suggestions and support for doctoral theses, project activities within companies, talks and discussions with undergraduates, research work, grants, inviting undergraduates to seminars, case studies and management business games. Only each company itself can decide which of these marketing efforts should be directed at which of Europe's universities and polytechnics.

Another important aspect of human resources management in European companies is the setting up of a uniform management remuneration system. The practice to date has frequently been for employees working outside their home country to receive the same rate of remuneration as local employees of the host country: salary and short-term benefits (e.g. vacation pay and sickness insurance) are patterned on the practice in the host country. Long-term benefits (e.g. pension schemes) are a matter for the home country to continue to control. So that employees abroad retain at least the same level of pay, the gross and net salaries at home are calculated, and the latter compared with the net salary received in the host country and based on the position filled by the employee there. If the calculation shows a disadvantage for the employee, this is offset by a supplementary payment to offset any loss in purchasing power. For people employed in other European countries, a mobility supplement frequently amounting to 10 percent of the remuneration to date, is often paid.

With the completion of the Single European Market, the harmonization of pay is of growing importance. This is a complex of problems that cannot be resolved from one day to the next. Nonetheless, we do observe a steady trend towards some kind of harmonization. This is, in part, a consequence of the growing harmonization of tax systems within Europe and, moreover, the prospects of a European currency.

Ever since the inception of the Exchange Rate Mechanism between the key European currencies, and the suppression of the rate of inflation to 2 to 5 percent (compared with 10 to 12 percent previously), the cost of living in the European countries has harmonized to a considerable extent, (except for Denmark, Portugal and Greece). And if salaries for managers working outside their home countries are based on the same, European-wide basket of commodities, instead of the national ones employed to date, a pan-European remuneration system will begin to take shape. And once European-wide assignments become a part of everyday managerial life, the question of relocation allowances for employees, working in London instead of Berlin for instance, will simply no longer arise. Management pay will consist of a basic element to which are added variable supplements determined by the performance of the individual and the profitability of the company and its divisions. Besides being affected by the profitability of the company, remuneration will also depend on targets set for the individual, and the degree to which these targets have been achieved. The levels of target achievement should be quantified and identified by company management. Particularly this variable element of remuneration, one measuring the success of a company, its divisions and the performance of the individual, is what young managers of tomorrow expect. They regard this not as a mere cost factor but explain that they see themselves as the driving force behind the success of a company, and that they therefore expect this to be acknowledged in the form of material rewards.

Personnel officers in European companies operating throughout the Single European Market will in future not only have to concentrate more closely on management and specialist staff at home but also on all the employees at the various European locations and branches. This includes providing access to information about the company and its divisions, a policy of continuous and frank information about the business situation and the progress of a company, its expenditure plans, the opportunities and risks in Europe, the labour conditions inside the various countries.

This policy of providing information must also explain any existing differences, why this is the case and how they can be overcome. Only by furnishing such kind of information to all employees in all the units of the organization can a company be sure that its people will identify with the business targets and strategies. Only thus will it be possible to integrate employees more tightly into efforts aimed at improving efficiency, developing the organization, total quality management, productivity and efficiency enhancement programmes or in other projects requiring co-operative leadership and creative potential.

Such efforts will only succeed within European countries if the mem-

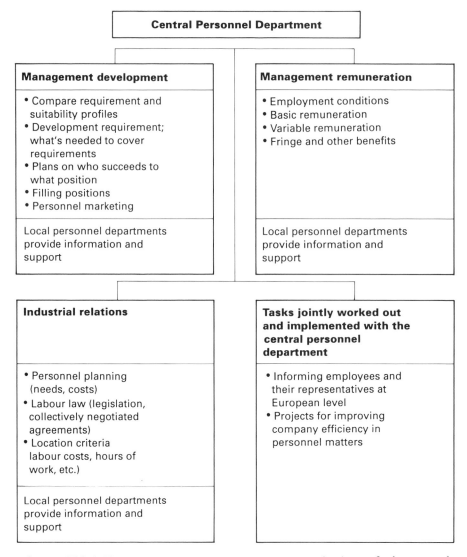

Figure T.2.4 Human resources management; organization of the central personnel department.

bers of the personnel departments at headquarters and in the local organization units, the branches, subsidiaries and affiliates work closely together. It is up to people at a local level to provide headquarters with the necessary information on human resources requirements within the organizational units, on promising management talent, on possibilities of recruiting undergraduates, on existing labour conditions and costs, on local laws and collectively negotiated agreements, on social systems and their benefits, and also on such questions as the cost of accommodation and all the other issues that need to be clarified whenever people move from one country to another.

Reciprocally, those at headquarters must also advise their colleagues at local level about the situation of the company as a whole and all the units within it. And, moreover, they should regularly invite these colleagues to meetings, participation in projects, and toegether with them, they should work out measures aimed at improving the efficiency of such European companies.

III. On the basis of the previous remarks, we can identify the following personnel-related functions for a company operating within Europe (fig. 4):

IV. The European related principles of personnel management in a company operating within the Single European Market can be summarized as follows:

1. All the employees must be given equal opportunity, irrespective of nationality. This applies particularly to promotion and remuneration. All that counts are skills, commitment and performance.

2. Companies operating throughout Europe must depoly their management and specialists throughout Europe.

    Top management at both headquarters and the affiliated companies abroad should include individuals trained in and experienced with conditions in other European countries.

    It should be the target of such companies to promote to top management positions those individuals who have successfully completed assignments abroad.

3. For the purpose of recruiting, screening and preparing management and specialists for European assignments, the company should carry out personnel development and personnel marketing measures on a European scale.

    Criteria for appointing individuals to positions of European significance should be, in addition to what is normally expected of qualified management, the ability and willingness to familiarize with foreign cultures, to communicate in foreign languages and to demonstrate mental and physical mobility.

4. The same remuneration principles should apply company-wide, Europe-wide. Rates of pay should be based on function and performance, and they should be competitive. Moreover, they will also be linked to the profitability of the company. Collectively negotiated rates will be taken into account as well as any local exceptions.

    Individuals assigned to positions outside the home country should be paid according to local rates plus some compensation for any additional expenses accruing.

    Long-term benefits (like company pension schemes) will chiefly depend on what has been agreed in the home country of the individual.

Short-term benefits (vacation pay, payment in the event of sickness) will follow the pattern of the host country.

5. If a company is to operate successfully in the Single European Market, it is essential that it adopts a single company language (most probably English). Individuals assigned to positions in other European countries should have a command of the local language. The company should assit the individual and his family in acquiring such language skills.

6. The advent of the Single Market, a frontier-free region permitting the free flow of goods, persons, services and capital, requires appropriate planning on the part of companies wishing to operate within this market. Personnel planning is an integral element of such corporate planning.

   Personnel planning should cover personnel requirements (quantity and quality), and the related personnel expenses. In this way, personnel planning makes sure that the company will have the human resources it requires for tomorrow's markets. Personnel planning should provide employees with information on existing and future jobs within the company so that they can adapt to these requirements in good time by acquiring the right skills.

   Personnel plans should be derived from the company's own corporate plans. The quantitative results should be translated into a qualitative requirement analysis as part of the company's plans for filling future vacancies. Taking into account any changes within the organizational structure, additional and minimum as well as replacement needs must be pinpointed and used as a basis for personnel planning activities.

7. The pros and cons of the company's various locations within Europe should be continuously reviewed. Such reviews should examine personnel and social criteria, labour costs, hours of work, absenteeism, the skills of the local workforce, social welfare and insurance schemes, local labour laws.

8. Personnel officers at headquarters and at local level should work together in all personnel measures of European relevance to the company. These include management development, management remuneration, personnel planning and personnel marketing, analyses of location (dis)advantages, the situation regarding European labour laws, working out and implementing efficiency improvement programmes, and other projects affecting personnel management and leadership. There should be a regular flow of information and mutual support.

9. Personnel officers at headquarters and at the local organizational units should make sure that there is a continuous and frank flow of information to employees and employee representatives on the business situation of the company and its prospects within the Single Market. Interaction with employees and their representatives should be based on mutual trust and comply with statutory and collectively negotiated rules and regulations.

CASE 1

Human resource management or personnel management?
Personnel policies in two district councils in England

LINDA KEEN

CONTEXT OF THE CASE

Significant changes occurred during the 1980s in the role of local government in Britain. Conservative government legislation imposed
extensive expenditure controls on local authorities, and required many
services, such as refuse collection, to be open to competition from private
sector contractors. Local authorities' manual workforces, known as
Direct Labour Organizations (DLOs), were required to operate essentially as businesses within each authority, and to meet stringent financial
targets. Traditional bureaucratic local authority management systems –
where centralized personnel departments enforced detailed control over
all departmental staffing practices – became too inflexible for operational
managers. In order to compete successfully with the private sector it was
necessary to achieve higher productivity and to remain within statutory
spending limits. Local authorities also found it difficult to maintain
their role as 'good' or 'model' employers, based on national pay and
conditions of service, life-time employment and stable, predictable career
paths.

BACKGROUND TO THE CASE

In addition to these pressures, both district councils in this case study
experienced labour market problems in the late 1980s, with skills shortages in professional sectors such as legal services, computing, architects,
etc. These groups were difficult to recruit because of the disparity in
incomes between the private and public sectors. Barset Council also
suffered from a shortage of clerical and secretarial workers due to local

Human Resources Management in Europe
Edited by Sarah Vickerstaff
Published in 1992 by Chapman & Hall, London. ISBN 0 412 45380 0

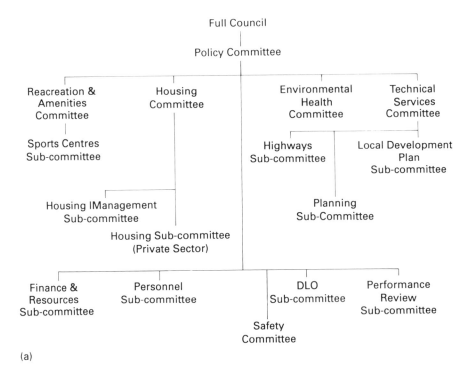

(a)

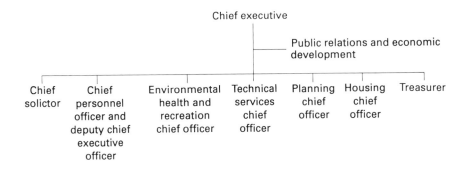

(b)

Fig. C1.1 Council structures of Barset and Foxton

    (a) Barset Council committee structure.

    (b) Barset Council organization structure.

    (c) Foxton Council committee structure.

    (d) Foxton Council organization structure.

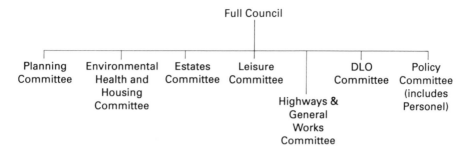

(c)

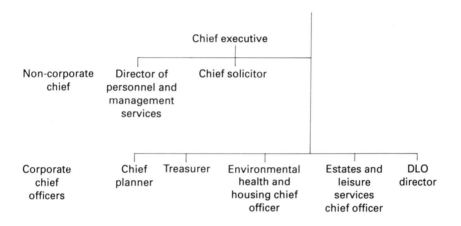

(d)

Fig. C1.1   (Cont.)

private sector competition, and the predicted fall in the number of young people entering the labour market was expected to exacerbate this problem. In both council areas, the local economy was booming, with low unemployment and high house prices, especially in Foxton. The population of each area was: Foxton, 126 000; Barset, 95 000.

The committee structure of elected councillors and the departmental organization of paid officials for each council, showing the usual range of district council services provision, is outlined in Figure C1.1. Following the retirement of all the chief officers during the 1980s, Foxton Council had taken the opportunity to reorganize, reducing the number of departments. Barset had an almost completely stable management team during this period.

Table C1.1   Political composition of each council

	Barset	Foxton
Conservatives	31	33
Liberal Democrats	9	11
Labour	5	5
Independent Labour	2	–
Liberal	1	–
Independent	1	–
Total	49	49

The political composition of the councils is shown in Table C1.1 The Conservatives, with a fairly right-wing ('Thatcherite') ruling group, under their new leader (a financial executive) had always controlled Foxton Council. The Barset Conservative ruling group, which had gained control of the previously 'hung' council in 1983, was decribed as 'left of right', under the leadership of a retired civil servant. The composition of each council's workforce was as follows:

Foxton: 650 staff; 350 manual workers in the DLO
Barset: 485 staff; 200 manual workers in the DLO

With the exception of the DLOs, decentralization of service operations to strategic business units or cost centres, had not taken place in either council.

THE PERSONNEL ROLE IN THE DLOs

Foxton had established its DLO as a completely autonomous business unit. The director had acquired full responsibility for all personnel functions and most other central services, to reduce his costs. He used advice from the Council Personnel Office for which he paid a small fee. His chief accountant acted as personnel administrator. Barset DLO was moving towards a similar model; the director had already acquired some independence from central personnel control, with control of recruitment for his own manual staff, and he was planning to take over more functions with a view to reducing his central charges.

To improve productivity and competitiveness, both DLOs had adopted local pay agreements, outside of the national bargaining structure. The directors had consulted extensively with the workforces, including a direct ballot in Foxton, plus consultations with union officials. The pay levels in both DLOs depended on the competitive tender price for each contract, as did the annual pay awards. Bonuses were still paid in Foxton, with profit sharing for the staff, but bonuses were being phased out in Barset: 'they're too expensive to run'. A profit-sharing element was planned for all the workforce, involving harmonization of manual and staff pay and conditions.

As well as maintaining contact with union representatives, both directors had increased direct communication with their workforces, including productivity circles in Barset. Both DLOs had introduced flexible working with core and peripheral workers, plus, in Barset, flexible functioning among all managers and some work teams. Both directors had also introduced rigorous computerized monitoring of worker productivity, sickness, absenteeism, etc. Despite describing his workforce as valuable 'human resources', which required regular maintenance like his vehicles, the Foxton director had felt compelled to cut his training budget to improve profitability.

Management/worker relations were generally good, pervaded by the mutual feeling that 'If we don't win contracts, we're all out of a job'; although one worker commented that the partnership idea was all very well, but, 'we don't earn the same, do we?'.

THE PERSONNEL ROLE IN EACH COUNCIL

The formally defined role of each council's Personnel Department is outlined using rather different styles.

Responsibilities of Barset Council Personnel Department

Barset Borough Council's Personnel Department incorporates a number of disciplines and responsibilities which, although quite different, complement each other and combine to provide comprehensive personnel service to the Authority. These disciplines include general personnel advice on industrial relations and employment law issues, trade union relations, conditions of service, training, management services (Work Study/Organization and Methods/Operational Research), recruitment, youth training scheme, payroll and health and safety.

(Barset Council, Annual Statement, 1989)

Foxton Council Personnel Department Mission

To ensure that the Council's strong human resource base is used to competitive advantage by establishing a climate which demands, and appropriately rewards, excellence from staff and which encourages individual growth, respect, initiative and commitment, in an organization with clear roles and accountabilities.

(Report to Council, 'Personnel – Into the 1990s', 1989)

The Foxton document (1989) represented a deliberate attempt (see below) by the chief personnel officer (CPO) to redefine his role and to introduce various policy initiatives, making extensive use of the current human resource management terminology. The Barset CPO's new policy initiative reports, also referred to staff as 'resources', but tended to be more succinct, sometimes including targets for monitoring performance in various personnel areas. Both CPOs were in their mid-fifties, and each had joined their council in 1974.

Table C1.2 Summary of the key differences between the personnel policies of each authority

Personnel policies	Foxton	Barset
Personnel Department responsibilities	Excludes payroll	Includes payroll, plus commercial training service for other authorities
Devolution to service departments	More extensive: chief officers responsible for staffing within budget, and one chief officer has appointed own personnel officer; more devolution is sought; PRP grades not formally monitored by central personnel; central training budget	Very little, although more involvement by line managers in training need analysis and provision; no demand for more devolution; PRP grades formally monitored by central personnel; central training budget
Devolution to DLO	Complete: DLO financial manager has personnel responsibility; central personnel used for advice	Partial: staffing and recruitment; more devolution being negotiated
Charging for central personnel	Traditional per capita basis	More rigorous system: per item or per time
CPO role in strategic planning	Very minor, but recent initiation of corporate mission and culture; not a full member of senior management team; no personnel committee; no formal corporate planning	Extensive: combines CPO role with deputy chief executive role; full member of senior management team; chairs own personnel committee; new strategic planning system
Recruitment and selection	More sophisticated methods planned; not yet implemented	Sophisticated methods already used; planning introduction of computerized monitoring
Training	Increased budget, new career grades	Increased budget, new career grades
PRP	Introduced in 1989 for senior grades only	Introduced in 1988 for senior grades, 1989 for all staff
Pay and conditions	Local pay/grades introduced in 1989; unilateral determination of annual pay award by council	Local pay/grades introduced in 1988; unilateral determination of annual pay award by consultants
Trade union relations	Essentially consultative	More of a partnership

Apart from payroll functions, which were allocated to the Treasurer's Department in Foxton, both personnel departments held essentially the same responsibilities, although the Barset departments also ran personnel consultancy and training services, on a commercial basis for other local authorities. Both councils retained centralized personnel departments. Formal devolution of personnel responsibilities to line managers in Barset (apart from the DLO) had not taken place: 'We basically have central-ization of both policies and practices and we don't devolve very much to the departments.' The chief officers, however, saw their relationship with Personnel (described as very positive) as more of a 'partnership', and it was clear that in some areas, such as training, there was increased participation by line management.

In Foxton, partly as a result of official policy decisions and partly because of unilateral action by two chief officers, devolution had pro-gressed further, with some responsibilities, such as staffing within establishment budgets, devolved to the chief officers. In the absence, until the 1989 document, of specific personnel policies in many areas, the chief planner (with the largest department) had developed his own personnel policies, and used a senior clerk as his own personnel officer: 'My department produces its own personnel documents – Personnel are not fast enough for us. We go ahead first and then we tell the personnel officer.'

Demands for reduced central service charges from the DLO in Barset had stimulated the council to introduce more rigorous costing systems, and personnel services were charged out to council departments on a per item or per time basis. Foxton was continuing with the traditional per capita basis (apart from the DLO) in response to vigorous opposition from chief officers to suggestions for change, although the new council leader had plans to force a re-examination of this issue. A summary of the key differences between the personnel policies of each council can be seen in Table C1.2.

THE ROLE OF THE CPOs IN STRATEGIC POLICY AND PLANNING PROCESSES

Following the failure of a complex corporate planning system introduced in the 1970s, Barset Council had introduced, in early 1989, a general corporate strategy for the whole authority, plus a series of informal strategy statements for each of the main service departments. The detailed planning of operations and implementation was devolved to individual chief officers. The chief executive had recently introduced a 'customer care' initiative throughout the council, which was to form the basis of a new corporate culture, with a corporate logo: 'The Way Ahead'. A full member of the management team (see Figure C1.1), with his own personnel sub-committee, the CPO (also deputy chief executive) was extensively involved in both corporate and departmental strategic planning, developing and monitoring personnel policies in various areas which were integrated with the chief officers' service strategy plans, and with the new corporate culture.

Foxton had never used formal corporate planning, and strategic planning took place largely on an individual department basis with limited overall corporate direction, corporate personnel policies or strong leadership from the chief executive. For example, the planning director had drawn up a comprehensive plan for his department, including a departmental culture and integrated personnel policies. The Foxton CPO stressed his junior status as a non-corporate member of the management team, the absence (unlike Barset) of his own personnel sub-committee, and was critical of the strong departmental, as opposed to corporate, culture which dominated the management team.

Following some criticism, in the late 1980s, of his rather reactive as opposed to proactive role, the CPO in Foxton had produced in 1989 a lengthy report entitled: 'Personnel – into the 1990s.' This paper suggested the introduction of corporate culture (welcomed by the new leader, and subsequently implemented under the CPO's direction). It also identified a new 'enabling and facilitating human resource management role' for the Personnel Department, while urging only very limited devolution of functions to the departments.

EMPLOYEE RELATIONS

Both authorities introduced new employment packages in the late 1980s. Foxton was considering the introduction of more sophisticated selection methods such as skills and psychometric tests. Barset has always extensively used skills tests, and the emphasis here was on extended use of psychometric tests, a new computerized system for monitoring recruitment procedures and labour turnover, and systematic checks on the progress of recruits on training programmes against their aptitude test results.

Both CPOs were considering various measures to attract women returners, older people and young people. Ten per cent of the Barset workforce were already part time and the numbers were increasing; the Foxton CPO was unable to supply numbers. Other measures included the usual benefits such as generous car provision, mortgage subsidies and good relocation packages. Training budgets were increased significantly in both authorities, with new training policies, special career training grades, and training initiatives to facilitate the introduction of each council's 'customer culture'. In addition, line managers became more involved in staff development, partly arising out of the new performance related pay (PRP) schemes. The Foxton council leader was, however, planning to investigate the cost-effectiveness of current training provision, and some Barset councillors were doubtful of the value of training.

Both councils had introduced PRP schemes: Barset for senior grades in 1988 and for all grades in 1989; Foxton for senior grades only in 1989. The Barset scheme (drawn up by a consultant) involved a more extensive, and more complex performance-linked pay component than Foxton's (designed by the CPO). The employee's line manager, advised by Personnel, carried out the appraisal in both councils, although the Barset CPO monitored ·the grades to ensure a normal curve distribution. The Foxton CPO, on the grounds of fairness and equity, had urged extension of the scheme to all staff, but the council had rejected this idea. The Barset view was that productivity-related pay rises were more cost-effective than simple across-the-board pay rises. Both CPOs were placing a new emphasis on the 'caring employer' image, with the introduction of various initiatives in the areas of health and safety (statutory obligations); equal opportunities (although these were not monitored); smoking policies; keep fit courses, etc.

Both authorities – Barset in 1988, Foxton in 1989 – had introduced local pay agreements outside the national collective bargaining frame-work, which had new extended grades for staff and manual workers. Both councils had communicated these proposals directly to the work-forces and ballots were held, securing staff agreement. Neither authority was involved in collective bargaining to determine the annual pay rise, which was guaranteed to at least meet the national settlement. Manage-ment consultants were used in Barset to set the annual increase based on comparisons with local private sector salary levels. In Foxton, the council determined the annual pay award, using an *ad hoc* advisory body to consult (but *not* negotiate) with the union. Relations were maintained with the union in each council through the usual formal and informal machinery. A 'partnership' model was generally considered to exist in Barset, with considerable emphasis on consensus decision making and cooperation between political parties, all sectors of the workforce and the local community. Foxton manifested a more formal style with more emphasis on 'the right of management to manage' and limited involve-ment in decision making by the union or the minority political parties.

DISCUSSION QUESTIONS

For sessions of 1–1½ hours:

1. What changes in personnel policies occurred in these two authorities in the late 1980s? Why do you think these changes were introduced?
2. How did personnel policies in the two DLOs differ from those in the other council departments?
3. What were the differences between the two authorities' personnel policies? Why do you think these differences existed?
4. Do you think the changes in personnel policies represent a move from 'Personnel Management' to 'Human Resource Management' in each authority?

For longer sessions:

5. What changes in personnel policies in each authority do you think might have taken place in 1990–92?
6. Using appropriate models from personnel texts, how would you describe the role of each chief personnel officer?
7. How would you account for the differences between the roles of the two officers?

SUGGESTED READING

Legge, K. (1989) Human resource management; a critical analysis, in *New Perspectives in Human Resource Management* (ed, J. Storey), Routledge, London, pp. 19–40.

Kessler, I. (1990) Personnel management in local government: the new agenda. *Personnel Management*, November, pp. 40–4.

Local Government Training Board (1988) *Personnel: the Agenda for Change.* 1988.

Sisson, K. (1989) *Personnel Management in Britain*, Chapters 1–2, Blackwell, Oxford. pp. 3–52.

PART TWO

Managing People: Motivation, Control and Work Systems

Organizations are social arrangements for the controlled performance of collective goals.

(Buchanan and Huczynski, 1985, p. 5)

The role of management in organizations is to ensure performance, this means the successful management of people and other resources. The quotation above reminds us that this is a social process and that it involves an element of control. Personnel management can been defined as people control as we indicated in Part One: human resource specialists are experts in ways of controlling employees and staff.

This may seem an unpalatable definition; however, much of personnel policy is geared towards effective control and motivation; for example, recruitment and selection procedures should be designed to guide selectors' behaviour, training will seek to improve and develop an individual's attitudes and performance; disciplinary policies may define acceptable and unacceptable codes of conduct within the workplace; machine layouts and job allocations may be designed to control the flow of work; compensation policies may seek to encourage certain features of performance by rewarding them; rules may govern the operation of certain work processes in order to ensure safety, and so on.

Some of these aspects of control are direct and personal, a supervisor overseeing the actions of another; others may be codified in rules and regulations with which the individual is expected to comply; others still may be machine controlled.

Knowing that personnel management and other areas of management involves controlling the efforts and actions of the managed does not, of course, tell us how that control will be exercised. Management is interested in motivating staff to work effectively. Performance management is typically achieved through a mixture of control and motivation mechanisms. In this part of the book we look at a number of cases which explore the relationship between the individual and the organization; the nature of different control mechanisms and the extent to which through the design of the organization, the style of management and the design of work it is possible to improve both organizational and individual peformance.

ORGANIZATIONAL CULTURE

In the 1980s there has been considerable interest in the notions of organizational culture and corporate culture and the extent to which successful companies foster cohesive organizational cultures which impact favourably upon corporate effectiveness and performance. Consideration of Japanese business success has led some to suggest that their performance is in some measure attributable to the sense of shared mission and cultural cohesiveness of large Japanese companies. (For a discussion of this issue see Briggs, 1991.) The idea of organizational culture is a difficult one; the more prescriptive management literature suggests that it can be created and manipulated by senior management in order to develop and sustain desired behaviours from organizational members. Others provide more sociological and psychological analyses of culture, suggesting that it is something embedded in organizational practices, that may be difficult to change or use. Some writers have stressed the fact that any organization is likely to have a number of 'cultures' at any one time. These may include, the 'official line': the espoused culture; the taken for granted assumptions about how things are always done, which may or may not be the same as the espoused culture, and various subcultures or counter-cultures among different groups, units, sections or professions within the organization. (For a discussion of the debates within the literature, see Lynn Meek, 1992.)

As this discussion suggests, organizational culture refers to the ethos, philosophy and taken-for-granted assumptions that organizational members or groups within organizations share. Corporate culture may be used to refer to deliberate attempts by organizational leaders to foster a particular image for the product, service, the management style and reputation of the company. For personnel managers the concept of organizational culture and its impact upon people management is further complicated by the fact that all organizations exist within wider social and cultural contexts. Hofstede (1980), among others, has tried to show how national cultures impact upon organizational expectations and designs. Personnel policies, either by design or by neglect, are critical in shaping the individual's and the group's perception of the organization and their roles within it. Through policies on discipline, absenteeism, grievances, training, career development, pay, etc., the organization signals to different groups how they are viewed and valued. Personnel policies set the tone, the nature of the regime. To give an example, there has been considerable debate in the 1980s about the harmonization of fringe benefits, espcially in a class-ridden culture such as Britain. Should entitlement to fringe benefits be used to reinforce and reproduce status distinctions and differences between groups within the enterprise, or, by harmonizing benefits does the organization wish to convey (whether successfully or not is another matter) that everyone is of equal worth?

ETHICS AND THE ORGANIZATION

In the 1990s organizations throughout Europe are likely to come under increasing pressure to become 'green', by virtue of government legislation and pressure from consumers and employees. The subject of business ethics has been receiving renewed attention in this environmentally conscious age. The public image of a company and its practice may not always coincide. At points like these the clash between the espoused culture and what employees know usually happens may create tensions between groups within the organization or put particular individuals in an ethical dilemma.

The way in which organizations respond to challenges to the 'normative order' are very significant in reproducing or undermining existing policies. Individual discipline cases present personnel managers with some of the most tricky issues. In addition to questions of fairness and equity, there is the need to maintain a consistent and reliable approach across all cases, and to be seen to do so; policy also needs to be framed in terms of the wider context of legislation and prevailing patterns of inequality in the society of which the organization is part.

Two of the cases in this section deal with issues of how to manage the relationship between the individual and the organization.

CONTROL, MOTIVATION AND WORK ORGANIZATION

Managers have long been interested in the relationship between work design, motivation, job performance and job satisfaction. The ways in which work is organized and tasks are allocated are rightly seen as forming a crucial site for control and motivation. Traditionally, in manufacturing industry, scientific management principles prescribed a clear definition of job tasks, rigid division of labour, tight supervision and payment-by-results systems to achieve productivity. This approach to job design and motivation issues is often called 'Fordism', reflecting its historical prevalence in the car-manufacturing industry. The 'scientific' approach to work organization can be seen to share similar assumptions to classical theories of bureaucratic organization. Both assume that there is a rational, technical and best way of administering the organization and designing the work.

Progressively these approaches have been challenged by both management and employees. Management theorists have used motivation theory to posit a different link between work organization, motivation, job satisfaction and job performance. Traditional 'Fordist' forms of work design embedded in hierarchical, bureaucratic forms of organization are seen to frustrate and diminish employee commitment and therefore performance. Often employees, on an individual basis, have responded to the boredom and routine of such work organization with absenteeism, poor-quality work and quitting. Collectively, workers have responded with militancy and calls for improvements in the quality of working life.

The argument of alternative approaches to job design is that if employees (a) are given the opportunity at work to develop interest and skills in the job, (b) are given a sense of responsibility and pride in the work outcomes, (c) receive regular and constructive feedback about their performance, and (d) have scope for social interaction, then they are more likely to enjoy their jobs and perform better. People at work today are less willing to accept arbitrary and unilateral management control. One way in which managers can seek to have an impact upon job motivation is through the way in which work is organized and the job tasks designed.

JOB DESIGN AND HIGH PERFORMANCE

In the 1980s in Europe the organization and design of work came under a number of different but related pressures. Technological developments in both manufacturing and services had a profound impact upon the jobs that needed to be done. Computer Aided Design (CAD) and Computer Aided Manufacturing (CAM) applications are changing job boundaries and transforming job tasks. Information technology has changed not only the face of office work, but also has profound implications for the structure of management within all organizations (Drucker, 1992). Assembly line systems, as well as being unpopular with workers, are seen to be less applicable and effective in new technological environments and in the context of changing competitive pressures and market demands. Teamworking systems seem increasingly to match technological demands and employee aspirations.

Many of these developments have been theorized together as constituting the development of a post-Fordist type of production system. In this new approach to job design the emphasis is upon teamwork, flexibility in work allocation, individual and group responsibility for productivity, quality and control.

Organizational theorists have linked these developments to changes in organizational design and structure, complementing the post-Fordist theories of the labour process with a vision of the post-modernist organization; that is, a less hierarchical, bureaucratic and authoritarian structure than has characterized major industrial and commercial organizations in the past (Clegg, 1990). It seems that in the 1990s, throughout Europe, the nature of organizations and the jobs within them are changing rapidly. Management is seeking what Buchanan (1992) has called 'high performance work design', i.e. organizational and work structures that are flexibile and adaptable to changing product demands and technological developments, which quarantee high-quality products and services. To achieve such work systems companies are recognizing the need to redesign the workforce in terms of their skills, expectations and commitment to the organization. The following cases provide readers with the opportunity to consider a range of motivation and control issues. Cases 2 and 3 concentrate on issues surrounding the individual and the organization. Case 2 gives an example of an ethical dilemma faced by an individual manager. This reminds us that organizational commitment may conflict with the individual's own beliefs or with other commitments in that individual's life. Case 3 explores a situation where a high status member of an organization transgresses both the written policies and the taken-for-granted assumptions on how to behave. How the organization deals with such issues has implications for the organizational commitment of other employees.

Case 4 considers a traditional example of control systems in a manufacturing setting. Readers are asked to consider how the design of work and related supervisory regimes impacts upon organizational climate or culture. The remaining three cases provide the opportunity to look at work organization and job redesign problems. Cases 5 and 6 – the chemical analysts and the camera plant – both involve situations in which management can identify problems in worker motivation reflected in performance deficits. The reader is asked to diagnose the problems and suggest possible solutions.

The last exercise in this section is taken from a very different political and cultural context than the other cases. It charts the development of the brigade system of work organization in Bulgaria. Once again the impetus for change comes from a desire to improve employee motivation in order to raise productivity and the quality of work. This last case gives readers an opportunity to assess the extent to which the different political and economic system in which the factories operated did theoretically and practically require different approaches and techniques from those applied in Cases 4, 5 and 6.

SUGGESTED READING FOR PART TWO

Briggs, P. (1991) Organizational commitment: the key to Japanese success?, in *International Comparisons in Human Resource Management* (eds C. Brewster and S. Tyson), Pitman, London, pp. 33–43.

Buchanan, D. A. and Hucynski, A. A. (1985) *Organizational Behaviour: An Introductory Text*, Prentice-Hall International, London.

Buchanan, D. A. (1992) High performance: new boundaries of acceptability in worker control, in *Human Resource Strategies* (ed. G. Salaman), Sage, London, pp. 138–155.

Cascio, W. F. (1991) Ethical issues in human resource management, in *Applied Psychology in Personnel Management*, Prentice-Hall International, Englewood Cliffs, New Jersey, pp. 437–451.

Clegg, S. R. (1990) *Modern Organizations*, Sage, London.

Drucker, P. F. (1992) The coming of the new organization, in *Human Resource Strategies* (ed. G. Salaman) Sage, London, pp. 128–137.

Gilbert, N. and Burrows, R. (1991) *Between Fordism and Flexibility*, Macmillan, London.

Hofstede, G. (1980) *Culture's Consequences: International Differences in Work-related Values*, Sage, London.

Lynn Meek, V. (1992) Organizational culture: origin and weaknesses, in *Human Resource Strategies* (ed. G. Salaman), Sage, London, pp. 192–212.

Schein, E. H. (1985) *Organizational Culture and Leadership*, Jossey-Bass, San Francisco.

Torrington, D. and Hall, L. (1991) *Personnel Management*, Chapters, 6–10 and 24, Prentice-Hall, Hemel Hempstead, pp. 87–162.

An ethical dilemma

JOHN SHELDRAKE

You are responsible for a division of a major chemical and pharmaceutical company and are based at its headquarters in London. Over the last two years there have been claims in the media that the incidence of child cancers in the population living around the company's Rotherham plant is far higher than in other areas of the country. In spite of the company's rebuttal of the claims, and the commissioning of an independent report which suggests that there may be many reasons for the child cancers, the children's parents are not satisfied and the local MP has now become involved.

As the Rotherham plant is part of your division you have been to visit it. During your visit you have found that certain short-cuts have been taken in some of the processes which have resulted in the escape of highly toxic chemical residues into the atmosphere. The production manager has done his best to ensure that procedures are tightened up and that the problem will not occur again. You have also found evidence that some of the operatives working on a particular process have died of cancer although all of them were heavy smokers and their deaths may not, therefore, have been connected directly to their work. Nevertheless, a doubt has been sown in your mind concerning the past safety record at the Rotherham plant and you at least half believe that the company may be responsible for the deaths of the children.

The case of the Rotherham children is now to form the subject of an investigative television programme which is due to be recorded next week. The president of your company has a high public profile and is prominent among the Green lobby. She is on the record as claiming that the company's products are environmentally friendly and among the safest of their kind in the world. She has wider political ambitions and the problems in Rotherham stand to be a severe embarrassment to her. She does not wish to appear on the television programme and has asked you to represent the company and to refute any linkage between the operation of the Rotherham plant and the child cancers. She has made it quite clear that if you successfully carry out this assignment you can expect to be rewarded with a directorship.

This is the dilemma. In your heart you believe that the operation of the

Human Resources Management in Europe
Edited by Sarah Vickerstaff
Published in 1992 by Chapman & Hall, London. ISBN 0 412 45380 0

Rotherham plant may well have caused the deaths of a number of children. You are therefore prompted to 'blow the whistle' and state this openly in the television interview. On the other hand, you feel a strong sense of loyalty to the company president who has so far prospered your career greatly. You also dearly want a directorship and have been working for this for the last 20 years. Further, you have an excellent standard of living and realize that if you do 'blow the whistle' you will no doubt lose your job and have the greatest difficulty in ever finding a similar one.

What course of action will you take?

SUGGESTED READING

Adams, S. (1985) *Roche Versus Adams*, Fontana Collins, Glasgow.
Donaldson, J. (1989) *Key Issues in Business Ethics*, Academic Press, London.
McHugh, F. (1988) *Business Ethics*, Mansell, London.

CASE 3

How to deal with antinormative behaviour by a high-status person: the case of a university president making obscene phone calls[1]

SANDRA SCHRUIJER and JIM TEDESCHI

BACKGROUND

Downsway University[2] is a prestigious and well-known university in North America. It employs approximately 400 faculty members. The total number of students amounts to 12 000 (45% men and 55% women). In the past Downsway University suffered from financial problems and a poor academic reputation. Since the appointment of Dr Jameson as president ten years ago, its financial position has improved considerably. Dr Jameson maintained a hectic schedule over a decade to woo the rich and famous to donate funds to the University. The endowment of the University increased from 5 million dollars to 20 million dollars. At the same time the quality of students was significantly enhanced. The average score on the Scholastic Aptitude Test for first-year students rose by 200 points. At the height of his success Dr Jameson abruptly announced his resignation because of 'physical exhaustion'. The real reason for his resignation soon received national attention in the mass media.

THE EVENTS

Several weeks after Dr Jameson's resignation, he was charged by police authorities with having made a series of obscene phone calls from a

[1] This case is based on several articles which appeared in the *Washington Post* and *The Chronicle of Higher Education* during the period of April 1990 and January 1991.
[2] The name of the university, as well as all names of the individuals mentioned in the text, are disguised.

Human Resources Management in Europe
Edited by Sarah Vickerstaff
Published in 1992 by Chapman & Hall, London. ISBN 0 412 45380 0

private telephone in his campus office. These charges were made after an extensive investigation. Police investigators had received complaints from adult day-care providers about a telephone caller who made sexually oriented remarks concerning children in their care. Then an obscene phone call was received by the wife of a police officer. She collaborated with officials and subsequent phone calls were taped. Electronic tracing found that the origin of the calls was a private phone in Dr Jameson's office. The duration of the conversations varied from 20 minutes to an hour. In these conversations Jameson discussed sexual fantasies and proposed engaging in sexual acts involving children. The calls have been described as obscene, containing smutty language. Police found no evidence that Jameson actually did any of the things he talked about in his phone calls.

On 24 May 1991 Dr Jameson pleaded guilty to the charges and was sentenced to two 30-day jail terms. The sentences were suspended provided that Jameson undertook psychological treatment and gave a regular report on his progress to the court. Although the maximum sentence for such an offence is 1000 dollars fine and one year imprisonment, the prosecuting attorney stated that this sentence was typical for obscene callers seeking treatment.

Immediately after his resignation Jameson was hospitalized and treated by the head of a sexual disorders clinic at a major university hospital. Upon release he continued in an outpatient treatment programme. Treatment revealed that Jameson was himself a victim of childhood sexual abuse by a woman close to him from the age of 8. A lie detector test established that he was telling the truth about the abuse. The aberrant behaviour began to occur following the death of Dr Jameson's father in 1988, a precipitating event that apparently activated repressed memories of childhood. He said he did not ask for help during this two-year period because he could not envisage how a therapist could help someone with a PhD and who was a university president. Therapy established that he was not a paedophile, and did not suffer from any other sexual disorder.

DR JAMESON

Jameson, 51 years old, received his BA from MIT in 1961 and his PhD in astronomy in 1969 from Harvard University. In 1974 Dr Jameson took a position as Professor of Physics at Downsway University. Three years later he was appointed as Provost of the University. He has been a president for the last ten years. Although his family background was modest, he soon established good relationships with the rich, powerful, and famous in the capital city of the nation. His success in improving the university's reputation and its financial condition gained respect in the academic community. In 1984 he published a book detailing the frenzied schedule he followed as a university president. Jameson is married and has two adult daughters; one from his present marriage, one from a former.

EPILOGUE

Jameson has stated that his personal background could not excuse his behaviour, but provided a context for his conduct. He appeared on a national television programme to discuss the problem of child abuse and publicly apologized to the victims of his phone calls for any pain suffered, stating that he deeply regretted his actions.

OPINIONS

During the time of investigation many opinions concerning the Jameson case were expressed. One of the victims was disappointed with Jameson's suspended sentence. She described Jameson as a very sick man.

Edward Reems, Chairman of the University's Board of Trustees, said 'There is a professional man and a private man. The private man has a problem, and the professional man has a great record.' As one third-year student expressed it, 'I feel bad for him,' he said. 'He's done a lot for the school.'

A member of the Board of Trustees had a different opinion. She said that Dr Jameson's actions had severely damaged the reputation of the University and would have a detrimental impact on enrolments and future financial gifts. She supported legal action to fire Dr Jameson, who was still a tenured professor in the Physics Department, for acts of moral turpitude. She argued that university officials had to give first priority to protecting the institution and its students.

Professor Smith, a faculty member at Downsway University, described the incident as a tragedy involving an illness that had befallen a very successful and popular man. In Smith's opinion Jameson's conduct should not disqualify him to be the University's president. He strongly argued that the University should hold Jameson's position available for him until his therapy again makes him fit to handle the responsibilities of that office.

AFTERMATH

On 13 April 1990 the Board of Trustees at Downsway University voted to fulfil the contract of Dr Jameson, which required them to pay him over $300 000 for the unfulfilled portion of the contract period. Furthermore, they offered him more than $600 000 (a total package of $1 million) if he would relinquish his tenure and leave the university. Dr Jameson indicated publicly that he would prefer to return to teaching than to take the money. The offer by the Trustees infuriated faculty and students, resulting in a demonstration on campus and a spate of angry letters. In December 1991 the million dollar offer was withdrawn. In January 1992, after almost two years furlough, Dr Jameson returned to the Physics Department and is now teaching at Downsway University.

DISCUSSION QUESTIONS

1. How well was the incident handled by university officials? Why?
2. What do you think would have been the best way for legal authorities to have dealt with Jameson's behaviour?
3. Was it a wise decision to allow Dr Jameson to once again teach courses to (under)graduate students? Why (not)?
4. Could Dr Jameson in your opinion be reappointed at some future time as a president of a university?
5. Discuss how students, faculty, victims, the wider community and the Board of Trustees probably feel about the fact that Dr Jameson is teaching again.
6. Do you think that Jameson's emotional disorders affect his professional functioning and indeed should have consequences for his (further) career? Why?
7. Would a European university have dealt differently with similar behaviour? Why?
8. Do you think the outcome of the case would have been different had it not involved a university president but rather a student, or administrative staff, or a president of a commercial institution?
9. Should the University have taken legal action to fire Dr Jameson for moral turpitude?
10. Do you agree that college presidents should be given tenure in academic departments and thus given the security of a position at the university no matter how they function as CEOs? Give your reasons.

SUGGESTED READING

Gatewood, R. D. and Carroll, A. B. (1991) Assessment of ethical peformance of organizational members: a conceptual framework. *Academy of Management Review*, **16**, 667–90.

CASE 4

The significance of control

JOHN SHELDRAKE

CONTEXT OF THE CASE

This case study is derived from a participant observation study conducted at a light engineering company formerly located in north London. The plant in question manufactured electrical components which were subsequently finished and assembled at other plants within the locality. The emphasis in the study is on control and specifically the control of human resources (i.e. people controls) although other control systems are mentioned in passing (Figure C4.1). The vernacular descriptions of some processes and practices have been used in order to retain the flavour of the workshop floor.

STRUCTURE OF THE PLANT

The people control system of the plant was devised to maintain compliance. The majority of workers were required to 'punch the clock' four times each day, i.e. morning, lunchtime, after lunch, evening. The penalty for more than 3 minutes' lateness was a 15-minutes deduction of pay (i.e. 'losing a quarter'). The penalty for more than three latenesses in a week was an unpleasant disciplinary interview with the works manager. Dismissal always followed persistent bad time keeping and persistent absenteeism resulted in the same outcome. Perhaps for this reason bad timekeeping and absenteeism in the plant were rare.

The workers enjoyed greater or lesser degrees of control over their work depending upon their individual seniority and skill. Broadly speaking there was a core of skilled men and a residue of semi-skilled and unskilled men, women and 'boys' – some 50 workers in all. The production control system was inspired by Taylorism and operated to minimize operatives' choice of task and also to maximize the division of labour. Ideally, the system was calculated to ensure that the next task an operative undertook was the one best calculated to achieve specific output objectives. Such tight control was not always possible, however, when small-batch production was being undertaken and other arrangements had therefore to be made. An example was the 'specials' section which

Human Resources Management in Europe
Edited by Sarah Vickerstaff
Published in 1992 by Chapman & Hall, London. ISBN 0 412 45380 0

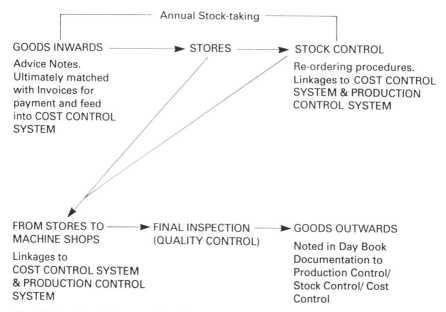

Fig. C4.1   Materials control and control interfaces.

operated in its own section of the plant and whose staff of four had substantial control over the pace of production.

All operatives were required to sign record cards on commencing a job and to sign off on completion. This activity was monitored by the appropriate supervisor (i.e. 'setter', chargehand or foreman) and also registered by a clerk. This process was known to be open to possible abuse, and falsifying entries on work record cards was likely to be treated as gross misconduct and result in dismissal. Not surprisingly, falsification (or at least its exposure) was a rare occurrence. The production times gathered from the work record cards were fed into the cost control system.

The operatives were largely concentrated into machine sections (e.g. 'autos', 'capstans', turning, milling, drilling, etc.) within open workshops. The open workshops maximized the possibility of visual supervision and meant that the operatives could not leave their positions without good reason. Partly completed components were moved from section to section by labourers (usually elderly men who occupied the lowest position in the wage/social hierarchy). The progress of components through the entire production process was monitored by the 'setters', inspectors and shop-floor expeditors.

OPERATIVES' RELATIONSHIP TO THE WORK

As has been noted, the operatives' control over the choice of job, and also the production process, was often negligible. This was often related to gender, with women doing the bulk of the repetition work. It is also accurate to say that no one (with the possible exception of the works manager) had a clear idea of what the components they were making were for. Nor apparently did they care. People spoke of an item or its code number (e.g. a batch of G2s or 5050s) and did not apparently consider it to be their business to know the end use. Nevertheless, there was substantial pride in the work, much of which was produced to very tight tolerances measured in 'thous' of an inch and also penalties for producing 'scrap'. The penalties stretched from a public dressing down by the immediate supervisor (referred to colloquially as a 'rollocking') to an unpleasant interview with the works manager and dismissal for incompetence. No sympathy for incompetence was forthcoming from the established workforce and only 'boys' fresh from school could 'scrap' several jobs and survive.

Fatigue and boredom were alleviated by morning and afternoon tea-breaks and occasional shouted conversations. Throughout the works the volume of noise was extremely high (literally deafening in places) and this was added to by pop music piped continuously through a Tannoy system. In several small workshops, attached to the large machine shops and under their own supervision (e.g. moulding, 'ebonites' and 'scratch brush and linishing') the generalized noise was accompanied by fumes, dust and the use of noxious substances. In the case of 'ebonites' (a resin-based material used for electrical insulation) the discomfort was extreme and the small group of workers involved negotiated their own specific piecework system within the general pay structure of the plant.

CONDITIONS AND MORALE

The company was not unionized and the plant did not possess a works council. The 'firm' was weakly paternalistic and many of the workers had long years of service. The works manager and the majority of the supervisors and 'setters', for example, had joined the company as 'boys' or apprentices. Many of the women workers had also been with the company for in excess of ten years. Labour turnover was low in a spite of a fairly tight labour market and plenty of alternative local employment. Some emphasis was placed on mutual loyalty between the company (which was a family firm) and the workforce, although this did not manifest itself very strongly except in the occasional presentation of long service awards and, as will be seen, the payment of profit-sharing bonuses.

Hours of work were relatively long (i.e. normally 9-hour days Monday to Thursday and 8 hours on Friday). Male workers were also expected to work on Saturday mornings and male and female workers often chose to work extra overtime if it was available. A 50-hour working week was not uncommon. Generally speaking the majority of workers seemed to be reconciled to, or even enjoy, being at work. This can perhaps be partly explained by the relatively small size of the organization and working relationships between the operatives (most of which described the plant as 'friendly').

COMPLIANCE AND COMMITMENT

The layout of the plant rendered techniques aimed at maintaining compliance relatively straightforward. Commitment was generated partly by selection procedures, partly by the early dismissal of 'misfits' and partly by pay arrangements. As has been noted, the bulk of workers 'punched the clock' and these were weekly paid. The élite of 'setters' had all begun their life in the plant by 'punching the clock' but had gradually been elevated to the 'staff'. The 'staff' were not required to clock in, were paid a monthly salary and also enjoyed certain distinctions such as different overalls and better seating at the annual Christmas dinner.

In addition to the opportunity of achieving elevation to the 'staff' (never actually achieved by a woman), all workers received a profit-sharing bonus. The formula for calculating this bonus was obscure but it was paid according to a personal code. It was usual for workers to improve their code over a period of years and thereby ultimately join the top bonus earners. All of the 'staff' élite, for example, received bonus at the top level. Pay bargaining was an individual matter conducted between the operative and the works manager, although its background was the going rate in the local labour market. Broadly speaking, pay levels were somewhat better than those prevailing in nearby plants, although working hours were somewhat longer.

Compliance and commitment were largely conditioned by a local tradition of factory culture and a generalized view among the operatives that factory life was inevitable. Briefly, a high degree of external social control operated and served to condition the success and extent of compliance and commitment within a particular plant. Figure C4.2 provides a systematized outline of the impact of compliance and commitment on the individual operative.

DISCUSSION QUESTIONS

In small groups of three or four, discuss the following issues:

1. How would you characterize the disciplinary regime in this company?
2. What implications does this regime have for the organizational or work culture of the firm?
3. Why do you think absenteeism and labour turnover have been consistently low?

Then consider the following problem:

In response to space constraints the company decided to relocate and found a suitable site in a semi-rural area 40 miles north-east of London. What problems, if any, would you foresee in the transfer of their traditional control strategies to the new location?

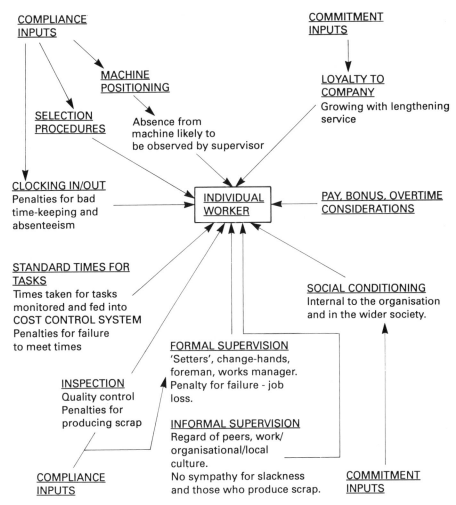

Fig. C4.2   Compliance and commitment.

SUGGESTED READING

Edwards, P. K. (1989) The three faces of discipline, in *Personnel Management in Britain* (ed. K. Sisson), Blackwell, Oxford, pp. 296–325.

Wickens, P. (1987) *The Road to Nissan*, Macmillan, London. Chapter 7, pp. 96–110.

Walton, R. E. (1985) From control to commitment in the workplace. *Harvard Business Review* 63 (March/April) pp. 76–84.

CASE 5

Omnipaint NV: job enrichment in the quality control laboratory

THARSI TAILLIEU

Your name is Tom Burke and about one year ago you joined the Phoenix Consulting Group in Amsterdam. You are a junior consultant there, and quite often you have been working with Arne Singer, one of the senior partners of the group.

This morning, when you entered the office, there was some consternation among the office staff. You learned that yesterday Arne Singer suffered a mild heart attack. His condition is stable, but he will be out for weeks. Through his wife, he has made an effort to instruct the office about his current obligations. His secretary has prepared a note for you and retrieved the file of Omnipaint, which is referred to in the note.

The Phoenix Consulting Group

OFFICE MEMO
From: Arne Singer
To: Tom Burke

Tom,
Could you handle the Omnipaint case for me? The report and feedback meeting is due next week. My secretary will give you my interview notes and the initial letter which was written by Clark, the director of the Quality Control Lab of the company.

I met Clark some years ago during a successful project in another site of Omnipaint. This time he wants an evaluation study of his own lab.

Make sure to properly discuss the pros and cons of both forms of job enrichment they experimented with: the dedication system and the co-ordinator system.

They seem quite open for advice, I believe you could suggest an approach which stepwise leads to optimal forms of job enrichment and teamwork.

I suggest you could use Hackman's The Design of Self-maintaining Workgroups as background for your thinking. Provide a copy to Clark, I am sure he will appreciate some background reading.

Thanks,

Arne Singer.

Human Resources Management in Europe
Edited by Sarah Vickerstaff
Published in 1992 by Chapman & Hall, London. ISBN 0 412 45380 0

The Phoenix Consulting Company

Mr Arne Singer
Senior Consultant.

Dear Mr Singer,

Following our telephone conversation this morning, I forward you the information which you requested about our company Omnipaint NV Let me express again how much I appreciate that you are willing to take this assignment.

Omnipaint NV is a chemical concern with several sites spread all over Europe. Headquarters are situated in Brussels, where most of the research and development is taking place, and which is also the site where the central quality control lab is located. The company produces paints, varnish, solvents, coatings and additives, in liquid as well as powder form, for its industrial and domestic clients (households).

The Quality Control Laboratory (hereafter called the lab) serves the research departments of the company and the production units elsewhere in Europe. Currently the most important clients are:

(a) the industrial research group, 8 teams, 120 researchers, headed by Director Büsch;
(b) the domestic products research group, 3 teams, involving 30 researchers and headed by Oevers;
(c) the pilot plant, directed by Barrachi, here in Brussels;
(d) the 8 production units which are scattered over Europe.

The lab is staffed by 28 chemical analysts of different educational backgrounds and specialization (40% are women). As a group they are able to perform about 800 different analyses. However, about 80% of the demand concerns routine analyses of fluids: wet chemical analysis. Each day from 100 up to 250 samples are deposited by clients, specifying a number of analyses per sample. The samples are coded and assigned by computer to a particular analyst. Each analyst has a repertory of analyses which he or she masters. The analyst collects the incoming work and performs it according to their own judgement. Urgency is indicated by using one to four stars on the daily computer printout. Results are obtained, coded and returned to the client through the computer system. The computer system also serves as the bookkeeping mechanism, in that the clients have to pay the lab services from their budget. To do so, a system of standard times per analysis has been developed over time.

The lab is divided into five sections, each headed by a manager. Most of the managers have served as analysts, from where they rose to their current positions (see lab layout). Mr Michat is manager of a group of analysts primarily performing wet chemical analysis ($n = 8$), while a second group doing similar work is managed by Mr Rogers. Mr Paulus is in charge of the group which operates the 'autoanalysers' ($n = 6$). His section contains automated machines capable of analysing large volumes (50 to 100 samples every two to three hours), analysing gas chromatography, absorption, molecular weight, etc. Mr Ivens heads a team of four people basically serving what we call the 'remote clients'. The work consists of samples which have been sent by other production units, and also the products of competitors on our markets. Mr Maher has the most recently installed group, four people, all of them technical engineers, who develop and adapt procedures, materials and methods of analysis according to demand of the research or other necessities. The managers are responsible for organization of work, coordination, external contacts, assignment of priorities, leading and evaluating of their work-force. Each of the managers has his own domain and follow developments of applied theory and instrument development in some area of chemistry relevant to the company's operations.

In the middle of 1990, a routine evaluation was held among the personnel. The survey data showed average satisfaction with work, hence indicating quite some opportunity for improvement. In particular some weak spots were: routine, lack of promotion opportunities, specialization and loss of all round knowledge, poor contacts with clients, unequal workload and little responsibility. Subsequent discussions led to a decision to experiment with job-enrichment, initially on a small scale but clearly with the intention to gradually involve the total lab. The experiment took place till the middle of 1991. The purpose was to assign analysts to particular research teams, in order to do all the work required by a team. We have experimented with two forms of job enrichment: (a) Miss Smith was *dedicated* to a research group (Coating-88) or Mr Oevers and has been doing until now all the analyses for that group. She seems to be quite satisfied with her working conditions, yet she is also an exceptional personality; (b) a second formula was developed. It consisted of appointing within the lab a *coordinator* for a particular group of clients. Mr Devel serves in this role (with mixed feelings) for the group of Barrachi. Mr Sarto has had a similar role for the group 'Heavy Duty Paints' of Büsch. After a couple of months the system seems to have collapsed. There has been quite some discussion about these experiments, not without heated arguments on all sides.

About six months ago, the experiments came to an end. We agreed to invite in a neutral outsider in order to evaluate the experience, and to make pro-positions whether to continue in the same or other directions. We have asked you to perform this task. Enclosed you will find an interview schedule with important informants from inside and outside the laboratory. They are quite willing to give you their information and insights.

We expect you to report as soon as possible your evaluation of both forms of job enrichment: what works and does not work in each case and why is that so. Which direction should we take for the future? We expect from you a plan concerning phases to proceed in order to get there. I should point out that effectiveness and efficiency are as important as a good organizational climate in the lab. Hence we expect you to preserve this vital balance in your proposals for job enrichment.

J. CLARK

Director, Quality Control Laboratory.
Omnipaint NV, Brussels

INTERVIEW SCHEDULE FOR MR SINGER OF PHOENIX CONSULTING GROUP

1. Mr Clark   Director, Quality Control Lab
2. Mr Michat   Manager, group Wet Chemical Analyses
3. Mr Sarto   Analyst (group Michat)
4. Mr Rogers   Manager, group Wet Chemical Analyses
5. Miss Smith   Analyst (group Rogers)
6. Mrs Carbonnel   Analyst (group Rogers)
7. Mr Paulus   Manager, group Instrumental Analyses

8. Mrs Donkers   Analyst (group Paulus)
9. Mr Ivens   Manager group 'Remote Clients'
10. Mr Devel   Analyst (group Ivens)
11. Mr Maher   Manager, group Methods & Techniques
12. Mr Barrachi   Director, Pilot Plant
13. Mr Büsch   Director, Research Industrial Products
14. Mr Oevers   Director, Research Domestic Products

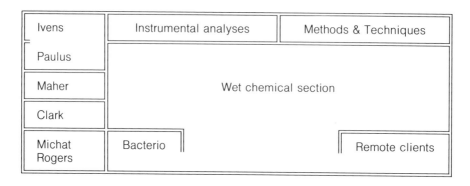

Mr Clark: director, quality control lab

CV: 40 years old, PhD Chemistry, Stanford, USA. Eight years with Omnipaint. First management job. Very friendly, gentleman's approach, does not look very assertive or persistent.

1. Very unclear what the outcomes of the job enrichment experiments are. Would like to continue in the direction of job enrichment and teamwork. Some analysts are motivated, others rather not. Maybe we should not involve all of them at the same time?
2. He feels resistance from the managers to continue with the experiments. It's likely they fear loss of responsibility through job enrichment. Clark has encouraged them but nobody takes initiatives; pretext: too much daily routine.
3. He has asked the managers (1988) to think about their own careers, and to choose an area of competence for their own development. Only Michat has reacted, and realistically works on a plan to become production manager within three to four years. The managers have grown into the hierarchy, but some might be less competent than the young analysts with regard to modern techniques, e.g. gas chromatography, autoanalysers.
4. Quality control is and will remain 80% routine activity. There are little opportunities for promotion within the lab. It might be possible to drop the strict connection between analyst and type of analyses by way of group work or rotation. It would require a lot of training to

guarantee quality work and not all analysts will be prepared to spend the effort.

5. There is a little contact between analysts and researchers (status!). In principle, contacts are possible, but it requires continuous effort by the analysts to remain informed about the status and developments of a project. Research teams frequently change projects and internal composition of members (average project takes 8 months). Hence installing a structure does not work very well. Also a small proportion of research (10%) is top secret.

6. Frequently we hear complaints from irregular clients. They are put at the end of the list (four weeks waiting time), and sometimes even the samples get lost. In such cases the clients come to Clark to ask for higher priorities, but it is impossible to overrule one's own managers and analysts.

7. Extremely seldom are there complaints about poor quality work (99% of the work is correct). Once in a while the researchers abuse double checks, or send 10 to 15 samples to get faster service (in that case it is worth while to load a piece of equipment and to start a separate run).

Mr Michat: manager, wet chemical group

CV: 34 years old, 20 years of service with Omnipaint. Has been a good all-round analyst. Manager for seven years. Aspires to become production manager at another site within three years.

1. Job: 50% external contacts, 50% within the lab. Played a major part in the development of the computer system for task allocation and bookkeeping for the lab. It was a massive effort, using full capacity of the lab computer and hard to make any more changes. The system works well, but the analysts have become lazy, e.g. they stick to their computer lists and never inspect the submission cards of the sample which gives background information. The information is available on cards but is no longer used.

2. The experiments were implemented too fast, without adequate preparation. We are continuously overloaded, with a backlog of about 600 hours which is never cleared up. There is always a rush to finish the most pressing work.

3. The priority system is abused, 50% or more of the samples are submitted with four star priorities, so the differentiation disappears. The research teams completely ignore the available work-hours of the lab, they annoy the analysts, eventually try to do some analyses by themselves, but most of the time they force the manager to mediate between parties (especially the groups of Büsch).

4. The coordinator role for three teams of Heavy Duty Paints of the Büsch section was an outright failure. The coordinator immediately got overloaded and had to force colleagues to do extra work. Too much work entered, and there were continuously priority fights

between the research managers. The analyst (Sarto) and his manager were caught in the cross fire. Nobody is now willing to do the coordinator's job. The research teams did not care for the coordinator anyhow.

5. Shows willingness to try something, but what? In any case no more coordinatorship, that would completely ruin the morale of the section.
6. Leaves has own analysts free to schedule their own work. Some work hard, other work less. They are individualists who perform their analysis according to own pace and mood. But they do deliver quality.
7. The group Michat performs work as much for Büsch as for Oevers. The distinction between the sections of Michat and Rogers is arbitrary. The sections contain the same types of analysts and they do similar work.

Mr Sarto: analyst, wet chemical group (Michat)

CV: 37 years old, 15 years of service as analyst.

1. Job: 100% routine analyses. Used to be a very competent all-round analyst. Due to the system of computer allocation, there are a number of analyses which he has not performed for years. Few promotion opportunities, and almost impossible to change jobs in the area.
2. Accepted the coordinator role for three teams of Heavy Duty Paints (Büsch). The system never worked. All the time when he turned his back, the researchers went to his manager to change priorities. The analyst did not have the power to make binding agreements and had to work for over thirty submitters. He was never invited to a meeting, nor informed about the nature or status of a project. All it meant was that he was forced to distribute work amongst his colleagues – which they almost always did not accept – and usually he had to do the real dirty stuff all by himself. Anyhow the colleagues were not interested in project information either.
3. Got bored and tired from the experiments. He simply wants to be left alone to do his own work.
4. Would appreciate some more variety in his work, and to have the opportunity to catch up with some developments. However, the computer is programmed in such a way that each receives only a particular type of analyses. The managers had so much trouble in programming the allocation rules that any change seems very unlikely.

Mr Rogers: manager, wet chemical group

CV: 31 years old, seven years with Omnipaint, manager for six months. Used to work in Packing, Control and Transport of finished goods. Still seems quite unfamiliar with the lab; reads a lot and works his way in.

1. Job: Spends a lot of time on computer registration and administration. Lets his analysts work autonomously. His section works as much for

Büsch as for Oevers, and quite often for Barrachi, especially when there is panic in the pilot plant. Then there is a massive effort to get difficulties resolved.

2. Shows himself definitely in favour of computer allocation of tasks. The volume is so large that otherwise it can never be done in an orderly fashion.

3. As potential for job enrichment: allow the analysts to work up to 10% of their time on method development and improvement. This cannot give immediate results however. Normally the analysts turn to the Maher group, whose people are more competent and better informed.

4. Loses a lot of time in solving priority fights between research managers and own analysts. The analysts neither can nor dare take a stand against the researchers for deciding on priorities.

5. Analysts are very often pressured by researchers who come to the lab to personally deliver samples and evade the procedure of priority setting.

6. Personally he would like to form three teams of two analysts to serve the complete group of Oevers. That would require that Mrs Carbonnel also takes her share of wet chemical analysis. That is very much the question. Moreover, probably nobody is willing to team up with her.

Miss Smith: analyst, wet chemical group (Rogers)

CV: 25 years old, five years of service, quite active, very charming and known as an extremely competent analyst.

1. Volunteered as dedicated analyst to the 'Coating-88' team. Is pleased about the experiment: working in a small team, knows the status of the projects, attends almost all progress meetings, determines priorities in collaboration with the team members. Good contacts lead to mutual respect, and fair share of the available working time. Information about the status of projects allows her to save up to 10% of the analyses, or to stop some in the process. There are far too many unnecessary analyses performed by the lab.

2. In order to work well, the dedication system requires the analyst to be very active in searching for information. Certainly not all analysts will show that commitment. This pays off: 80% remains routine, but 20% of the time is now spent on some research for method variants. Usually she reports back on all work of 'Coating-88' within two or three days after submission.

3. The coordination system is not good at all. The analyst has to do all the work: distributing samples amongst colleagues, collecting results, reporting back to the teams, and policing his peers. It is, on the other hand, very convenient for the researchers to handle all their work through one person in the lab.

4. She is very much in favour of organizing the wet chemical section into teams. For instance, the Rogers group could be divided into three

dyads to be dedicated to the research teams of Oevers. The problem, of course, would be Mrs Carbonnel, who declines to do wet chemical analysis. Smith would love to learn Bacteriology, also to keep the work going when Carbonnel is absent.

5. Overall she finds the managers quite soft: they seldom intervene and have little authority. Most have neglected their skills and knowledge and are not well aware of new developments. Maher is the exception, but he will be promoted very soon, there is little doubt about that.

Mrs Carbonnel: analyst, wet chemical group (Rogers)

CV: 42 years old, unmarried, exclusively French-speaking, very argumentative and difficult to get along with.

1. Job: For ecological reasons, bacteriological analysis has become important in the lab. Has spent some time in Paris (Pasteur Institute) to learn bacteriological methods of analysis. The research has to take place in a well-equipped and totally isolated work space. She is not too busy and determined to protect her turf. Most of the time she can keep busy for a whole day. Let the others mess around with the wet chemical analysis stuff.

2. Has no desire to be included in a team. She only wants to further develop the bacterio research. The others are completely ignorant in that area. The work requires diligence and accuracy, and is best performed by one single person.

3. The lab is an organizational jungle. Her own manager (Rogers) does not even know his own job, and is totally unable to evaluate her work. Has serious question on how the bonuses will be distributed at the end of the year. She feels unappreciated for her special skills, and has never received any financial compensation for it. Given their incompetence, favouritism is the way in which managers give promotions and bonuses.

4. She visibly dislikes the presence of an adviser. She seems very suspicious about the possibility that something happens to her bacterio job.

Mr Paulus: manager, group instrumental analyses (Autoanalysers)

CV: 45 years old colonial career in technical education system. Manager for two years, after a year of specialization on gas chromatography in the UK.

1. Job: Leads a team of six people in charge of a diversity of automatic machines to handle large volumes of analyses. The section occupies a separate space in the lab. The group consists of three men (technical engineers) and three women (analysts). Quite often the men and women quarrel about unequal workloads. The women are not all

that busy and often have waiting times during the execution of the analyses. It happens that they spend the waiting time by knitting, and they usually decline when instruments are to be calibrated or fine-tuned.

2. Has been marginally involved in these useless experiments. Due to the nature of the work, and the physical separation, he, de facto, already has a team. The use of coordinators or dedicated analysts for his team means that an extra link is introduced for supplying the work.

3. Maintains little contact with the research teams. They do not respect the weekly available work-hours of the lab and almost certainly want to perform an excessive number of analyses.

4. Michat and Rogers are far too little involved with their people. They are continuously busy with the computer, and ignore everything else. Little wonder that everybody does what he or she likes down there.

5. Whatever happens, he will not allow his group to get broken up or to have to leave its own physical location. It is pleasant to work with a small team in a confined area. The central area of the wet chemical section is too big, far too noisy and too impersonal to feel at home. It's impossible to have any contact with other people there.

Mrs Donkers: analyst, group instrumental analyses (Paulus)

CV: 23 years old, two years with Omnipaint, training as chemical analyst.

1. Job: Serves and maintains the autoanalysers for large volume work. This involves filling and cleaning every two or three hours. It's busy work but between runs there is always some time to read or talk with colleagues. Some of the men take time out for a smoke as well. Because they go outside, you cannot see them.

2. There are quite often tensions between men and women in the section. They consider us as uninterested, but forget that they have a more advanced specialization. Donkers is very hesitant to do maintenance work on the instruments (fine-tuning and calibration). The work is very delicate and the manuals are usually nowhere to be found.

3. By far she prefers to remain in the instrumental analyses group. It is not too large, has its own separate workspace, and the work is pleasant and not too difficult.

4. The manager is rather authoritarian and in fact dishonest. It is known in the group that he uses data by the analysts to write his own reports, without mentioning the sources. You always have to be careful as to the nature of the work he assigns to you.

Mr Ivens: manager, group 'remote clients'

CV: 42 years old, 20 years of service on all possible jobs in the lab. Became manager five years ago.

1. Job: Responsible for processing of samples which have been sent by other European sites, and for the analysis of all competitive products by other firms (40% of the analyses of competitive products are done by himself). Not too much time pressure. Given the special nature of the work, this section already more or less operates as a team in their separate work space.
2. Contacts are made only by phone, mail or fax, so we have little hassle about priorities. We arrange our work according to our own taste. Ivens considers his own group to be the most all-round and flexible. Analysts share work and help each other out whenever the pressure mounts.
3. Devel is coordinator for the pilot plant of Barrachi. Devel is a very competent analyst. Given that no one volunteered in the other sections, he stepped forward for the job. It is terrible. Every fortnight on Tuesdays and Wednesdays the pilot plant tests all European products. If something goes wrong, all plants in Europe might be halted to produce a particular product. So it happens that 100 or more samples immediately have to be analysed. Delays can cost a fortune. Devel then begs his colleagues for priority and finishes most of the last-minute work by himself. People avoid him during these days. In fact that coordinator job belonged to the sections Michat or Rogers, but their people declined.
4. Ivens favours the idea of continuation of the experiments to get something going in the lab. He openly prefers to keep his own team intact. He would appreciate it if Devel could be relieved of the co-ordinator role for Barrachi.

Mr Devel: analyst, group 'remote clients' (Ivens)

CV: 26 years old, six years of service, excellent analyst.

1. Job: 70% of the time working for indirect clients. Usually they enquire by phone about the work, so there are few difficulties about priorities and the time pressure is low.
2. Volunteered to take the job of coordinator for the pilot plant of Barrachi. It takes up 30% of the time. Especially on Tuesdays and Wednesdays when the pilot plant tests all European products. When everything turns out to be normal, it takes two half days of analysis work. Barrachi then demands absolute priority for testing or retesting his samples, eventually two or three times. Devel is forced to make the tour of all analysts of Michat's and Rogers' sections to ask them to reschedule some of their work. He gets a tremendous amount of resistance. Quite often he has to do the most annoying or time-consuming leftovers by himself. It is obvious that his colleagues go out of their way to avoid him on those days.
3. The coordinator role is very handy for the researchers. They can address themselves to one person who handles all their work. The coordinator serves as a distribution centre within the lab, and has to

patrol his colleagues. It is horrible work; you can see why nobody of Michat's and Rogers' sections wanted to do it.

4. It would be desirable to give the analysts more time to do some research for small improvements of methods and techniques, say 15% of the time. In any case, we have to get rid of the coupling of every analyst to a limited list of analyses as it is now. Why not simply pool our lists and work as a team?

Mr Maher: manager, group methods & techniques

CV: 29 years old, PhD Chemistry, three years service as manager, good reputation as chemist.

1. Job: Has a team of four qualified technicians (technical engineers) in charge of the development of new instruments and the study of variations of analytical methods in order to follow the research developments. Given that addition of any new additive can render an existing procedure unreliable, a lot of vigilance and testing is required.
2. The group works as a team, each of the members takes the lead for some of the research projects and provides assistance and advice to colleagues, whenever necessary.
3. Our biggest problem is up-dated and accurate information. Quite often research teams inquire for procedures which they never use (although we spend weeks developing them), or a project shifts course without us being informed.
4. There is a tremendous opportunity with regard to job enrichment. The computer system has become a hindrance for contact between analysts and researchers. The analysts have no contact, do not know the projects, have no idea what is urgent or necessary and perform a lot of unnecessary and senseless work. It is absolutely vital that something should be done about it, most likely in terms of dedicating analysts to perform all the work of particular teams. This, however, requires training, and our group is able to provide that.
5. It is possible to let analysts spend a certain percentage of their time on method improvement. It would require good coaching by their managers. The past has shown that they spend two or three weeks on a three-day job. The research teams know that and they prefer to come to our section.
6. In particular, the managers have failed to fight obsolescence. They are quite busy, but sometimes poorly informed. Take, for instance, the people in Paulus's section. They claim to know more about gas chromatography than their boss. It's sad to see that none of them can really get to the finesses of their instruments. They are very good at routine work, but they are far from flexible with their equipment.

Mr Barrachi: director, pilot plant

CV: 45 years old, director for five years, prior to that position he spent 15 years in the lab, in almost every position.

1. Job: Leads the pilot plant which synthesizes all new products. In addition to that, every 14 days the pilot plant manufactures some batches of all products of other European sites as a test on quality and standardization.
2. The pilot plant is the third largest user of the lab. Would prefer to have a couple of analysts for himself, but Clark refused repeatedly because of objectivity of analyses (he cannot be blamed for that).
3. On Tuesdays and Wednesdays, products are tested for standardization. Normally it takes two half days of analysis work. When the results do not conform to expectation, absolute priority has to be given to the pilot plant, otherwise we might have to stop the production in other countries. The loss could rapidly run into millions.
4. On such occasions, Barrachi personally comes down to the lab to demand and, when necessary, to threaten Clark and his people to give priority. Given that he knows most of the analysts personally, he considers himself quite successful in this role.
5. The coordination system works excellently. A single person distributes the samples, collects the results, eventually finishes the work and reports back. The nature and urgency of the work brings an amount of tension with it. He himself is under strong pressure from the other sites during such days. Everyone fights for their own corner, or do they?
6. Dedication of some analysts to the pilot plant would be a good idea, but it is not all too clear how to do it. The work comes all of a sudden on those days, then he needs three or four analysts. A permanent team is not necessary.
7. As long as the lab delivers fast and good service, the internal organization of the lab is of lower importance to Barrachi.

Mr Büsch: director, research industrial products

CV: 50 years old, 20 years of service, globe trotter, research director for ten years.

1. Job: Head of eight research teams, totalling 120 people, composed of all possible nationalities. Projects move fast (7 to 8 months) and the team composition changes. Mostly researchers stay one or two years in Brussels on projects.
2. The lab serves the research department. Because of scale factors (equipment and instruments) and because of the routine nature of the analytical work, a centralized laboratory was installed for all research teams. The internal organization of the lab is generally unknown to the outside, and in fact that is purely internal business.
3. There is fierce competition for analyses. Irregular users are delayed: waiting times of four to six weeks have been reported. If you do not insist, you get no help. This situation is intolerable and hampers the progress of the projects.

4. The analysts probably hide samples to test the reality of priority indications of some clients. If they hear no protest, they consider that client definitely second rank.
5. The coordinator role is a good solution. You only have to deal with a single person who is responsible for all your work. In that way the analysts cannot send you back and forth as they usually do.
6. The dedication of an analyst to a research group is not very realistic. Why should a research group spend extra effort to inform an external person? Communication within changing teams is difficult enough. Moreover, some of the analysts barely understand what it is all about, and some projects are even secret. To counter bias, it is generally better that they do not know the expected results.
7. The quality of the work delivered is very good. However, they resist double-checks, as if it is not allowed to check and make sure when the results do not conform to the team's expectations.
8. Büsch has had no direct contact with the experiments. To prepare this meeting he has obtained information from the project leaders.

Mr Oevers: director, research domestic products

CV: 35 years old, six years of service, energetic and visibly on the fast track in Omnipaint.

1. Job: In charge of three teams of researchers working on normal household products. The projects change quickly, and so do the teams. Oevers puts considerable effort into following his teams, and fostering teamwork within his groups.
2. He personally leads 'Coating-88'. The team works well and is obtaining remarkable results. Initially he had to overcome some resistance from his researchers to integrate Miss Smith into the team. Miss Smith, however, is a very attractive young lady, open, communicative, and incredibly active. That has certainly helped. Oevers takes care that she is kept informed, and that the research teams agree among themselves on priorities before she is put to work. Her contribution has had the effect that 10 to 15% of the analyses are not needed, or can be cancelled on the basis of first results.
3. Oevers would prefer a system of dedicated analysts for each of his research teams. It requires a lot of effort, discipline and agreements on both sides, but outcome is worthwhile. The question is how many characters of the calibre of Miss Smith are there among the analysts? At least he is prepared to continue with the system of dedicated analysts.

DISCUSSION QUESTIONS

This case is presented as a consulting assignment. In the teaching situation the case can be worked through in the following ways:

For a session of 1–1½ hours:

1. The case as a whole can be given to small groups to work on, who in turn present their analyses and recommendations.

For a longer session:

2. The case can be run as a role play exercise. Some participants take the roles of the Omnipaint staff. The other participants act as Mr Singer, the consultant, and interview the Omnipaint team. Having collected the case information via the interviews, the participants, working in small groups, formulate an analysis and recommendation.

In both forms of discussion it is vital that participants have read and prepared the material thoroughly in advance.

SUGGESTED READING

Hackman, J. R. (1983) The design of work teams, in *Handbook of Organizational Behaviour* (ed. J. Lorsch), Prentice-Hall, Englewood Cliffs, New Jersey.

Robertson, I. T. and Smith, M. (1985) *Motivation and Job Design: Theory, Research and Practice*, IPM, London.

Work redesign at the production department of a camera plant

SANDRA SCHRUIJER

THE PRODUCT GROUP CAMERAS

The Product Group Cameras, which is part of a large electronics firm, develops, produces and sells cameras for professional and semi-professional use.

THE PRODUCTION DEPARTMENT

Product

The production department produces three different types of cameras. The sub-department called 'existing business' produces two types which have been in production for some time now. The other sub-department produces the most complex and new camera, the so-called CA77.

Operational activities

The operational activities to be performed in the production of the cameras are: (a) assembly of the circuit boards and wiring, which is carried out by female assembly workers, (b) assembly of the circuit boards, wiring and other components into a complete camera; an activity carried out by male assembly workers ('end-assemblers'), and, finally, (c) measurement and electronical adjustment of components and of the camera in its entirety. These activities are executed by male technicians. These three categories of activities form the basis of the production of each camera. However, the way in which these different activities are integrated in the production process, and how and by whom certain activities are carried out, differ for the older products on the one hand and the CA77 on the other.

Human Resources Management in Europe
Edited by Sarah Vickerstaff
Published in 1992 by Chapman & Hall, London. ISBN 0 412 45380 0

Structure

Apart from the existing business and the production of the CA77, two other sections belong to the production department: Pilot Production, which tests the feasibility of the production of new cameras, and Special Production, which deals with the customers and their special wishes concerning the product. The following staff departments are added to production: Logistics (including Entry Control and Production Planning), Purchase, Quality Control, Configuration Control and Administration.

The production department is managed by a department head. In total 128 employees work at the production department; 71 directly and 57 indirectly.

THE CA77

Background

The CA77 and its accompanying new production process arose out of a need to survive in an increasingly competitive market. The Task Force CA77 consisted of employees from development and production who intensively worked together for two years to develop the new product and process. To ensure high product quality, it was considered important that the availability of direct feedback was incorporated into the process, so that inspection control was built in as much as possible. The philosophy was, furthermore, that each employee was to be given responsibility for his or her own work so as to foster commitment to the job and the department.

Production process

Production occurs in flow. On the basis of an order, a list of all the circuit boards and wiring is composed and subsequently attached to a 'materials car', on which all the necessary circuit boards are deposited. Each assembly worker makes the circuit board next on the list when it is her turn and puts her name on it, behind the circuit board she assembled (which is required for the feedback). This implies that each assembly worker is capable of making all the different circuit boards which are part of the CA77. Thus, the assembly workers as a group produce the required circuit boards. After soldering the circuit board it is tested by the assembly worker with the help of a specially designed computerized tester. This device indicates whether errors are made in the assembly of the circuit board and, if so, where. Errors are corrected by the worker, the board is tested again, etc., until the tester reports no further errors. Those who make the wiring receive direct feedback via an electronic system which informs the assembly worker directly when a wire is assembled incorrectly.

After the assembly of the circuit boards and wiring, the next group of assemblers, 'end-assemblers', produce a total camera of the boards and wiring, and functionally test the wiring. If necessary, these 'end assemblers' provide feedback to the assembly workers.

Subsequently, the components are pretested and adjusted by the technicians. Finally, technicians carry out the end- and functional test in which the camera as a whole is tested. The technicians feed back to the assemblers in case of errors.

A daily 'flow meeting', in which the assembly supervisor, process facilitator (formerly the quality inspector; see later), an assembly worker, a technician, and technical assistant take part, monitors whether the production activities match the planning, so that in case of deviations direct action can be taken.

Structure

The CA77 department consists of nine assembly workers assembling the circuit boards, and three assembling the wiring (these assemblers have no vocational training; their pay scales vary between 20 and 25 with the majority in 25). The nine end-assemblers received vocational training; their pay scales also vary from 20 to 25 with the majority in 25. All the assembly workers are managed by one assembly supervisor. The technicians ($n = 10$) went to technical college; their pay scales vary between 30 and 40. The CA77 project manager plus five other (technical) employees also belong to the department. The technicians are managed by the test-room supervisor.

PROBLEMS OF THE CA77 DEPARTMENT

Modifications

A major problem concerned the department's inability to realize the production planning: only 40% of the planned number of cameras were produced. The cause of this lies outside the production department: a large number of modifications in the product design created many disturbances in the production process.[1] These modifications imply that assembly work and/or testing must be done differently and hence can cause severe delays. In addition, (adequate) information concerning modifications does not always reach the assembly workers in time. Due to the lack of adequate information, and due to the fact that a fair number of assembly workers are newly recruited, modifications are inappropriately executed. Lack of time is the underlying reason for not sufficiently training new personnel. Finally, it is not possible to test recently

---

[1] This problem, the origin of which is external to the production department, will be treated as a given. No attempt will be made in this paper to address the origins of the problem.

implemented modifications using the computerized tester. This means that errors are exported to end-assembly and the testing department, and that no immediate feedback is available, which impedes learning.

Supervision

The assembly workers are satisfied with their supervisor. He is seen as someone who listens to his subordinates' criticisms, ideas and suggestions and they generally like the way he gives them responsibility for their work. The technicians, however, are rather dissatisfied with their supervisor: they feel that he should listen to them more and exhibit a greater interest in their opinions and ideas and actually act in line with these. They want a greater say in important decisions and need to be informed more. They have the impression that their supervisor emphasizes quantity at the expense of quality.

Pay

All three groups complain about their pay and the pay system. These complaints are particularly evident among the technicians and the end-assemblers. They refer to the limited promotion possibilities and the relatively low salary in relation to the complexity of the work and in comparison to colleagues working for other companies. The female assembly workers are generally slightly positive concerning their pay.

Summarizing, the female assembly workers are satisfied to very satisfied with their work; the end-assemblers satisfied and the technicians somewhat dissatisfied. In order to understand these differences it is necessary to describe briefly how the work at the production department has changed over time.

CHANGES IN THE WORK AT THE PRODUCTION DEPARTMENT OVER TIME

The way it was

Most of the employees working at the CA77 department were already producing cameras. The work, however, was different. Cameras were produced in batches. Assembly workers produced series of identical circuit boards and did not test these themselves. Several times a day a sample of an individual's assembly work was subjected to quality inspection. Special controllers visually inspected the assembled circuit boards. The end-assemblers also worked in batch. The assembled products were stored and only much later assembled into a complete camera. The technicians measured series of the same circuit boards. These boards, as well as other assembly work, could still contain many errors since the visual inspection was not very accurate. Moreover, adequate feedback to the person responsible for the error was, due to the leadtime (up to 6 months!), impossible (who produced the item?), and unfruitful (no learning can be achieved).

The atmosphere at the department was quite hierarchical; the supervisor was responsible for work done by his or her subordinates. Executing work was strictly separated from controlling it. Also, the assembly of circuit boards, of the wiring, end-assembly and testing were activities which were both geographically (technicians worked in special little compartments) and socially separated: hardly any contact existed between these groups.

The work as it is now

With the new camera and production process, the work of the assemblers and technicians changed considerably. The philosophy is that employees should be given responsibility and direct feedback. The female assembly workers obtain immediate feedback via computerized testers of circuit boards and wiring. Errors can be corrected immediately. But the assembly workers receive more than immediate feedback: their jobs are enriched too! Apart from carrying out the assembly activities, the workers also inspect their own work. And in actual fact this inspection is work that used to be done by the technicians.

Assemblers are themselves responsible for the quality of their work; a responsibility which is enabled by their current relationship with the staff who prepare the instruction manuals. In the past no direct communication was possible; now the assemblers go directly to those responsible for the instructions and booklets in case of uncertainties. Also their pay has changed: assembly workers used to be paid according to scale 15 or 20. Scale 25 was virtually impossible. Now assembly workers either receive scale 20 or 25.

The end-assemblers' work also changed, although to a less considerable extent. They assemble in flow and activities are rotated. The end-assemblers test the wiring functionally with the aid of a computerized tester before assembling it into the camera. Feedback is received from the test room. They, too, are held responsible for their work as manifested for example in their participation in the planning and execution of their activities. The pay structure has changed for them as well: in the past, scales 15, 20 and 25 were applied to end-assemblers. Now they are paid according to scale 20 or 25 with a majority in 25.

For the technicians, however, not all changes are positive. Circuit boards are practically flawless by the time cameras arrive in the test room. Therefore the technicians' work no longer involves finding causes of malfunctioning of circuit boards, but consists predominantly of adjusting the boards, which is a routine activity. Another change is the location of their work: previously in special compartments, now in the production hall next to the end-assembly. No changes in pay have taken place.

DISCUSSION QUESTIONS

1. How high is the motivation and satisfaction of assembly workers, end-assemblers and technicians in the current situation? Explain.
2. How can the motivation and satisfaction be improved within the present production philosophy?
3. Is there anything which could have been done to prevent the problems within the test room?
4. Evaluate the managerial style of the two supervisors. Are they in line with the new philosophy? Could you suggest any changes in the supervisory style?
5. Discuss the ways in which each of the three groups receive feedback. What are the differences? Are there ways to improve the quality of feedback?
6. How can the production department better cope with the disturbing impact of modifications in product design?
7. Can you conceive of any problems with respect to the interface between the CA77 department and the 'existing business'?
8. Which organizational changes need to take (have taken) place in order to make the new philosophy plus accompanying production process a success?

SUGGESTED READING

Cherns, A. (1987) The principles of sociotechnical design revisited. *Human Relations*, **4**, 153–62.

Hackman, R. J. and Oldham, G. R. (1980) *Work Redesign*, Addison Wesley, Reading, Mass.

Wall, T. D. and Martin, R. (1987) Job and work design, in *International Review of Industrial and Organizational Psychology* (eds C. L. Cooper and I. T. Robertson). Wiley, Chichester.

Walton, R. E. (1985) From control to commitment in the workplace. *Harvard Business Review*, 76–84.

CASE 7

Redesigning the organization of work in eastern Europe

JOHN E. M. THIRKELL and DIMITRINA DIMITROVA

INTRODUCTION

From the late 1970s the improvement of economic performance and productivity was a central problem for the countries of eastern Europe and this continued through the 1980s. Whereas in the west the path to improvements in economic performance was regarded as requiring industrial restructuring and improved forms of company management, in eastern Europe the issue of restructuring was largely excluded by the political commitment to full employment. Similarly, the decentralization of industrial management would have required a surrender of central control that, at the political level, was then deemed unacceptable.

This constraint in practice excluded the western approach that managements should be held responsible for the development of organizational and labour relations strategies to improve the performance of their enterprises. Instead management's primary responsibility remained that of carrying out instructions from higher levels. In this context there was more emphasis on the need to improve the motivation and discipline of workers than the creativity and motivation of managers. In the socialist countries great managerial resources were devoted to the 'Scientific Organization of Work' as the application of Taylorism to the design of tasks and incentive payment systems was termed. However, researches by sociologists and others led to the questioning of the assumption that improved worker performance was simply a problem of industrial engineering. Thus the leading Soviet sociologist Tatiana Zaslavskaya argued that this required a much wider recognition of the 'human factor' through the development of structures and mechanisms for worker participation and involvement.

From the late 1970s the major change in the organization of work was the shift from what were termed 'individual' forms of work to the new 'collective' forms. Essentially this meant that workers were paid on the work done by the team or group instead of the work done by the individual. The allocation of the team's earnings to its members was

Human Resources Management in Europe
Edited by Sarah Vickerstaff
Published in 1992 by Chapman & Hall, London. ISBN 0 412 45380 0

done internally within the team. In the Soviet Union, Bulgaria and Czechoslovakia the new teams were termed 'brigades'.

LABOUR RELATIONS STRATEGY IN BULGARIA

In Bulgaria, from which the two case studies are taken, the decision to make the brigade the generic structure of work organization was taken by a special conference of the Communist Party in 1978. This meant that all enterprise managements had to organize their workers into brigades. Over the next seven years the introduction and diffusion of brigade organization was the principal component of labour relations strategy at the national level. A series of regulations and laws were introduced setting out the design criteria for the brigade as a unit of organizational structure and the mechanisms that were intended to make it operate. There were several main criteria for the design of the brigade: techno-logical, accounting, size and self-management. Their application deter-mined the brigade's boundaries, size and composition – that is, which workers (which jobs) should be included in a brigade, which should be outside in another brigade or in no brigade. The accounting criterion meant that the brigade should be a cost centre with its own accounts for the costs of labour, materials, energy and depreciation and, ideally, should be able to compare these costs with its contribution – that is, the results of its work in terms of what it produced whether it was a machine, a single unit, a part or a service. The technological criterion meant that the brigade should be based on a complete technological (production) cycle of a measurable intermediate or final product, thus combining the accounting criterion. The accounting and technological criteria were most easily satisfied by larger brigades covering perhaps a department or other unit responsible for producing a final product. These criteria therefore conflicted with the two other criteria of size and self-management (autonomy). The criterion of size drew on the findings of psychologists and sociologists of work and organization that smaller groups are socially more integrated. This was consistent with the self-management criterion in that smaller groups are more able to manage themselves and take rapid decisions to solve immediate problems. The self-managing brigade had three internal institutions: the brigade assembly, comprising all the members of the brigade as the final auth-ority in decision making; the brigade leader and the brigade council, composed of representatives of the brigade, both elected by the brigade assembly. The principal monthly mechanism which made the brigade assembly work, in the sense of involving the active participation of the members, was the distribution of earnings according to what was termed the coefficient of labour. This provided criteria for the distribution between the brigade members of the brigade's earnings for the month. The proposals for the distribution of earnings were prepared by the brigade leader in consultation with the brigade council, and these pro-posals had to be voted by the brigade assembly. Other mechanisms included agreements with management and between brigades in sequential production processes.

The process of strategy formulation in Bulgaria was initiated from the top and imposed on the managements of enterprises with only limited consultation with enterprises. Consequently, most managements implemented the national strategy mechanically, carrying out the orders from the top. The two cases set out here are untypical in that the managements of both enterprises used the pressure from the national level as an opportunity to develop labour relations strategies which they saw as necessary for increasing the efficiency of their enterprises. These cases are intended as illustrations of questions relating to organizational design, labour relations and the management of human resources with particular reference to the design of work units (teams) and the mechanisms to make them work.

METALS

This enterprise, opened in 1969, is located in one of the oldest industrial centres in Bulgaria. In 1985, the workforce totalled 3000 and there were three main production departments and auxiliary departments producing equipment and spare parts.

The economic problems of the plant were seen as deriving from poor labour relations and management of human resources expressed in low utilization of machinery, high labour turnover and absenteeism. The initiative in strategy formulation was taken by a small group of three key individuals in the management team, who saw the identification of the workforce with the means of production – their machines – as the key strategic issue. This meant that workers should feel a sense of ownership of their machines and equipment and a corresponding sense of responsibility. The management team judged that this would require a transformation in the relationships between the different levels of the organization: between management at the top and the middle level of the department and between them and the workers at the base. Management strategy was related to two general design criteria, in addition to that of accounting: first, that brigade organization should be as complete as practicable, including the widest possible range of occupations found within the enterprise; second, that brigades should be relatively small – for example, a brigade for each shift rather than covering two or more shifts – thus implementing the social criterion. By 1985, 98% of the workers had been organized into 46 complex brigades and 30 specialist brigades. Complex brigades were made up of workers of different skill grades and were usually engaged in direct production. Typically they had 15–25 members. Specialist brigades were smaller and composed of perhaps 8–10 maintenance or ancillary workers.

At the base of the enterprise the implementation of the first, accounting criterion led to the inclusion of clerical and lower level administrative personnel within production brigades, instead of servicing the operational management of the department as in the previous structure. Restructuring was not confined to the base: attempts were made to apply a form of brigade organization to managers at the levels of the department and enterprise.

Management judged that the dynamic of 'pressure from below' – that is, upwards from the brigades – was a necessary element for the success of their strategy for involving the workforce. They also envisaged the brigades organizing operations, competing between themselves and generating lateral as well as vertical pressures. Management recognized that to make the structure work as they intended a comprehensive set of mechanisms was necessary. They therefore designed a system of contracts and other mechanisms. There were contracts between complex brigades, between complex and specialist brigades and between brigades and departmental management and also between departments. The general content of these contracts was essentially similar: management agreed to provide the brigade with the machines and materials needed for the planned task; the brigade was liable for deductions from its wage fund if failure to meet the targets was judged to have been its responsibility. Contracts between brigades required the supply of semi-finished products or services. In cases of disputes over responsibilty between brigades or between brigades and departmental management there was provision for arbitration.

MATERIALS

Materials was a plant in the textile sector. The critical event which triggered the process of redesigning the organization was a serious fire which destroyed part of the factory and led to the dispersal of many of the workers. The managing director faced the problems of reconstructing the building, restoring production levels and attracting back workers who had left. At Materials, there was a radical restructuring of the middle level of management with the abolition of the departmental level. The structure of the enterprise thus became one of two levels, the brigade and the enterprise thus conforming to what has been called 'the clothes hanger' model of enterprise organization. This abolition of the middle level of management was a central feature of the Director's strategy for enterprise development. He restructured the way in which work was organized and remunerated. The main factory was rebuilt as a single large hall with the stores located in the middle. The production process was the responsibility of two large brigades, one of 300 and the other of about 200 located on either side of the store from which raw materials were taken and to which finished or semi-finished products were returned and accounted for. In effect the accounts showed the workers 'buying' materials from the stores and 'selling' finished or semi-finished products to the stores. The main change in managerial structure was that the middle level of management was abolished and most managers at this level were transferred down into the two brigades, or in few cases became members of the management brigade of about 60 members at the top of the enterprise. These structural changes were intended to resolve the issues of linking the interests of managerial staff to the overall results of production, and of increasing productivity and quality through material interests and extended collectivity in production. The restructuring resolved these issues: previous production levels were achieved with fewer workers and quality control and earnings increased. The inclusion of managerial and engineering staff in the brigades had, unforeseen consequences for the dynamics of brigade organization: in these big brigades with large brigade councils the influence of the engineers was perceived by the workers as predominant, and this led to the trade union organizers in the brigades assuming a much stronger role in representing worker interests than in smaller, less qualificationally differentiated brigades where 'direct' democracy was more common.

DISCUSSION QUESTIONS

1. What are the advantages and disadvantages of large and small work teams?
2. Is it appropriate to try to integrate lower levels of management and clerical workers with production workers by a common organizational structure? When a work team comprises workers of different levels of skill and qualification and perhaps supervisors or lower management, what internal tensions may develop and how might they be overcome?
3. Is the creation of strong work groups with the capacity to assert their interests potentially dysfunctional for management?
4. Has the concept of 'pressure from below' – that is, of an organization of work which leads to work teams or groups pressing management at higher levels – any relevance for Western management?

SUGGESTED READING

Petkov, K. and Thirkell, J. E. M. (1991) *Labour Relations in Eastern Europe: Organisational Design and Dynamics*, Routledge, London.

PART THREE

Employee Resourcing

'Recruitment is the biggest single challenge facing personnel managers in the 1990s' (Curnow, 1989). So began an article reviewing the British Institute of Personnel Management's latest survey of recruitment and selection practices among British firms. It has always been important for companies, of all sizes and in all sectors, to obtain the right quantity and quality of staff to meet their needs. The costs of poor recruitment and selection can be significant. They range from a failure to find the required employees with the attendant implications for meeting output targets; through taking on inadequate staff who may have a deleterious effect on quality and morale; to high labour turnover and recurring recruitment, selection and possibly training costs. For companies dependent upon the 'know how' and flair of managers and professionals, poor recruitment can mean the difference between organizational success or failure. These issues are not new; however, many would argue that finding and choosing new employees is becoming increasingly difficult and ever more vital. In Europe as a whole, skill needs are changing in tune with technological innovation, and the need for new and updated skills in eastern European industry will be critical in the next decade.

In addition, demographic changes are effecting the labour supply in many countries; declining numbers of young people and ageing populations are challenging traditional recruitment strategies. The countries of eastern Europe are experiencing the need to develop genuinely free labour markets and the problems of retaining newly mobile workers.

In many western European societies the number of women working outside the home has continued to increase. Among EC countries Denmark, the UK, Portugal and France head the league table with women accounting for over 40% of the total workforce. Spain, Ireland and Greece have the fewest women working outside the home, but even in these countries women now account for just over 30% of the total workforce (Hootsmans, 1992, pp. 186–8). With increasing numbers of women in paid employment the pressures on governments and individual companies to address equal opportunities issues is building up.

Labour markets are increasingly internationalized, making it important for companies to be aware of what is going on outside their usual catchment areas. This requires an understanding of labour mobility patterns; the different systems of qualification pertaining in European countries; and a sensitivity to the complex problems of managing a multi-cultural workforce.

Many textbooks, such as this one, now use the term 'employee resourcing' rather than the more traditional 'recruitment and selection' in connection with these issues. It is tempting to assume that this is just more jargon. However, it can be defended because it forces us to see this area of human resource policy as wider than simply finding and choosing new employees. There are always a number of ways in which an organization can meet its labour requirements: by recruitment, transfer, retraining, labour substitution/mechanization, overtime working or raising productivity. Finally, and least desirably, in the absence of the required staff the company may need to modify output targets. Thus, the notion 'employee resourcing' encourages us to remember that there are different possible responses to staff vacancies. This may be particularly vital if we are entering a period in which the labour supply is changing, skill needs are turbulent and the legal framework more exacting. The company that can be imaginative in these circumstances is likely to compete well for that scarce resource: the ideal employee.

HUMAN RESOURCE PLANNING

The prerequisite for good employee resourcing is understanding the organization's needs at the corporate, job and individual levels. Human resource planning is the means by which the organization can begin to develop a systematic approach to identifying its labour needs. In practice, human resource planning is often maligned as a set of over-complicated statistical techniques that try to predict an essentially unpredictable future. Which Berlin-based companies in the middle 1980s were drawing up plans for the implications of re-unification on local labour markets? Even if the future is uncertain there is no excuse for not understanding the profile of the existing workforce and, at minimum, considering the extent to which this workforce can meet requirements in the short to medium term.

Definition

Vickerstaff (1989) gives the following three-fold definition of human resource planning:

1. To meet future labour/staff needs.
2. To utilize existing human resources more effectively.
3. To integrate and monitor human resource policies.

The value of human resource planning is not in the attempt to produce all-embracing plans but in the discipline of considering, comparing and evaluating different possible responses to employee resourcing issues. At its best, human resource planning systems should raise the quality of decisions made, as knowledge and understanding of the organization's current position and possible future directions improve. It also implies the

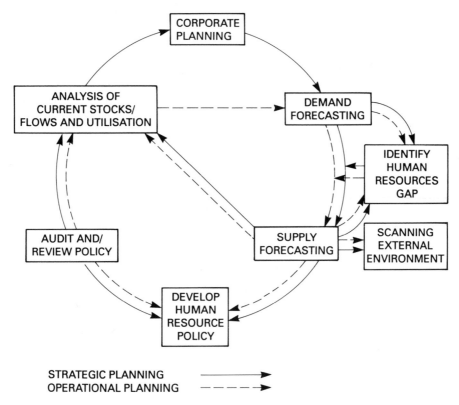

Fig. P3.1   A framework for human resource planning
Source: S. Vickerstaff (1989).

need to coordinate human resource planning activities with business planning more generally.

Human resource planning can begin by analysis of current stocks and flows of employees within the organization. By focusing on current patterns of productivity – labour turnover, absenteeism, promotion, transfer, retirement, etc. – an organization can begin to assess the short-run implications of its existing workforce and identify future possible issues such as career blockages and succession problems. This kind of analysis can make the organization think about the adequacy of its current employee resourcing policies.

The framework for human resource planning (Figure P3.1) indicates schematically how short- and long-term planning activities can be integrated as part of a continuous planning, review and evaluation of the human resource management effort.

LABOUR MARKETS AND LABOUR SUPPLY

With the changes in labour supply mentioned above it will become increasingly important for organizations to understand labour market trends both within and across national boundaries. A very noticeable feature of labour markets within Europe in the 1980s is the increase in part-time work in almost all countries. Linked to this have been related tendencies for other 'non-standard' forms of employment, such as temporary work, fixed-term contracts and self-employment to increase in some countries (OECD, 1991, pp. 44–53). These trends are typically discussed in terms of the competitive pressures on organizations to reduce labour costs, respond to technological innovations and in general react flexibly to changing market contingencies. As Teague (1991, p. 3) has commented: 'Throughout the 1980s it was fashionable to regard the European labour market as suffering from inflexibilities and rigidities.' These rigidities were seen to arise from labour and social welfare legislation and trade union influence through collective bargaining arrangements: management's room for manoeuvre was constrained. Some European countries, for example, Italy and Germany, have modified legislation to make the employment of non-standard forms of labour easier (OECD, 1986, p. 107). In Britain, legislation on trade unions was part of a strategy to increase flexibility in the labour market (Beaumont, 1990).

Part-time work has continued to increase as a proportion of total employment in many European countries. The term 'part-time work' covers a considerable range of work situations, in terms of the hours worked and whether the work is temporary or permanent. Text 3 provides figures on part-time employment in Europe and highlights the tendency for women to predominate in this category of work. The recruitment, selection and retention of part-time workers raises particular human resource management problems which are explored in Case 8.

RECRUITMENT AND SELECTION

Ideally, recruitment and selection should be a process that flows from the organization's ongoing human resource planning and job evaluation

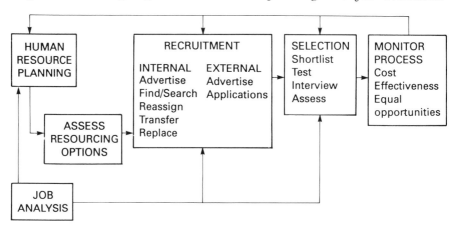

Fig. P3.2 The recruitment and selection process.

activities. Figure P3.2 shows schematically how the different parts of the process are linked together. Human resource planning activities should allow an organization to keep under review, and to forecast, the labour requirements. Analysis of stocks and flows of staff will aid identification of replacement needs. Job analysis, involving the review and assessment of the responsibilities, tasks, skills requirements and necessary aptitudes for jobs, aids the development of job descriptions and personnel specifications where relevant. Planning and analysis together contribute to understanding the numbers, qualifications and skills that are required.

Assessing resourcing options requires the organization to consider the different ways in which it might meet a given need for staff; for example, whether to recruit from among the existing staff or whether to search for new recruits. Research on recruitment and selection processes reveals that companies remain traditional in their approaches, through advertising in the press and using employment agencies for recruitment, while the interview remains pre-eminent among selection techniques. The key issues at the recruitment stage are costs, targeting, effectiveness and image. The organization seeks to attract suitable applicants at a reasonable cost. Information given to potential recruits is important for framing realistic expectations and as marketing material. Equally, information gained from applicants at this stage is crucial in enabling the organization to begin the selection process.

Cartoon: 'We think you'd make an ideal manager – but unfortunately customers find a bald head and moustache more reassuring.' © 1986 Geoffrey Dickinson, from the *Financial Times*, 14/2/86.

The interview has been much criticized as a predictor of future performance, but managers remain wedded to it (Cascio, 1991, pp. 271–7). The tendency for untrained interviewers to rely on 'gut feelings', which typically means their prejudices and stereotypes, has been much criticized from an equal opportunities perspective. (See the cartoon, reproduced with permission, from *Financial Times*, 14 February 1986.)

Large companies have been more willing to experiment with new techniques, especially in the recruitment of managers. Psychometric tests, personality tests, in-tray exercises, aptitude tests have all increased in popularity. Assessment centres, which use multiple selection methods in an attempt to increase the validity and reliability of decisions, have gained in importance. However, techniques such as these are often outside the price range of small companies. Equity and fairness are increasingly demanded by job applicants in the recruitment and selection process, and equal opportunities issues are increasingly receiving attention in legislation and company practice. With more and more women working in paid employment outside the home, issues of discrimination in the workplace have a higher visibility.

The cases in the rest of this section look at a number of different aspects and techniques of employee resourcing. Text 3 looks at the growth and pattern of part-time employment in a number of different countries. The discussion issues arising from the text focus on why part-time work is increasingly prevalent and poses questions about the implications of part-time work for personnel policies. Case 8 looks at the recruitment difficulties of a small firm and asks readers to consider imaginative and cost-effective strategies for securing the required workforce. Case 9 considers equal opportunities issues; it reminds us that selection is a two-way process, not only is the organization trying to choose but so is the individual. Recruitment is the first point of contact for the applicant and therefore first impressions begin with the advert, recruitment material and reputation of the organization. Text 4 and Case 10 consider the application of particular selection methods. In the first of these the use of graphology (handwriting analysis) is discussed along with other methods. In Case 10 we look at the development of an assessment centre technique for the identification and selection of managerial talent, in a context where the skills required of managers were changing.

SUGGESTED READING FOR PART THREE

Beaumont, P. B. (1990) *Change in Industrial Relations*, Routledge, London.

Cascio, W. F. (1991) Recruitment and initial screening, Chapter 12, in *Applied Psychology in Personnel Management*, Prentice-Hall International, Eaglewood Cliffs, pp. 249–77 New Jersey.

Curnow, B. (1989) Recruit, retrain, retain: personnel management and the three Rs. *Personnel Management* (November), pp. 40–7.

Curran, M. M. (1988) Gender and recruitment: people and places in the labour market. *Work, Employment and Society*, **2** (No. 3, September), pp. 335–51.

Dowling, P. J. and Schuler, R. S. (1990) Recruitment and selection of international employees, Chapter 3 in *International Dimensions of Human Resource
Management*, PWS-Kent Publishing Company, Boston, pp. 47–78.

Hootsmans, H. (1992) Beyond 1992: Dutch and British corporations and the
challenge of dual-career couples, in *Dual-Earner Families* (eds S. Lewis, D. N.
Izraeli and H. Hootsmans), Sage, London, pp. 185–203.

OECD (1991) *The OECD Employment Outlook*, OECD, Paris.

OECD (1986) *Flexibility in the Labour Market*, OECD, Paris.

Scullion, H. (1992) Attracting management globetrotters. *Personnel Management*
(January), pp. 28–32.

Teague, P. (1991) Human resource management, labour market institutions and
European integration. *Human Resource Management Journal*, **2** (No. 1, Autumn),
pp. 1–21.

Torrington, D., Hall, L., Haylor, I. and Myers, J. (1991) *Employee Resourcing*,
Institution of Personnel Management, London.

Vickerstaff, S. (1989) Human resource planning, in *Human Resource Management*
(ed. C. Molander), Chartwell-Bratt, Bromley, Kent, pp. 22–41.

TEXT 3

The growth of part-time work in Europe

Tables T3.1 and T3.2 give comparative figures on part-time working from the *OECD Employment Outlook*, 1991. These figures show that part-time work, especially for women, has been on the increase over the 1980s in most countries. The term 'part-time' covers a wide range of different employment situations, in terms of hours worked and degrees of job security. The advantage of part-time work for both employer and employee is often seen to be the greater flexibility it offers. The employer can better match fluctuations in demand by employing part-timers to cover peaks without necessarily offering long-term secure employment. Employees may value the opportunity to work part time as a means of balancing the demands of paid employment and domestic responsibilities, such as childcare. However, part-time work has typically been seen as low status, marginal employment; with the attendant implications for pay and career prospects.

DISCUSSION QUESTIONS

1. Why has part-time work increased in a number of European countries?
2. Why are women typically over-represented among the ranks of part-time workers? How would you begin to explain different participation rates for women in different European countries?
3. What are the implications of increasing numbers of part-time workers for personnel policy in the following areas:
   - recruitment and selection
   - labour utilization
   - training
   - equal opportunities?

SUGGESTED READING

IDS (1990) *Part-Time Workers*, IDS Study No. 459, Incomes Data Services, London.

Cook, A. H. (1992) 'Can work requirements accommodate to the needs of dual-earner families?', in *Dual-Earner Families International Perspectives* (eds S. Lewis, D. N. Izraeli and H. Hootsmans), Sage, London, pp. 204–20.

Table T3.1 Size and composition of part-time employment, 1979–1990[a] (percentages). From OECD Employment Outlook 1991 © 1991 OECD

| | Part-time employment as a proportion of | | | | | | | | | Women's share in part-time employment | | |
| | Total employment | | | Male employment | | | Female employment | | | | | |
	1979	1983	1990	1979	1983	1990	1979	1983	1990	1979	1983	1990
Australia	15.9	17.5	21.3	5.2	6.2	8.0	35.2	36.4	40.1	78.7	78.0	78.1
Austria	7.6	8.4	8.8[b]	1.5	1.5	1.6[b]	18.0	20.0	20.0[b]	87.8	88.4	88.8[b]
Belgium	6.0	8.1	10.2[b]	1.0	2.0	1.7[b]	16.5	19.7	25.0[b]	88.9	84.0	89.6[b]
Canada	12.5	15.4	15.4	5.7	7.6	8.1	23.3	26.1	24.4	72.1	71.3	71.0
Denmark	22.7	23.8	23.7[c]	5.2	6.6	9.0[c]	46.3	44.7	41.5[c]	86.9	84.7	79.4[c]
Finland[c]	6.7	8.3	7.2	3.2	4.5	4.4	10.6	12.5	10.2	74.7	71.7	67.8
France[d]	8.2	9.7	12.0	2.4	2.6	3.5	16.9	20.0	23.8	82.2	84.4	83.1
Germany	11.4	12.6	13.2[c]	1.5	1.7	2.1[c]	27.6	30.0	30.6[c]	91.6	91.9	90.5[c]
Greece	–	6.5	5.5[c]	–	3.7	2.9[c]	–	12.1	10.3[c]	–	61.2	65.7[c]
Ireland	5.1	6.6	8.1[c]	2.1	2.7	3.8[c]	13.1	15.5	17.1[c]	71.2	71.6	68.2[c]
Italy	5.3	4.6	5.7[b]	3.0	2.4	3.1[b]	10.6	9.4	10.9[b]	61.4	64.8	64.7[b]
Japan	15.4	16.2	17.6[b]	7.5	7.3	8.0[b]	27.8	29.8	31.9[b]	70.1	72.9	73.0[b]

Luxembourg	5.8	6.3	6.5[c]	1.0	1.0	2.0[c]	17.1	17.0	15.1[c]	87.5	88.9	80.0[c]
Netherlands[d]	16.6	21.4	33.2	5.5	7.2	15.8	44.0	50.1	61.7	76.4	77.3	70.4
New Zealand	13.9	15.3	20.1	4.9	5.0	8.5	29.1	31.4	35.2	77.7	79.8	76.1
Norway	25.3	29.0	26.6	7.3	7.7	8.8	50.9	63.3	48.2	83.0	83.7	81.8
Portugal	7.8	–	5.9[b]	2.5	–	3.1[b]	16.5	–	10.0[b]	80.4	–	69.8[b]
Spain	–	–	4.8[b]	–	–	1.6[b]	–	–	11.9[b]	–	–	77.2[b]
Sweden	23.6	24.8	23.2	5.4	6.3	7.3	46.0	45.9	40.5	87.5	86.6	83.7
United Kingdom	16.4	19.4	21.8[b]	1.9	3.3	5.0[b]	39.0	42.4	43.8[b]	92.8	89.8	87.0[b]
United States	16.4	18.4	16.9	9.0	10.8	10.0	26.7	28.1	25.2	68.0	66.8	67.6

[a] For sources and definitions, see Annex 1.B OECD *Employment Outlook 1989* and Annex 1.C OECD *Employment Outlook 1990*, except as indicated below for the Netherlands.
[b] Data are for 1989.
[c] Data are for 1988.
[d] Break in series in 1985.
[e] The 1990 data for male employment include conscripts, contrary to the situation for earlier years.

Sources: Australia: Australian Bureau of Statistics, *The Labour Force Australia.*
Austria: Central Statistical Office, *Mikrozensus.*
Belgium, Denmark, France, Germany, Greece, Ireland, Italy, Luxembourg, the United Kingdom: EUROSTAT, *Labour Force Sample Survey.*
Canada: Statistics Canada, *The Labour Force.*
Finland: Central Statistical Office of Finland, *Labour Force Survey.*
Japan: Bureau of Statistics, *Labour Force Survey.* Data refer to non-agricultural industries.
New Zealand: Labour and Employment Gazette.
Netherlands: Data were provided by the Central Bureau of Statistics.
Norway: Central Bureau of Statistics, *Labour Market Statistics.*
Sweden: National Central Bureau of Statistics, *The Labour Force Survey.*
United States: U.S. Department of Labor, Bureau of Labor Statistics, *Employment and Earnings.*

Source: OECD (1991).

Table T3.2 Size and composition of self-employment,[a] 1979–1989 (percentages). From OECD Employment Out-look 1991 © 1991 OECD

	Self-employment as a proportion of									Women's share in self-employment		
	Total employment			Male employment			Female employment					
	1979	1983	1989	1979	1983	1989	1979	1983	1989	1979	1983	1989
North America												
Canada	6.7	7.1	7.2	7.2	7.8	7.9	6.0	6.2	6.2	35.4	37.5	39.0
United States	7.1	7.7	7.5	8.7	9.5	9.0	4.9	5.6	5.8	29.3	32.3	35.5
Japan	14.0	13.3	12.0	14.6	13.7	12.8	12.9	12.6	10.8	34.5	36.6	35.8
Central and Western Europe												
Austria	8.9	8.1	6.6	–	–	–	–	–	–	–	–	–
Belgium	11.2	12.3	12.9	12.6	14.1	15.5	8.8	9.2	9.0	28.0	28.4	28.5
France	10.6	10.5	10.5	–	–	–	–	–	–	–	–	–
Germany	7.7	–	8.4	9.4	–	–	4.8	–	–	23.1	–	–
Ireland[b]	10.4	10.7	13.0	–	–	–	–	–	–	–	–	–
Luxembourg	9.4	8.8	7.4	–	–	–	–	–	–	–	–	–
Netherlands	8.8	8.6	7.8	–	–	–	–	–	–	–	–	–
Switzerland	–	–	–	–	–	–	–	–	–	–	–	–
United Kingdom	6.6	8.6	11.5	9.0	11.1	15.7	3.2	5.1	6.3	19.4	24.9	24.6

Southern Europe												
Greece[b]	32.0	27.9	27.4	34.0	32.8	33.1	25.7	15.2	15.1	19.9	15.3	17.2
Italy	18.9	20.7	22.4	21.7	24.1	26.3	12.8	13.5	15.1	20.8	21.2	23.3
Portugal	12.1	17.0	17.2	–	–	–	–	–	–	–	–	–
Spain	15.7	17.0	17.6	17.1	18.2	19.2	12.5	14.1	14.1	23.5	24.9	25.8
Turkey	–	–	–	–	–	–	–	–	–	–	–	–
Nordic countries												
Denmark	9.2	8.5	6.9	–	–	–	–	–	–	–	–	–
Finland	6.1	7.0	8.7	7.9	9.1	11.4	4.2	4.9	5.9	33.1	34.2	33.5
Norway	6.6	6.8	6.4	8.9	9.6	8.8	3.4	3.2	3.5	21.4	21.0	25.8
Sweden	4.5	4.8	7.1	6.2	6.5	10.1	2.5	2.9	3.9	25.4	28.9	27.0
Oceania												
Australia	12.4	12.1	12.3	13.9	13.6	14.5	10.0	9.7	9.2	29.3	30.8	31.1
New Zealand	9.5	–	14.6	–	–	–	–	–	–	–	–	–

[a] Non-agricultural, excluding unpaid family workers.
[b] 1988 in place of 1989.
Source: OECD Labour Force Statistics, 1969–89, Paris, 1991.

Source: OECD (1991).

Road Safety Ltd: the recruitment of non-traditional sources of labour supply

SARAH VICKERSTAFF

CONTEXT OF THE CASE

Road Safety Ltd is a small British firm located in the south of England. The company manufactures flexible road signs and road safety equipment. Its products are sold to the police and other emergency services in the main, although they also do business with a variety of other customers. In general, road safety issues can be expected to become increasingly important in the 1990s, so the potential market for the company's products is an expanding one. The company operates in a tight labour market; unemployment levels are below the national average in the area and this is combined with regional shortages of skilled workers.

BACKGROUND TO THE CASE

The business is 15 years old, the company is in a reasonably healthy financial position following a takeover by the present owners a few years back. The firm currently has some 33 employees, five of whom are outworkers in the garment department. Quality is a very important issue for the road safety industry. The Department of Transport specifies a very large number of quality standards. Other European countries also specify their own standards which typically vary significantly from each other. This lack of harmonization in road safety standards is one of the main problems associated with moving into other European markets. There will be new standards across Europe for 1993, the company is unsure how large a part British standards will play in this. It is thought that the German regulations may play a more dominant role. Thus, for Road Safety Ltd, 1993 is currently seen as a potential threat rather than an opportunity, especially when the language barrier is taken into account.

The growth strategy of the business is to increase the production of high-quality equipment in an expanding market. Senior managers of the company recognize three major constraints on further growth, these are:

- the high cost of borrowing and difficulties with obtaining capital;

Human Resources Management in Europe
Edited by Sarah Vickerstaff
Published in 1992 by Chapman & Hall, London. ISBN 0 412 45380 0

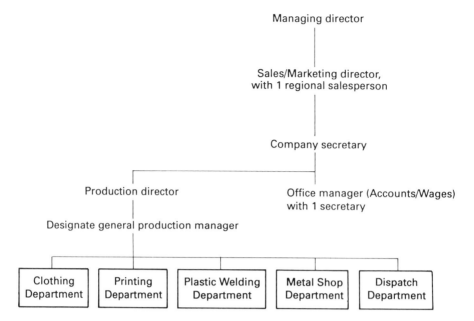

Fig. C8.1   Details of the workforce at Road Safety Ltd.

- the space constraints of the existing premises;
- recruitment difficulties and the prevailing context of skill shortages.

THE FIVE DEPARTMENTS

The departments are shown in Figure C8.1.

Clothing: This department is responsible for manufacturing reflective clothing of all types. It consists of a department head, 2 full-time seamstresses; five outworkers.

Printing: This department prints the badges and road signs onto the appropriate reflective material. The work is done in conjunction with the welding and employees often have experience in both departments. It consists of the department head, a cutter, 2 printers, 1 badge printer and 1 trainee printer.

Plastic Welding: The main task of this department is welding the road sign material ready to have the metal stands attached to them. It consists of the department head and 4 welders, all of whom joined the company in the last year.

Metal Shop: The work done here is mainly the making of different stands for the road signs the company produces. It consists of the department head, 1 full-time and two part-time employees.

Despatch: Department head plus one other.

The staff currently employed at Road Safety Ltd is shown in Table C8.1.

Table C8.1 Staff currently employed by Road Safety Ltd

	Males	Females	Totals
Full time	13	8	21
Part time	2	4	6
Youth Trainee (YT)	1	–	1
Outworkers	–	5	5
Totals	16	17	33

THE CASE PROBLEM

The company suffers from recruitment difficulties. The main areas of work are in making garments, printing, cutting and welding the plastic for signs and badges, making metal stands for road signs, dispatching goods to customers and general administration and management. There are shortages of skilled screen printers and plastic welders in the local labour market.

The majority of the current workforce are people with strong local connections and Road Safety Ltd is very much a part of the community. This is clearly an important consideration with regard to the recruitment and retention of staff, and especially the ease with which the company can employ outworkers.

Road Safety Ltd is very interested in recruiting women returners from the local area. They see this source of potential employees as possessing particular skills; married women typically are thought to display very high accuracy in plastic welding and are generally reliable. With a view to encouraging women returners the company has given some consideration to the introduction of job sharing, since the hours involved might be more attractive to this group. In an interview the managing director commented: 'I would love to employ more women and more women returners . . . but it's getting hold of them . . . it is convincing women, I think, of the possibilities.' Labour shortages remain a major constraint on further growth. The company realizes that it must develop a strategy to secure a stable and sufficiently skilled workforce in order to expand as it wants to.

CURRENT POLICIES

The company is involved in Youth Training[1] and usually employs at least one trainee. The company uses induction training for new employees as

[1] Youth Training is the successor to the government-sponsored Youth Training Scheme. It is a training scheme for 16–18 year olds, in which companies receive an incentive to employ and train young people. The scheme does not guarantee the young person a full-time job after the period of the traineeship.

the mainstay of its on-the-job training. The cost of training off-the-job is very high and this, combined with the pressure of work, makes it difficult to consider releasing people for courses. The majority of the company's labour needs are semi-skilled. Review of training is done very briefly, there are no job descriptions and no existing appraisal scheme for staff. Newer staff in welding, printing and the metal shop seek help and advice from supervisors as and when necessary.

The company has advertised locally for plastic welders hoping to attract women returners but has been unsuccessful. Many new employees are found through informal methods, e.g. word of mouth of existing staff, other links with the local community.

Management believes the best means of resourcing its skill needs is either to train or retrain existing staff and/or to recruit and train unskilled staff.

DISCUSSION QUESTIONS

You have been asked as external consultants to help the company devise a strategy for recruiting and retaining workers, with a particular emphasis on the possibility of employing women returners. The managing director has asked specifically that you make recommendations in the following areas:

1. Previous attempts to attract mature female applicants have been unsuccessful; how should the company go about reaching this non-traditional source of labour supply?
2. In what ways might the company modify current working practices to provide an environment attractive to female staff?
3. As training on the job for new employees is the linchpin of its skill strategy, how can the company assess whether any changes are necessary to its current induction programmes?
4. Are there other possible strategies for recruiting and retaining the necessary workforce that the company has not thought about?

In making your recommendations you should have particular regard to the fact that the company does not have a personnel department as such and does not have the resources to introduce expensive recruitment and selection techniques. The scope for expanding the organization's expenditure on training is also limited.

SUGGESTED READING

Watson, T. (1989) Recruitment and selection, in *Personnel Management in Britain* (ed. K. Sisson), Basil Blackwell, Oxford, pp. 125–48.
Curran, M. M. (1988) Gender and recruitment: people and places in the labour market. *Work, Employment and Society*, **2** (No. 3, September), pp. 335–51.
IRS (1990) *Effective Ways of Recruiting and Retaining Women*, Industrial Relations Service.
Vickerstaff, S. A. (ed.) (1990) *Training and the Small Business*, CBS/KEN.

Recruitment and integration of women in the Dutch Royal Air Force

SANDRA SCHRUIJER

INTRODUCTION

The Dutch government aims at providing equal opportunities for men and women in its organization. It strives at realizing a proportional representation of women. Naturally, this applies to the Dutch Army and hence to the Air Force as part of the Army.

The government's policy in this respect has not been fully successful yet: women are still strongly under-represented in the Air Force. A likely cause for this state of affairs is the technical nature of many jobs within it. In view of the relatively small number of women with a technical education it may well prove to be impossible to realize a proportional representation of women in the Air Force in the short term. Therefore it has been decided to strive for an increase in the overall percentage of women. The target for 1989 was for 5% of the total number of soldiers serving the Air Force (approx. 20 000) to be women. The stated percentage for 1993 is 8%.

In this case we shall address the recruitment strategies of the Air Force aimed at increasing the number of female staff. In particular, we shall have a closer look at the Air Force's recruitment material designed for this purpose. This material is used to raise questions concerning the effectiveness of the recruitment strategies, but also more general issues concerning the integration of women in the Air Force.

ACTIVELY RECRUITING WOMEN TO JOIN THE AIR FORCE

Although the target for 1989 has not been reached, the Air Force is determined to try to employ 8% women in its organization by 1993. To this end a positive action plan has been formulated which aims at (a) actively recruiting women, and (b) increasing the commitment of current female soldiers to the Air Force. Measures which belong to the first

Human Resources Management in Europe
Edited by Sarah Vickerstaff
Published in 1992 by Chapman & Hall, London. ISBN 0 412 45380 0

category are, for instance, increasing external recruitment at the expense of internal recruitment, stimulating horizontal (re)entry, positive discrimination in selection procedures, training of women with insufficient education, regional placement. The second category includes measures like creating the possibility of part-time employment, providing childcare, enabling parental and maternity leave, implementing placement policies which coordinate the placement of partners, offering guidance in integration processes.

As part of the attempt to actively recruit women, several brochures and a cassette tape have been developed which are directly addressed at women. We shall have a look at the cassette tape, some specific brochures, and at two general booklets which are meant to inform both men and women.

RECRUITMENT MATERIAL

Cassette tape

On the cassette tape nine interviews with women working for the Air Force are recorded.[1] The tape is sent to women expressing interest in joining the Air Force. Issues raised are: why join the Air Force, how is it to be a woman among men, the basic military training, the content of work, and femininity. The interviewees work as officer head personnel, corporal telephonist, corporal chauffeur, officer helicopter pilot, sergeant guided missiles, corporal administration, corporal steward, officer traffic controller. One interviewee just started her basic training.

The following reasons are mentioned for having joined the Air Force: freedom and independence, desire to fly, social contacts, curiosity, variety of work, excitement, security, desire to work in a male environment, and higher pay, better starting position and promotion possibilities as compared to non-military jobs.

The basic military training is described as tough and requiring a good physical condition. They reported that it was initially very strange to be in a male environment (many of them were the only female). As they stated, it was equally strange for men. As one interviewee remarked: 'As a female you are intruding in the image men have of the Air Force.' Nevertheless, they all felt accepted and were not isolated. They held their own attitude responsible for this. One interviewee completed her training with another woman and found that very supportive. The training they underwent was similar to the men's although demands for certain sports activities were lowered. Some interviewees mentioned that they had to

---

[1] *Nine Women about their Work in the Air Force*, produced by the Dutch Royal Air Force, 1987.

perform at least equally well as men since, being female, they felt they were paid extra attention to.

A question asking for the characteristics of a successful woman in the Air Force elicited the following answers: motivation, persistance, flexibility and good verbal qualities. The interviewees felt that no concessions were required concerning their femininity. Wearing a uniform was seen as no problem and even convenient by some.

The impression the tape conveys is that (a) the Air Force provides many opportunities (for women) careerwise, (b) the basic military training is physically demanding but not unfeasible, (c) working for the Air Force is challenging, interesting, and a good experience, (d) women are accepted provided they have the right attitude and motivation, (e) the Air Force does not require women to give up their femininity, (f) possibilities for dual-career couples within the Air Force exist.

Brochures for women

Two brochures have been issued which are specifically written for women. The first one is called *Air Force Magazine for Young Women*. Its text is based on six of the above-mentioned interviews. Photographs showing them at work, at home, and during a sport activity, are added.

A second brochure provides general information for women. It states that women are as equally suitable as men for jobs with the Air Force and that therefore all 45 functions within the Air Force are in principle open to both sexes. Career opportunities are equal for men and for women. 'It is ability that counts and not whether you are male or female.' Three different ways in which women can be employed are described: (1) an orientation period of two to three years, (2) a contract lasting for four to six years, and (3) a contract of unlimited duration. The first alternative is only open to women, not to men. Women are informed that the basic military training is tough but not unattainable. It says that the Air Force strives to place several women in one class and that it may even be possible to have a class in which the majority consists of women. After the basic training further professional education is provided. Four photographs are included which depict female soldiers in action. Furthermore, five citations, ostensibly provided by women already in the Air Force, are included. To give a few: 'Take the example of an ascending F-16. That single moment encapsulates everything one is confronted with when working in the Air Force: action, discipline, perfect team work, excitement, job knowledge, ambition. Whether you are a man or a woman.' 'Of course, you enter a man's world. And it is fully up to you whether you are accepted or not. Be yourself. Then you will get along fine.' 'In the normal work contact one interacts in an unconstrained way. But when it comes to the crunch of the matter, your "stripes" tell you clearly where the boundaries are. That in itself already means that opportunities for Air Force men and women are equal.'

General brochures

We looked at two brochures which are intended to inform men and women. The more elaborate of the two[2] does not address either men or women specifically. The issue of gender is only raised when discussing selection criteria: for men a minimum height is required of 1 m 60 and maximally 1 m 99, whereas the minimum height for women is 1 m 55. All pilots need to measure between 1 m 63 and 1 m 93. The text, moreover, mentions that women can join for a period of two to three years. It adds that women are equally valued as men in the Air Force and that no typical male occupations exist within it. Thirteen colour pictures are included, depicting 37 individuals in uniform. Of these 37 soldiers, four are visibly female.

The second (smaller) general brochure[3] includes a special section for women in which a statement is made that the Air Force wants to employ more women and that all positions are open to both sexes. Again, the possibility of a short-term contract is mentioned. Readers are informed that a special brochure for women and a cassette tape are available. The different requirements concerning the height of men and women are stated. Eighteen pictures of individuals whose gender is clearly visible are incorporated. Five pictures depict both sexes; seven pictures depict only women. One picture shows a male and a female fighter pilot.

DISCUSSION QUESTIONS

1. Do you think that the measures aimed at recruiting and committing women to the Air Force are effective? What are the problems some of these measures may elicit?
2. In your opinion, how successful are the brochures and the cassette tape in stimulating women to apply for a job with the Air Force? Why?
3. Can you think of ways to improve the Air Force's strategy to recruit women?
4. Discuss the advantages and disadvantages of positive discrimination. What are the differences between positive discrimination and positive action?
5. What are the (dis)advantages of being the only woman among men in a training class or in a department? How will the men and the woman feel and behave? Compare this solo-status to being in pairs and to a situation in which the number of men equals that of women: what are the attitudinal and behavioural consequences?
6. Which jobs will be very hard/very easy for women to enter in the Air Force? Why?
7. Under what conditions is it in your opinion appropriate to differentiate between men and women in the Air Force? Why? (Discuss, e.g. job content, work conditions.)

[2] Published by the Personnel Department of the Dutch Royal Air Force, August 1989.
[3] Published by the Personnel Department of the Dutch Royal Air Force.

8. Which stereotypes concerning men and women are likely to exist in the Air Force? Can you think of situations which would elicit negative stereotypes and attitudes between the sexes? How can one combat negative stereotypes and attitudes?
9. Discuss the phenomena of women entering male-dominated occupations and men entering female-dominated occupations. What are the similarities and the differences?

SUGGESTED READING

Cheatham, H. E. (1984) Integration of women into the US Army. *Sex Roles*, **11**, 141–53.

DeFleur, L. B. (1985) Organizational and ideological barriers to sex integration in military groups. *Work and Occupations*, **12**, 206–28.

Edwards, J. (1988) Moral dilemmas of positive discrimination. *Social Policy and Administration*, **22**, 210–21.

Kanter, R. M. (1977) Some effects of proportions on group life: skewed sex ratios and responses to token women. *American Journal of Sociology*, **82**, 965–90.

Tajfel, H. and Turner, T. (1979) An integrative theory of intergroup conflict, in *The Social Psychology of Intergroup Relations* (eds W. G. Austin and S. Worchel), Brooks/Cole Publishing Company, Monterey, California.

Williams, C. L. (1989) *Gender Differences at Work: Women and Men in Nontraditional Occupations*, University of California Press, Berkeley.

TEXT 4

Different European perspectives on selection techniques: the case of graphology in business

GLORIA MOSS

INTRODUCTION

In many ways, human beings are rather strange creatures. Practices which are normal in one part of the world, are condemned in another and there are few guides as to what constitutes normal or abnormal behaviour. In Tibet, for example, it is quite common for several brothers to share the same wife, whereas in Britain this would be greeted with public outcry in one of the tabloids. In parts of Germany, foxhunting is forbidden, whereas in Britain it is trumpeted with pomp and circumstance. In France, government ministers and MPs would be admired for having attractive mistresses, in Britain it is a cause for resignation. One can be forgiven for being a little confused as to what is the right thing to do.

The situation with graphology is rather similar. In some countries, it is held in high esteem and used extensively in recruitment and selection. This is the case in many parts of continental Europe. It is taught in universities and is a well-respected discipline. In other parts of the world, however, it is treated with ridicule and derision, and is associated with the occult and the psychic. This is the case with Britain where graphology is still greeted with scepticism and disbelief by the majority of people.

Why is this? We shall look at the origins of graphology and discuss how, and to what extent it is used in various parts of the world. We shall also take a brief look at some of the other methods of personality analysis available and explore the evidence for their effectiveness. We shall end with a brief look at the basic principles of handwriting and an analysis of some samples.

ORIGINS OF HANDWRITING

The origins of handwriting analysis lie in continental Europe. The first surviving treatise on the subject was written in Italy by the physician

Human Resources Management in Europe
Edited by Sarah Vickerstaff
Published in 1992 by Chapman & Hall, London. ISBN 0 412 45380 0

and professor, Camillo Baldi, in 1622 and was entitled 'The means of recognizing the habits and qualities of a writer from his handwriting'. The torch then passed, two centuries later, to France where a learned French abbot, Jean Hippolyte Michon (1806–81), published two important books on the subject and coined the word 'graphology'. He went on to establish the French Society of Graphologists and a flourishing school of French followers, among whom was Crépieux-Jamin.

Towards the end of the century, developments shifted to Germany. Wilhelm Preyer, a university professor of medical physiology, undertook experiments at the University of Berlin, which showed that writers who had lost the use of their writing had developed the same characteristics with the new hand – or sometimes foot, or even mouth – which they exhibited before their accident. He said that handwriting was a form of 'brainwriting' and that we saw in handwriting a mirror of the patterns of the brain. Preyer was followed in Germany by Dr Wilhelm Klages who began to see in handwriting the expression of human personality as a whole.

From Germany, developments moved to Switzerland where Swiss graphologists began making significant contributions to the subject in the mid-1920s. One of these, Max Pulver, a Swiss writer and philosopher, linked graphology to new discoveries in psychology and showed how writing could echo both conscious and unconscious drives. He showed therefore that graphology could reveal the whole person, and not just the person projected on the surface.

HOW HANDWRITING ANALYSIS IS USED

We have seen from the brief historical sketch above the graphology had its origins in continental Europe. There has never really been a British tradition of graphology, although there is now a thriving British Institute of Graphologists and a growing body of professional experts. This is largely due to the arrival of graphologists from abroad – Robert Saudek, Hans Jacoby, Eric Singer and Frank Hilliger, the founder of the British Institute of Graphologists.

It need not therefore surprise us if graphology is given short shrift in Britain. The tradition does not exist there. A look at the different tools used in recruitment reveals this. A survey by Industrial Relations Review and Report (IRRR, 1991) showed that employers are using a variety of methods to recruit their staff (Shakleton, 1991): interviews, 100%; references, 97%; psychometric tests, 58%; literacy/numeracy tests, 57%; ability/aptitude tests, 48%; assessment centres, 30%; and graphology, 1%.

In France, by contrast, the picture is rather different: interviews, 100%; graphology, 77%; and references, 11%.

The use of psychometric tests, which has doubled in the past two years in Britain, has not yet hit France. Graphology holds a much more important place there. Big companies like St Gobain, Elf Aquitaine,

Crédit Lyonnais and Peugeot use it, and it has an interesting place in the selection process. At St Gobain:

> elle est en général utilisée pour des postes de cadre et toujours après la sélection faite par interviews. Elle permet d'apporter un éclairage complementaire, notamment quant aux aptitudes à communiquer, convaincre, animer d'autres personnels, aux qualités relationnelles difficiles à apprécier dans un interview. (Direction de la Gestion des Cadres)

The above response came from a survey of European companies carried out by the author this year. The results showed that 80% of the respondents used graphology, and of these 40% used graphology 'all the time' and 40% 'sometimes'. Only 20% did not use it at all.

The same survey revealed that a large number of companies regularly use graphology. These include Ciba-Geigy and Hoffman–La Roche. Other companies that are known (independently of the survey) to use graphology include Crédit Suisse, Sandoz, Swissair, as well as all the banks and insurance companies. Some companies employ graphologists full time, but others use cabinets of graphologists. In fact, so common is graphology in Switzerland, that candidates will often be asked to supply their own graphological report (from a well-known cabinet) to an employer, and be expected to foot the bill.

So, graphology is used extensively in decisions about recruitment, promotion and team compatibility. Other countries where graphology is regularly used include Germany, Belgium, Holland, Israel and America. In Israel, it has been used by manufacturing and military industries, as well as by textiles and cosmetic companies like Helena Rubinstein. In America, graphology is widely used in the courts, not just in evidence, but increasingly to analyse the handwriting of an opponent and also to help decide who the jurors should be. Each lawyer can choose six out of 30 potential jurors and lawyers often use a graphologist to help select out those who are likely to be hostile to their case.

As far as Britain is concerned, it does, as we have seen, use graphology, but at the moment most companies are either shy of using it or shy of admitting that they do. To give an indication of the sort of attitude that is found, let me quote the remarks of a personnel director of a 2500 person company, refuting the use of graphology (the company is referred to here as X):

> . . . I must emphasize that X does not utilize, has not utilized, and is not likely in the future to utilize graphology in any part of our evaluation of existing or potential employees.

The same knee-jerk reaction against graphology is seen in an article in *New Scientist* (Farnham, 1991). The author, a psychologist, equates graphology with astrology each time he mentions it:

> . . . both graphology and astrology are falsifiable . . . astrological and
> graphological readings have other attractions, particularly for people
> who are anxious or insecure.

At no point does the author examine the case for graphology or even
show that he has an appreciation of how it works. To conflate graphology and astrology in this way is confusing. There is in fact nothing
in common between astrology and graphology except the fact that they
are both methods of describing personality. Their methodologies and
assumptions are entirely different.

This kind of paranoid response is typical of reactions in Britain. Why
are these attitudes found? One reason, it could be argued, is prejudice
and ignorance. Most people do not know how graphology works and
therefore, quite reasonably, are resistant to the subject. Once one shows
people how and why it works, attitudes swiftly change.

Another reason perhaps for people's antagonism lies at the graphologists' own door. Their tendency to make inflated claims for their
art/science has not helped their cause. Graphology can uncover many
aspects of personality make-up, but it cannot predict how an employee
will act in any given situation. Again, graphologists, like many professional groups, are not always good at explaining their art to the lay
person: it can be difficult for a non-expert to understand the reasoning
behind graphology. And finally, graphologists are often their own worst
enemy because not only do they have enemies outside the profession (e.g.
many psychologists) but they also have enemies within. In Britain, there
are two rival examining bodies offering qualifications in graphology: the
British Institute of Graphologists as well as the Academy of Graphology.
Graphologists do not speak with a single voice in Britain.

Despite these problems, there are some staunch defenders of graphology in Britain. These include S. G. Warburg (which has used handwriting analysis since it was founded in 1946), as well as other city
banks and commodity brokers. They use graphology as it is used by
continental companies, i.e. as an aid to recruitment, promotion and team
compatibility.

WHAT DOES GRAPHOLOGY CLAIM TO BE ABLE TO DO?

Graphologists the world over claim to be able to describe personality
from a sample of handwriting. They talk in terms of character traits (e.g.
impulsive, tenacious, good concentration levels, quick mind) and so are
of that school of thought who hold that personality is fixed and can
be described. They are not among the situationalists who believe that
personality can only be defined in relation to experiences. Nevertheless,
they would be unlikely to hold that what was said of a person at a single
moment in time, would be true forever more. Handwriting will change
and so will the personality. So, from a company's point of view, it would
be advisable to recheck a person's writing every two or three years.

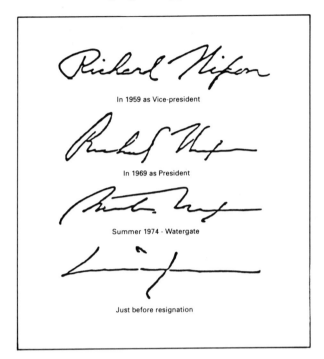

In 1959 as Vice-president

In 1969 as President

Summer 1974 - Watergate

Just before resignation

Fig. T4.1   The writing of Richard Nixon.

The changes that can take place in writing are shown vividly in this writing of Richard Nixon (Figure T4.1). You will see that the signature changes from a confident start (large, well-formed letters) to a sinewy line (this form is known as a 'thread'). The signature is said to illustrate the public self, the self that is projected to the outside world, and we can see here that he is slowly disappearing from this arena.

Some graphologists will not only talk in terms of fixed traits of personality, but will also suggest the unconscious drives that motivate that person. Many graphologists follow the Jungian model of personality and are able to describe people in terms of the four functions of personality:

Most people would be said to have a primary function (that function which predominates) and a secondary function (that which is second in importance). In addition to this, there is said to be an opposite function (the function opposite the primary function on the chart) and this is the area in which problems will arise. It is the area from which a person's inferiority derives, and is embedded deep in the unconscious.

So, by saying for example that a person is the 'Thinking' type, one knows immediately that this person will deal easily with facts and figures but that he or she may have problems on the 'Feeling' level. Graphologists would also be able to identify the secondary function, in this case either intuitive or sensory.

To conclude. Graphologists claim to be able to describe personality at a single moment in time and also to be able to describe areas of weakness and vulnerability. They also claim to be able to describe what is 'hidden' and can reveal something of the unconscious motives of a person.

WHAT IS THE EVIDENCE FOR GRAPHOLOGY?

A very large number of tests have been carried out to check the validity of graphology. In a paper published by the British Institute of Graphology, and written by Margaret Gullan-Whur (1991), no less than 212 studies are described. The reader is referred to this document as well as to a short article in *Personnel Management* (Fowler, 1991a) for a detailed account. We shall try to provide a brief overview here of some of the main work.

Studies cover issues of reliability as well as of validity. These are measured on a scale of 0 to 1.00. To remind readers of the measures which are normally tested, these are:

Reliability
1. Internal consistency: The extent to which the measure is consistent throughout the length of the test.
2. Inter-rater reliability: The extent of agreement between assessors.

Validity
1. Face validity: Whether test looks as though it is measuring what it is supposed to measure.
2. Construct validity: Extent to which the test measures a particular construct.
3. Predictive validity: Extent to which test helps make judgement about a desired outcome.

What is the evidence of graphology on these measures? Taking them in turn:

Reliability

Internal consistency   Tests for this go back a long way. According to Alan Fowler (1991a) Harvey, in 1934 found a median correlation of 0.77 in the characteristics of the handwriting of 50 subjects tested two months apart. Squire, in 1967, put the figure even higher at 0.9. Again we find a few years later, in a study by Wallner (1975), that variables appeared in an individual's handwriting with equal quality in all specimens produced within a particular period of time. Sonneman and Kernon (1962) also showed that there was consistency between two samples by the same writer.

It should also be said that it is extremely difficult to falsify one's handwriting since there are so many variables that would need to be altered.

Inter-rater reliability   Studies for inter-rater reliability are all consistent in pointing to high levels of inter-judge correlation. Galbraith and Wilson (1964) asked three graphologists to look for five personality traits in specimens of handwriting. The average correlation was 0.78. Hofsommer *et al.* (1965) again took three graphologists and asked them to rate 322 foremen for leadership qualities. They achieved a coefficient of 0.74.

Validity

Face validity   No tests have, to the author's knowledge, been done on this. If they had, it is suspected that graphology would come out rather badly. If a graphology test is done properly, then the handwriting produced is no different from that of everyday handwriting. This does not look in any obvious way like a test.

Again, people might argue that graphologists gain all their insights by reading the script. Rafaeli and Klimoski (1983) concluded that 'script content has little effect on graphologists' assessments'. In fact, graphologists are trained not to read the content of the hand-writing they are analysing.

Construct validity   This is another difficult one. To establish whether graphologists are able to measure a particular construct or not suggests comparing their constructs with those found by other means. So, we are talking about the tests which compare graphologists' ratings with those of psychologists, or graphologists' ratings with those of supervisors', etc. In both cases, there is a risk that the results are meaningless since the comparator's evaluation may itself be low in validity. If personality tests have the low validity coefficient of 0.15, as the British Psychological Society suggests, then failure to agree with these results could be read in a positive way.

To give a taste of the studies that have been done, there are those by Crumbaugh and Stockholm (1977) in which significant results were obtained by people who knew subjects and tried to match the evaluations to the people they knew.

Again, in studies by Lemke and Kirchner (1971), where the comparator was the 16 PF, and Lomonaco and Harrison (1973), where the comparator was the TAT test, there were significant but low correlations. In the Cox and Tapsell study (1991), the comparator was a variety of assessment techniques. Correlations were either extremely small or negative.

Predictive validity   The studies seem to divide into two groups, which show that (a) graphology is a good predictor, or (b) it has no predictive validity at all.

(a) Studies with good validity

Psychometric assessments seldom reach beyond 0.3. What about graphology? In some studies, higher correlations have been found. Sonneman and Kernan (1962), for example, obtained high correlations of 0.54 to 0.85 in a comparison of graphologists' predictions and those of managers. In a 1989 study by Williams and Stuparich, the graphologists were asked to predict, from a group of 88 newly recruited insurance sales agents, those who would be successful and those who would not. Measured against future results, their predictions were extremely accurate.

(b) Studies with low validity

Zdep and Weaver (1967) attempted to identify the people who would make successful salespeople from a list of traits that the graphologists associated with high sales performance. The graphologists had been shown the handwritings of successful salespeople but they were not successful in identifying the high fliers.

How does one explain the difference in these results? I suggest that there are two reasons. Firstly, some graphologists are quite simply better than others at describing personality. Graphology is only as good as the graphologist doing it and a poor graphologist will produce poor results. Again, another factor that will control success is whether it has been possible to identify those factors which determine success in the job. This is not always easy. As Christopher Molander (1991), Professor of Personnel Management at Bradford University and Chairman of the British Institute of Graphology, has said:

> it is quite simply not possible to list – never mind statistically control – all the variables which will lead to the perceived success of someone in a job. Many of these variables are external to the individual . . . inaccurate job descriptions; changing market conditions; technological innovation; the characteristics of the boss and subordinates and general working conditions are but a few of the factors which affect job performance.

Conclusion

Some of the evidence for reliability and validity is good; some less good. One must conclude with Michael Dixon (1991) that 'the case for graphology as a gauge of working abilities remains non-proven either way' at the moment. One must wait for further work to be done.

OTHER METHODS OF PERSONALITY EVALUATION

Employers recruiting staff these days are faced with a whole battery of resources that they can use. If anything, they are spoilt for choice. They can choose between:

Interviews   (100%)
Psychometric tests (58%)
Intelligence tests (48%)

The percentages show the proportion of companies in Britain who use these methods. We shall examine the evidence for the first two, since the usages are so high.

INTERVIEWS

Do interviews work?

As we saw above, all employers seem to be using the interview to select staff. So, how successful is this as a method of selection?

One thing on which, probably, most people would agree, is that they are good at interviewing and understanding other people. This would explain why it is the most popular method of recruitment.

There is a lot, in fact, to be said in favour of interviews. One has the opportunity to see the candidate, to see if one actually likes him or her, to check on certain facts and test the candidate's reactions. These are all valuable things. And the value of the interview is enhanced if the interviewer uses a system of structured questions to test different qualities needed on the job. This is the 'situational' interview which probes critical incidents likely to be found on the job, and which is therefore 'criterion related'. The structured approach also allows the responses of one candidate to be compared with those of another.

The good news is that a very high proportion of UK employers are using situational interviews. Of the sample of 171 employers in the report referred to above (IRRR, 1991), 81% include situational-type questions.

The bad news is that, despite all these good points, interviews are still vulnerable because of the subjective nature of much of the evaluation. Let us look again at the evidence. What does it show?

It shows that, overall, the validity coefficients are not very high. Four well-known studies produced validity coefficients of 0.11, 0.13, 0.19 and 0.30. Recent work with situational interviews revealed validity coefficients of up to 0.35 only. This is probably the best that one could expect of interviews.

Why is this? Why are interviews such a poor method of people evaluation? Mostly, it has to be said, because interviewers are fallible and easily influenced by a number of factors. Researchers have uncovered many of these and the catalogue of factors makes interesting reading. The first points are all concerned with the reliability of interviews. As we shall see, there are a number of problems.

1. *Test–retest reliability* (the ability to obtain the same results on different occasions). Robert Half has shown that you will not be rated as highly if you were interviewed on a Monday as if you were interviewed on a Wednesday. If you are the first person to be interviewed, you are three

times less likely to be hired than the last person on the list. ('The Robert Half way to get hired in today's job market.') This shows that there are other factors which will affect the results of the test.

2. *Internal consistency.* This is likely to be low since all the evidence shows that people are either very bad listeners, or do not believe what they hear. In one study, recruiters asked 20 questions about what a candidate had said in a short interview and, on average, half got it wrong (*New Scientist*, 31.1.85). The evidence shows that most interviewers are very poor listeners and make up their mind about the candidate in the first few seconds of the interview. They will spend the rest of the interview hearing and believing what they want to, rather than what is actually said, often to confirm their initial impression. The evidence shows that even if people do listen, they will be more likely to believe the candidate if they are behaving in a way which is inconsistent with the role they are applying for, than if they behave in a consistent manner (Jones *et al.*, 1961).

3. *Inter-rater reliability.* In an early study by Hollingsworth, 57 candidates were interviewed by 12 sales managers. Every candidate received a wide range of rankings from the 12 managers.

Validity

Face validity   Most people expect to be questioned before they start a job and one strong point about the interview is its high face validity. What could be more normal than an employer sitting down to talk with a potential employee?

Construct validity   The order in which you hear information will have an important bearing on the conclusions that you reach. It seems that the first things you hear about a person will stick, despite what follows. The work of Asch bears this out. Asch read a list of traits describing somebody to two groups. He then asked each group to describe the characteristics of that person. So, Group I was told that the person was 'intelligent, industrious, critical, stubborn and envious' and Group II was given the same list of traits, but in reverse. How did the two groups rate the person?

Group I said: 'This person is intelligent. He is stubborn only because he knows what he is saying.' Group II said: 'This person is emotional. He allows his bad points to cover up his good ones. His good qualities are taken over by his bad.' So much for objective evaluation.

Prior assumptions about a candidate will also influence that conclusions one reaches. Kelley's work at MIT in the 1950s shows this strikingly. He told a psychology group about the new psychology teacher they were going to have. Both groups were told that he was a graduate student, had three terms of teaching experience, was 26, and was married. Then, one half, Group I, was told that he was 'a rather *cold* person, industrious, critical, practical and determined'. The other half was told that he was 'a rather *warm* person, industrious, critical', etc. When, at the end, the students were asked to rate him, those in Group II rated him as more sociable, popular, human and humorous than those in Group II. All because of one word.

Conclusion

Where does this leave us? It shows us that although the interview is greatly used, it needs to be used with great caution. The interview provides an opportunity to get to know somebody and to probe about the past and attitudes to the job. The interviewer nevertheless needs to be aware of all the problems that can beset the interpretation of what is actually (eventually) heard.

PSYCHOMETRIC TESTS

What do they reveal?

About 58% of UK firms employing more than 2000 people now regularly use personality assessments as part of the selection process. The figure for ability and aptitude tests is around 75%. As Christopher Molander has said:

> The evidence for the validity and utility of the latter (ability and aptitude tests) in good employment practice is beyond serious statistical dispute. It is however the area of personality assessment in which most growth has been in recent years and which is causing real concern to the British Psychological Society. (Molander, 1991).

Certainly, there has been a big increase in the use of psychometric tests in recent years. According to the IDS 1991 survey on recruitment, more than 53% of those employers using personality tests introduced them in the last two years. The growth is by no means restricted to the number of employers using them. It is also seen in the abundance of tests now on the market. From the first personality questionnaire used in the First World War to predict breakdown in conflict, we now have over 5000 different tests in English to choose from. As Raymond Cattell, the psychologist, said, they are 'the prolific rabbits of the psychometric world'.

Undoubtedly, psychometric tests have a great deal to offer the selector of people. How are the tests divided up, and how does one distinguish the good test from the bad? We shall attempt to answer these questions briefly. Anybody familiar with testing should pass over this section, and move on to the next.

Types of test

There are two kinds of test. The normative test and the ipsative test. The normative test measures the extent to which a trait is present in a person and presents this as a norm against a wider sample of the population. It does not tell you about the relative strength of those characteristics in a particular person. Ipsative tests, on the other hand, do just that. They will tell you about a person's relative strength in, say, leadership measured against the person's tendency to like to break the rules. They won't tell you how this relates to the population norm, however, which makes it difficult to compare one person with another.

1. Examples of normative tests include:
   (a) The OPQ Model. A number of different versions.
   (b) Cattell's 16 PF. This measures 16 personality factors.
   (c) The Myers–Briggs Type Indicator. Based on Jung's personality types.
   (d) The Eysenck Personality Inventory. Measures introversion/extroversion and stability/neuroticism.

2. Ipsative tests include:
   (a) Gordon Personality Inventory
   (b) The PPA (Thomas International). Measures dominance, influence, security, conformity.
   (c) The PAPI (Kostick Perception and Preference Inventory)
   (d) The OPQ model. Two of the versions of this test.

One of the issues over which the controversy surrounding psychometric questionnaires has focused is the question of the Normative v. Ipsative test. Critics of the latter tend to point to the fact that candidates are forced to choose between personality characteristics which are scored on different scales. In other words, you are not offered a choice of degree with respect to one particular personality characteristic, but are forced to make a choice between one or more unrelated characteristics. And there is the nub.

Another issue which has set commonrooms alight is the question of sample size. Charles Johnson and Steve Blinkhorn have questioned whether sample sizes in validity tests were large enough.

Finally, with an increasing number of employers using personality testing, the issue of repeat performances on the tests rears its ugly head. One recent study by the chartered psychologists Kerr Brown Associates, showed that 25% of the students in the sample said that they had been tested more than once on the same test. The study said that improved scores could be expected with repeated testing (*Personnel Management*, September 1991).

We do not wish to enter the debate on any of these issues. Suffice it to say that we believe that the usefulness of a test does depend on whether it:

(a) allows you to compare one individual with another;
(b) allows you to measure the relative presence of different characteristics in a person – in this sense, one would like a test to be both normative and ipsative;
(c) will produce the same results on repeated use with one individual (test–retest validity).

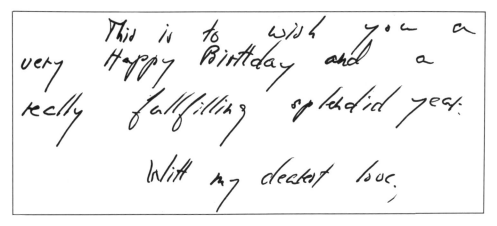

Fig. T4.2 Large, spaced writing.

HOW DOES GRAPHOLOGY WORK?

In this final section, I shall attempt to illustrate the rationale behind graphology and show some of the qualities of management personality it can bring out. I cannot unfortunately in a short space offer a comprehensive view of the subject but there are many excellent books available if you want to read further.

Please note that none of the features described below can be looked at in isolation. One cannot draw conclusions about handwriting without looking at how a number of different features relate together.

Spacing

Spacing holds the clue to understanding graphology. The way people express themselves on paper, the layout and the spacing they use will tell you something about them. If the words are large and well spaced out, this indicates somebody who likes space and has plenty of confidence (Figure T4.2). If the words are small and huddled close together, then this is somebody without a dominant ego who craves the company of others. The same kind of symbolism applies to space. The left side of the page which one leaves behind as one writes, represents the past; the right side which beckons one towards it, represents the future. A writing which keeps close to one side will show a predisposition in favour of either the past or the future in the way that person solves problems and approaches life. (See Figure T4.3(a) and (b).)

Individual letters

Every sign has a meaning which can be worked out in logical way. An 'i' dot which is put straight above a stem is one sign of a careful person

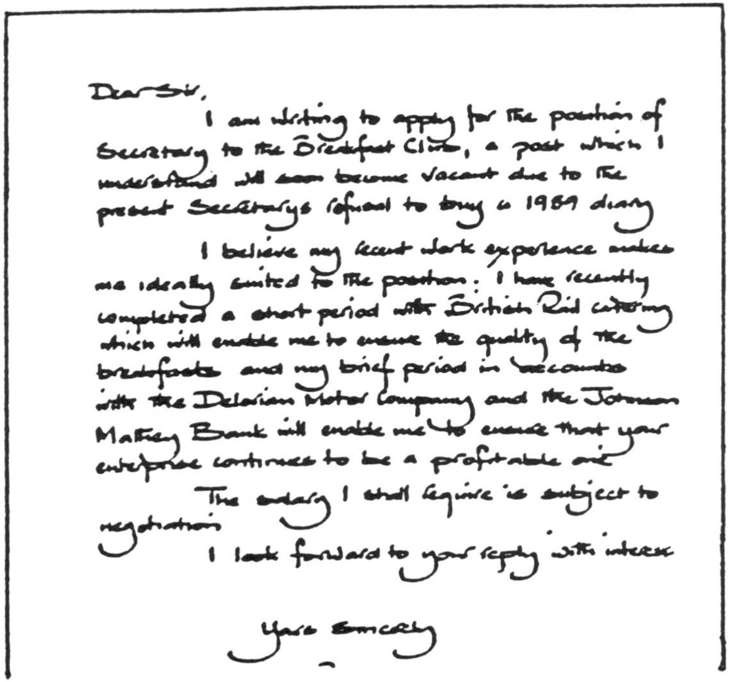

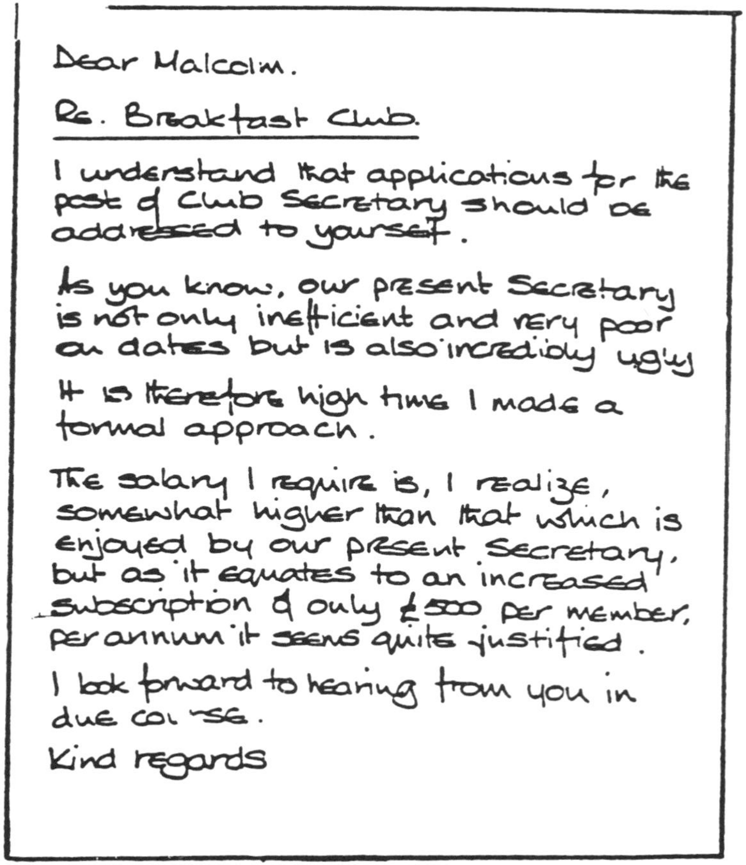

Dear Malcolm,

Re. Breakfast Club

I understand that applications for the post of Club Secretary should be addressed to yourself.

As you know, our present Secretary is not only inefficient and very poor on dates but is also incredibly ugly

It is therefore high time I made a formal approach.

The salary I require is, I realize, somewhat higher than that which is enjoyed by our present Secretary, but as it equates to an increased subscription of only £500 per member, per annum it seems quite justified.

I look forward to hearing from you in due course.

Kind regards

(b) Narrow margins.

Dear Sir,

I am writing to apply for the position of Secretary to the Breakfast Club, a post which I understand has now become vacant due to the present Secretary's (forced to say a 1989 diary)

I believe my heart dark experience makes me ideally suited for the position. I have recently completed a short period with Dublin Rail society which will enable me to ensure the growth of the breakfasts and my brief period in Ireland with the Dublin Metro Company and the Johnson MacKay Bank will enable me to ensure that your enterprise continues to be a profitable one.

The salary I shall require is subject to negotiation.

I look forward to your reply with interest.

Yours sincerely,

(a) Wide margins.

Fig. T4.3 Handwriting margins

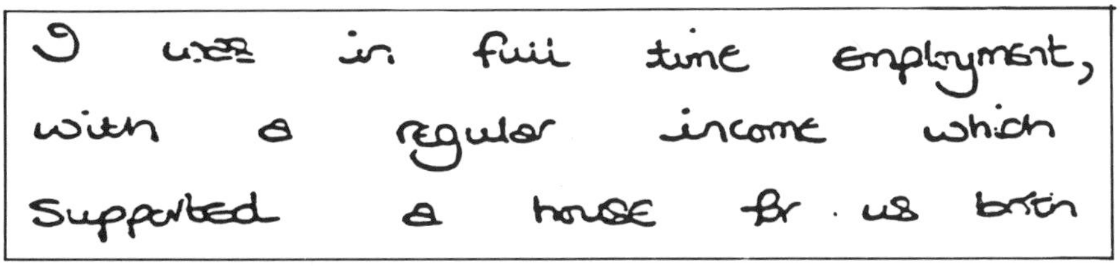

> I was in full time employment,
> with a regular income which
> supported a house for us both

Fig. T4.4 'i' dots straight above the stem.

(Figure T4.4). Some people will leave out 'i' dots altogether, which could be one sign of a maverick disposition.

Please remember as we said above, that no single feature of handwriting should ever be examined in isolation. The graphologist will need to examine a large number of traits and look at their relationship to each other before any conclusions about the writer can be reached.

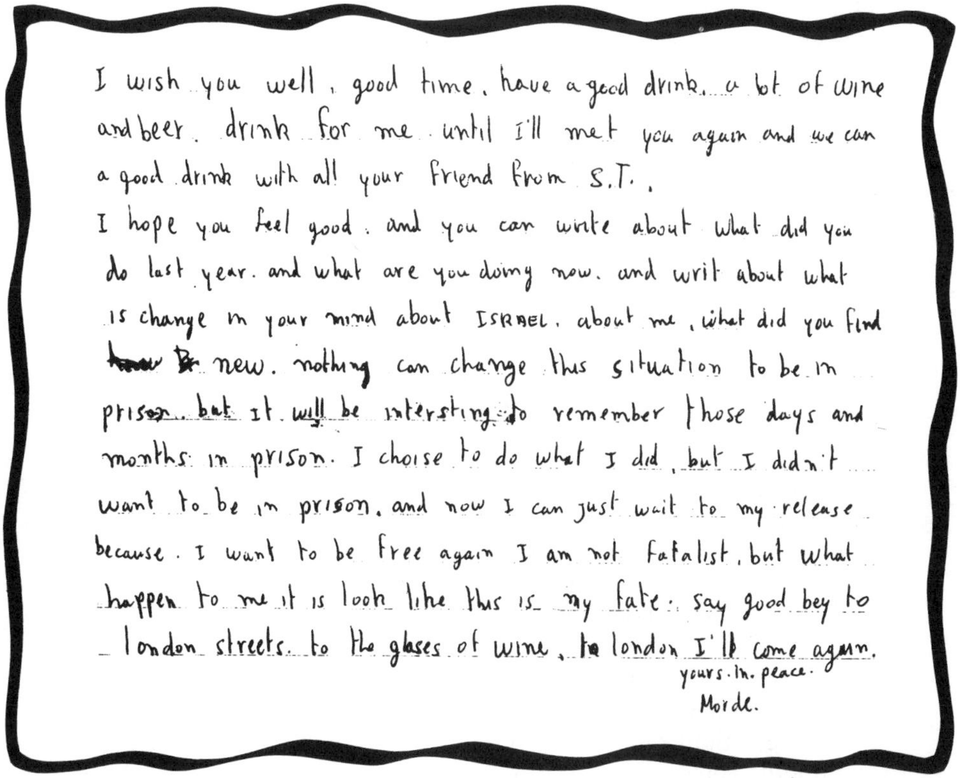

> I wish you well, good time, have a good drink, a lot of wine and beer. drink for me until I'll met you again and we can a good drink with all your friend from S.T.,
> I hope you feel good. and you can write about what did you do last year. and what are you doing now. and writ about what is change in your mind about ISRAEL. about me, what did you find new. nothing can change this situation to be in prison, but it will be intersting to remember those days and months in prison. I choise to do what I did, but I didn't want to be in prison. and now I can just wait to my release because. I want to be free again I am not fatalist, but what happen to me it is look like this is my fate: say good bey to london streets. to the glases of wine, to london I'll come again.
> yours in peace.
> Morde.

Fig. T4.5 Disconnected writing.

Connectedness

A person who links all the letters together and produces what is known as 'connected' writing is likely to try and do the same with facts and find connections and group them together. A 'disconnected' writer may be less concerned to bring things together and more interested in seeing things as a disonnected series of facts, much as a child views the world before they are taught 'joined up writing'. The writer may have a more naive view of the world, in which events are not seen as part of a logical series of patterns, but as one-off events.

This may explain two things. The high degree of connectedness among MENSA members (Paterson, 1967) and the low degree found in a writer like the Israeli Mordechai Vanunu who revealed Israel's nuclear secrets to the world. An article by the journalist who wrote the scoop story revealing the secrets of Israel's arsenal, shows that Vanunu was a man driven by an inner need to express the truth, without any thought of gain or of the harm it would do himself or his country. He was sentenced to 18 years' imprisonment for treason and espionage and after five years wrote to the journalist whose writing led to his sentence:

> . . . my suffering is temporary. I don't need prize Nobel [he had been nominated for one], all I want is my freedom, to live in my own philosophy. The main point is that I did what I want to do and that it is good for all the human kind . . .

This innocent, childlike view of the world seems to be expressed in his writing (Figure T4.5).

The three zones

Another major principle of graphology is the three zones. Letters can occupy one or more of these zones:

Upper

Middle

Lower

The upper zone, the zone reaching upwards, will tell you something about how a person uses his or her intellect. Very high upper lengths would indicate somebody who enjoys rational approaches to problem solving. A short upper zone does not indicate lack of intelligence but a lesser reliance on a 'thinking' approach. So, people working together with these different features (if they were backed up by other signs in the handwriting) might find life frustrating. The middle zone, corresponding to the middle zone in the body, will give you information on a person's sentiment. Generally speaking, a large middle zone betokens a person with warmth and feelings. The lower zone, corresponding to the lower parts of the body, will tell you something about a person's energy levels and sex drive.

A glance at somebody's handwriting will tell you which is the predominant zone or whether they are all of roughly equal strength. A graphologist will then examine the shapes (e.g. rounded or angular) and movements (e.g. rightward or leftward tendency) in each of the zones, and describe the tendencies in more detail.

Signature

The signature is a very informative part of a person's handwriting. According to many graphologists, it represents the 'public' person, the person projected to the outside world. The private or real person is seen in the body of the handwriting and a very interesting exercise is to compare the handwritings in the two cases to see if there is any divergence.

For example, compare Figures T4.6 and T4.7. As you will see, the signature projects more confidence than you can see in the rest of the handwriting. Or again, Figure T4.8 shows the handwriting of a headmistress. The signature shows decision and speed; the rest of the writing shows caution. This latter is the real self. Looking at the signature is a very quick way of seeing through the mask and seeing the kind of tensions that exist in the personality.

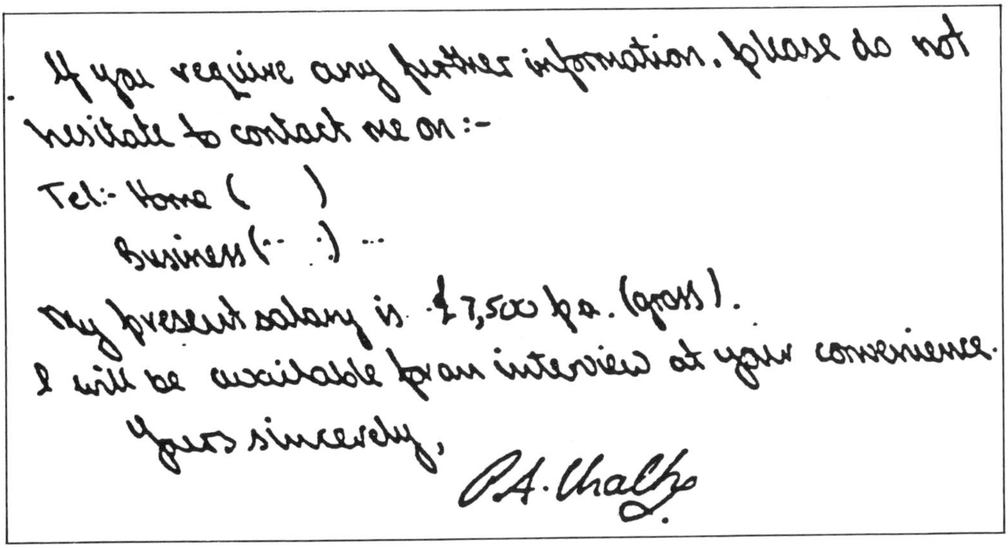

Fig. T4.6

Dear Malcolm.

Re. Breakfast Club.

I understand that applications for the post of Club Secretary should be addressed to yourself.

As you know, our present Secretary is not only inefficient and very poor on dates but is also incredibly ugly

It is therefore high time I made a formal approach.

The salary I require is, I realize, somewhat higher than that which is enjoyed by our present Secretary, but as it equates to an increased subscription of only £500 per member, per annum it seems quite justified.

I look forward to hearing from you in due course.

Kind regards

Fig. T4.7

I recommend  as a child of integrity + ability who, I believe, would give credit to any school whose philosophy includes the value of the person's self esteem + human relations.

Yours faithfully,

Fig. T4.8   The handwriting of a headmistress.

Conclusions

It is difficult in a short text to convey any of the rich complexity of graphology. However, we hope that the reader will have gained an appreciation of why a study of handwriting should cast light on personality, how graphology is used in Eruope, and what validity it has as an assessment technique.

Graphology is a powerful aid to personality assessment in modern personnel management, and efficient personality assessment is crucial in optimizing group compatibility programmes. Although British companies are latecomers in examining the uses of graphology, a number of our foremost public and private sector firms are now showing an interest in its uses.

REFERENCES

Bartram, D. (1991) Addressing the abuse of psychological tests. *Personnel Management* (April).

Cox, A. and Tapsell, J. (1991) Graphology and its validity in personnel assessment. Paper presented at BPS Conference, Cardiff.

Crumbaugh, J. and Stockholm, E. (1977) Validation of graphoanalysis by global or holistic method. *Perceptual and Motor Skills*, **44**.

Dixon, M. (1991) An egregious miscarriage of justice. *Financial Times* (6 March).

Fletcher, C. (1989) A test by any other name. *Personnel Management* (March).

Fowler, A. (1991a) An even handed approach to graphology. *Personnel Management* (March).

Fowler, A. (1991b) How to conduct interviews effectively. *Personnel Plus* (August).

Furnham, A. (1991) Hooked on horoscopes. *New Scientist* (January).

Galbraith, D. and Wilson, W. (1964) Reliability of the graphoanalytic approach to handwriting analysis. *Perceptual and Motor Skills*, **19** (No. 2).

Gullan-Whur, M. (1991) Research papers relating to the validity and reliability of graphology. British Institute of Graphologists.

Harvey, O. (1934) The measurement of handwriting considered as a form of expressive movement. *Character and Personality*, **2**.

Hofsommer, W., Holdsworth, R. and Seifert, T. (1965) Problems of reliability in graphology. *Psychology and Praxis*, **9**.

Hubbard, G. (1985) How to pick the personality for the job. *New Scientist* (January).

IRRR (1991) *The State of Selection*, Industrial Relations Review and Report. April.

Jones, Davis and Gergen (1961) *Journal of Abnormal Psychology*, **63**, 302–10.

Lemke, E. and Kirchner, J. (1971) A multivariate study of handwriting, intelligence and personality correlates, *Journal of Personality Assessment*, **35**, 1971.

Lomonaco, T., Harrison, R. and Klein, F. (1973) Accuracy of matching TAT and graphological personality profiles. *Perceptual and Motor Skills*, **36**.

Molander, C. (1991) The predictive power of personality assessment. Paper presented at BIG Symposium, Cambridge, p. 2.

Paterson, J. (1967) Handwriting survey. *Mensa Journal* (March).

Rafaeli, A. and Klimoski, R. (1983) Predicting sales success through handwriting analysis: an evaluation of the effect of training and handwriting sample content. *Journal of Applied Psychology*, **68**.

Robbins, W. (1991) Betrayal. Mordechai Vanunu – the man who revealed Israel's nuclear secrets. *New Moon* (December).

Shakleton (1991) Quoted in Carrington, L. (1991) *Personnel Today*, 5–18 Feb.

Sonneman, V. and Kernon, J. (1962) Handwriting analysis: a valid selection tool? *Personnel Administrator*, **39**.

Squire, H. (1967) *Graphology as a Method of Selecting Employees*, Ohio State University.

Smith, M. and Abrahamsen, M. (1992) Patterns of selection in six countries. *The Psychologist*, 5, 205–7.

Wallner, T. (1975) Hypothesis of handwriting and their verification. *Professional Psychology*, **6**.

Williams, H. and Stuparich, G. (1989) Validity and reliability of handwriting analysis. Paper presented at BIG Symposium.

Zdep, S. and Weaver, H. (1967) The graphoanalytic approach to selecting life insurance salesmen. *Journal of Applied Psychology*, **51**.

DISCUSSION QUESTIONS

In the light of the text on graphology, consider the following questions:

1. Why do you think attitudes towards graphology differ markedly from one European country to another?
2. Compare the reliability and validity of graphology to other selection techniques. To what extent is the proven effectiveness of different techniques reflected in their popularity?
3. Why are such techniques as the interview – which are commonly seen to have low predictive value – still widely used?
4. What applications can graphology have in personnel management?

SUGGESTED READING

Hoban, E., Prag, N. and Moss, G. (1992) *The Uses of Graphology in Business*, Mercury Books.

Cascio, W.F. (1991) *Applied Psychology in Personnel Management*, Chapters 7, 8 and 9. Prentice-Hall International, Eaglewood Cliffs, New Jersey, pp. 123–187.

CASE 10

Developing the best managers? An assessment centre for general managers in the NHS

DAVID PERKINS and TONY SNAPES

INTRODUCTION

South East Thames Regional Health Authority (SETRHA) is part of the British National Health Service (NHS) and is responsible for the provision of services to 3.2 million people in south-east England. These services are planned together with the local health authorities, hospitals, community health services, and the family doctors within the region which includes south-east London, and the counties of Kent and East Sussex. In all, approximately 73 000 staff are employed and, of those, around 15% are employed in a managerial capacity.

The 1980s saw the introduction of commercial models of general management following a report by Sir Roy Griffiths which, as one of its proposals, included a move from functional and professional management to general management. The new general managers were expected to take personal responsibility for service achievements and to make up for the deficits of functional management, which was widely felt to be slow and unresponsive with considerable discussion but little action. General management would make it quite clear who was in charge in each part of the service and who could be called to account.

The implementation of general management in SETRHA required a new culture led by distinctive managers with new competencies. This case concerns the process set up to find staff from within the service to fill the roles of general manager.

INTRODUCING GENERAL MANAGEMENT IN SETRHA

The Griffiths Report gave few clues to the Human Resources Department when it came to finding appropriate people to fill the general management positions. At the top level of district and regional general managers there was no dearth of applicants, and using traditional procedures posts were advertised, interviews undertaken and appointments made subject to confirmation by the Secretary of State for Health, which emphasizes the extent of political influence within the service.

Human Resources Management in Europe
Edited by Sarah Vickerstaff
Published in 1992 by Chapman & Hall, London, ISBN 0 412 45380 0

The Human Resources Department made its first important decision, which was not to fight the established procedures for this top level of posts but to focus on creating a reservoir of individuals from all the functional areas who would make credible candidates for Board level positions in the first instance and then for general manager positions. Where appropriate, advice was given to appointment panels for the top general manager positions, but the main focus of attention was at the operational or unit level, i.e. hospital, community services, and care of the long-term and mentally ill. Altogether, these services employed 73 000 staff (headcount).

The South East Thames Regional Health Authority has responsibility for:

1. *Family Health Services*   Five authorities cover the services offered by general practitioners, dentists, opticians, and the staff employed by them providing a first level service to the whole region.
2. *Hospital and Community Health Services*   15 District Health Authorities with the full range of hospital and community services for the acutely ill, mentally ill and handicapped, elderly, and the full range of public health and health promotion services. Also included in this category are teaching hospitals and highly specialist medical services.

DEFINING GENERAL MANAGEMENT

While there are clear models of general management in the private product and service sectors the same could not be said of the public sector. Public servants are subject to political control, or, in the case of the NHS, control through politically appointed authorities of lay and professional members. Health service managers were involved in the implementation of policy decided ultimately by others. Even when the role could be clearly described, it was not clear what skills would be required to perform effectively.

The approach taken was to work with a wide range of managers within the service to identify the range of competencies it was thought might be required in this new role and then to create a process of assessment centres to see if individuals with such skills, or the potential to develop them, could be found within the service. Limited resources were available and it was thought appropriate to concentrate them on managers whose potential had been rigorously assessed.

IDENTIFYING COMPETENCIES

While there were many sources of generic competencies, the nature of health service management made many of them inappropriate. Additionally the HR Department was in no position to impose its own views on top managers in the service who were at liberty to take or reject its findings. The process undertaken to identify competencies was designed, therefore, to generate a raft of managerial support strong enough to ensure that the whole process could be carried through.

After obtaining the public support of the Regional general manager, a process was implemented to determine competencies with a structured sample of 30 managers within the Region. Trained interviewers used a combination of Repertory Grid Analysis, Critical Incident Analysis, and expert panels to identify and test the competencies described below.

LIST OF AGREED COMPETENCIES

Criteria for identification of those with aptitude for general management – GMTS II

1. PEOPLE ORIENTATION
Promotes team working and cooperation. Takes others' interest and views fully into account. Supports and enables staff to achieve their objectives. Manages in an open manner, establishing good relationships with a wide range of staff.

2. PERSONAL SKILLS
   (a) *Communication Skills*
      (i) Oral – Expresses complex issues succinctly. Spoken communication is clear, confident, enthusiastic and appropriate for audience.
      (ii) Written – Expresses complex issues succinctly. Written work is clear, concise, well researched, grammatically correct and appropriate for the audience.

   (b) *Interpersonal Skills*
      Shows skills in listening and empathy. Recognizes threads, identifies lines of agreement and keeps order. Negotiates sensitively, keeps in mind key objectives and outcomes. Consults and takes account of a wide range of opinion.

3. PERSUASION/INFLUENCE
Able to influence people and 'win the day'. Persuades people to accept and implement controversial decisions. Assists others to see issues in a wider context.

4. LEADERSHIP
Takes control and manages a situation. Draws on strengths and weaknesses of others. Acts as catalyst giving direction and energy to team. Gives clear instructions.

5. PERSISTENCE IN GOAL ACHIEVEMENT
Hard-working, accepts responsibility, and follows through issues to completion. Routinely meets tight deadlines. Willing to confront difficult issues with energy to resolve them. Accepts organizational goals and shows high level of personal commitment. Continues to pursue goals despite setbacks.

6. CONSISTENCY UNDER PRESSURE
Accepts pressure and always meets deadlines. Keeps sense of humour and resilience. Remains accessible to staff.

7. CREATIVE RESOURCE MANAGEMENT

Thinks independently and has original ideas. Finds entrepreneurial solutions but recognizes organizational culture. Manages creatively in crisis. Creative use of budgets enables achievement of goals. Able to respond to shifting priorities by changing use of resources.

8. PRIORITY AND OBJECTIVE SETTING

Sets clear priorities. Recognizes implications of priorities for organization and staff. Delegates and monitors progress towards objectives. Takes short-term action in light of major objectives.

9. PROBLEM ANALYSIS

Is able to grasp a complex problem quickly. Uses information and analysis effectively to identify options. Considers solutions to problems that are entrepreneurial and new and appreciates possible outcomes. Tackles difficult as well as easy problems.

10. PLANNING AND ORGANIZING

Thinks ahead and plans practical actions to achieve objectives. Recognizes needs and takes action to meet them. Ensures staff are aware of and pursuing plans.

11. DECISION MAKING

Makes quick decisions without unnecessary consultation or delay, recognizing where further information/support is necessary. Recognizes implications of decisions for long-term goals. Willing to make unpopular decisions if necessary.

A critical requirement of the competencies we identified was that they needed to be identifiable by objective observers in real situations and by trained observers in the simulated exercises that make up an assessment centre. In essence, they needed to be not only behavioural but also to have a high level of face and inter-observer validity.

The resulting competency statements were strongly challenged, by the assessors in particular, at the developmental stage but remained acceptable for the duration of the assessment process, a period of 3 years and 6 months.

FROM COMPETENCIES TO COMPETENCE

With an agreed set of competencies for the target posts, the next steps of Assessment Centre design, assessor training, and candidate nomination commenced. The Assessment Centre had to meet the following requirements:

1. The whole process needed to be regarded as valid and professional by managers within the region and by all participants.
2. The process had to be seen to benefit even those managers who were not selected for accelerated development to general managerial positions.
3. The assessment of individuals within the Centre had to be undertaken

by trained assessors drawn from among the senior managers within the region who needed to be persuaded that the process was worth while and who had to perform at a high level of objectivity in making their assessments.
4. The Assessment Centre had to prove attractive to ensure ongoing nominations and not frighten prospective candidates.

Assessor training and workshop development took place together, enabling assessors to act as an expert panel in assessing the face validity of the assessment instruments. Assessors needed to learn and practice some basic skills, specifically behavioural observation, and distinguishing between observed behaviour and the assessment of that behaviour against the competencies. One of the principle assumptions of the process was that observation and assessment needed to be separated as far as possible to ensure that judgements took account of observed evidence and to minimize as far as was possible the effect of individual assessor bias.

ASSESSMENT CENTRE DESIGN

The Assessment Centres, entitled Career Development Workshops in order to foster a positive set of expectations, had two components: the assessment process which came first; and the career development process which followed. The process ended with the first stage in the feedback process in which the assessors, after due consideration, shared their agreed findings with each participant. This immediate feedback prevented problems arising from prolonged uncertainty for candidates. Assessors were required to complete their written reports before leaving the Centre to ensure that subsequent stages could continue promptly.

The Centres lasted for 48 hours and were residential. While the assessors were considering their observation data and preparing for the assessor conference to agree recommendations, the participants took part in a self-assessment workshop using a range of introspective methods to consider their career progress to date and their preferences for the future. This component was 'insulated' from the rest of the workshop in that the leader was not party to any of the data from the assessment part of the workshop.

Assessment exercises were chosen to meet the requirements of the competency framework with the deliberate intention that each competency should be addressed by two or more sources of data in order to prevent undue influence arising from one poor, or indeed exceptional, exercise. Table C10.1 shows the exercises set against the competency framework showing how each exercise contributed to the whole.

MAKING DECISIONS

The decisions made by the Centre were important to the candidate for a number of reasons. While performance review processes were in

Table C10.1

F = Focus * = Primary data source ○ = Secondary data source	Numerical/verbal tests	Interview	Analysis and scheduling exercise	Assigned role exercise	Non-assigned role exercise
People orientation		F			*
Oral communication		*	*	*	*
Written communication			*		
Interpersonal				*	*
Persuasion/influence		*	*	*	*
Leadership				*	*
Persistence			○	*	*
Consistency under pressure		F	○	*	
Creative resource management		F	*		*
Priority and objective setting			*		
Problem analysis	*		*		
Planning and organization			*		
Decision making			○	*	*

operation, these were not consistent in their implementation. Neither were they regarded as objective in their judgements. For many candidates the view of the assessors was likely to have an important positive or negative effect on their perceptions of their own managerial skills and, as important, their aptitude for future promotions. Many were currently working within a professional function, e.g. nursing, and a move towards general management would imply managing a number of discrete functions or a particular service component outside their own personal experience.

The views of the assessors were made known to the individual and their manager together with preliminary thoughts from the assessor as to how the individual's personal competencies and management contribution might be best developed. These were later developed into personal development plans. Thus the assessment process might result in valuable career development opportunities for an individual 'recognized' as having the aptitude for a more demanding managerial position.

Line managers accepted that under normal working conditions they were not always able to make a good judgement about the managerial capabilities of their staff. They often had received little management training, or else the members of staff were in jobs which they performed comfortably and which offered little scope for job expansion.

Finally, decisions were important since entry to the accelerated development scheme implied investments made from the regional level which were not otherwise available to candidates. Membership of this cohort promised new opportunities for advancement.

RESULTS OF CAREER DEVELOPMENT CENTRES

Outcomes for individuals

We were fortunate in that we were able to evaluate the scheme. By mid-1990, 60 individuals had gone through the career development workshops and 16 had been accepted onto the scheme. All 16 were followed up, as were a sample of those not accepted. The scheme was designed to identify and develop individuals with managerial potential in the short term, and thus the individuals who had been on the scheme for two years were the focus. On the follow-up some 40% of the 1988 intake had achieved the target level role in two years, well ahead of schedule, and another 25% reported that it would occur soon.

All had experienced significant role changes into management and reported considerable personal development, the most significant source was the challenge of a managerial role and the most helpful development support, a mentor.

Other key support came from a programme that emphasized self-awareness and personal role exploration. Coming to terms with the role and identifying a personal management identity was frequently quoted as a key challenge. Formal training in managerial techniques was reported as less helpful!

Interestingly, the manner of many of the participants seemed to have changed over the period of the development programme. They were, by and large, now very confident and physically poised young men and women! The scheme appeared to have had a substantial motivating effect on participants. As one person put it: 'without the scheme I would have left the service'.

The workshop seemed to have had a useful career planning and motivating effect on those accepted onto the scheme. The objective feedback was valued in particular. Seventy-five per cent of the individuals not accepted onto the scheme had taken up some form of development since the workshop. The career planning and personal planning had still stayed with them and a number of them were continuing with planned job changes to broaden experience and continue into management.

On a financial note, the majority of those accepted onto the scheme recorded substantial personal salary increases, ranging from two-thirds to a doubling of salary over the training period.

Outcomes for the organization

In the light of the scale of SETRHA described above, the identification of 15 potential top managers was a valuable contribution but not likely to solve succession problems alone. It did, however, demonstrate that the methods used had considerable positive effect and they have since been expanded and developed at regional level and also within operational units.

The development of assessor/managers shows that the skills of assessment have wide currency in day-to-day management situations fostering closer and more reflective observation of manager behaviour and a stronger interest in planned manager development.

The experience of planned personal manager development also showed that the medium-term interests of the organization and the individual often require that the short-term operational interest must, to some extent, be sacrificed. For instance, the movement of a manager into a new post for development purposes might mean that short-term arrangements have to be made to replace the individual and to ensure that the current workload is covered and also that, in the new post, it might take some months for the manager to reach optimal levels of performance.

A frequent complaint was made that the focus of attention and resources towards small numbers of 'high-flyers' is at the expense of the vast majority of managers for whom development opportunities were more limited. The extent to which such methods can be extended within the organization without losing their effect is an empirical question for which results are, as yet, not available.

Investment in manager development has a price: whether the investment pays off will be seen in future years.

DISCUSSION QUESTIONS

1. Is this approach to manager development likely to improve opportunities for women and other disadvantaged groups, to increase organizational mobility, or promote effective recruitment to general management positions?

2. What appear to be the costs and benefits of such an approach? Could it be adapted for use in other organizations?
3. Are there any dangers inherent in such an approach?

SUGGESTED READING

Cascio, W. F. (1991) Managerial selection, in *Applied Psychology in Personnel Management*, Chapter 14, Prentice-Hall, London, pp. 307–37.

Seegers, J. J. J. L. (1992) Assessment Centres for identifying long-term potential and for self development, in *Human Resource Strategies* (ed. G. Salaman) Sage, London, pp. 273–302.

Sadler, P. (1989) Managerial development, in *Personnel Management in Britain* (ed. K. Sisson), Basil Blackwell, Oxford, pp. 222–46.

Woodruffe, C. (1990) *Assessment Centres: Identifying and Developing Competence*, Institute of Personnel Management, London.

PART FOUR

Human Resource Development

THE EUROPEAN PERSPECTIVE

Training and development policies have attracted considerable comparative interest in the 1980s as many have suggested the link between effective training and organizational performance. Within Europe there are many different systems of training. The approach to training in the various countries can be differentiated in terms of the prevailing legislation, the role of government and the social partners in training policy and institutions, and the attitudes and expectations of individuals (Drake, 1991).

These differences are reflected in the nature, scope and comprehensiveness of vocational qualifications in different countries. There are considerable variations in the numbers of young people who continue into further and higher education; the numbers of school leavers taking apprenticeships; and the range of training and qualifications that adults at work are able to aim for. The link between a well-qualified and skilled workforce and high-quality products, efficiency and capacity for innovation is increasingly being made (see, for example, Finegold and Soskice, 1988).

In the post-1983 European Community, with the expansion of businesses within Europe and greater labour mobility among professional, managerial and possibly skilled manual or intermediate skilled groups, the question of how someone is qualified takes on new significance. As we saw with the personnel profession, the typical routes to positions as personnel or human resource managers varies in the different European countries. If we take another example, that of accountants (see Text 5), it is easy to see why the issue of common qualifications across Europe is both an important and a thorny one.

Notwithstanding the different institutional supports for training in different countries, organizations have the key role in developing their human resources and making the best use of the talents and aptitudes that their workforces possess. Thus the management of training is a critical aspect of human resource management, in fact Keep (1992, p. 321) has gone as far as to say:

Companies that, for whatever reasons, are inclined to treat their employees simply as a cost or commodity, and who hence fail to invest in training and development activity, cannot meaningfully be said to be practising human resource management.

A SYSTEMATIC APPROACH TO TRAINING AND DEVELOPMENT

Employee resourcing and human resource development are necessarily linked parts of the human resource management process. Training can often be an alternative strategy to recruitment for meeting labour requirements. Through training and development activities the organization is seeking to improve upon its human capital and maximize the value of its investment in staff. Training in this light is a vital part of the performance equation; well-trained employees make better products, serve the customer more effectively, and are likely to have more ideas about how to change the process and the product to improve quality and efficiency. However, the benefits of a well-trained workforce can only be realised if the training effort is properly managed. Training of itself is not necessarily beneficial, but appropriate training is, if it is effectively given to the right employees.

Training and development activities may be focused upon relatively short-term needs such as providing good induction for new employees; they may be continuous in terms of providing the training and experience needed to acquire particular job-related skills; they may be more long term in the sense of a programme of skills updating in preparation for the introduction of new systems or processes, or to develop the next generation of managers that the organization will need.

Organizations facing particular pressures from labour or product markets or from technological change may need to upgrade and increase their investment in training activities in order to meet business objectives. For example, the manufacturer of road safety equipment in Case 8 may need to invest in extra training if new European quality standards are introduced.

Organizations need to develop a systematic approach to the identification and evaluation of training needs, what is often in English called a Training Needs Analysis (TNA). A TNA may need to address a number of different levels: the organizational level in terms of business strategies and their related impact upon skills requirements; the job level at which the tasks to be performed and the required performance levels condition the skills needs; and the individual level, at which current and desired performance and rated potential determine the necessary training and development requirements.

Identifying training needs at these different levels ties into other human resource management processes. At the organizational level human resource planning activities feed into the analysis of the numbers and qualities of employees needed in the medium to long term. In a large organization in a stable environment the main focus may be on career planning and succession issues; in a technologically turbulent context the accent may be upon predicting longer term skill needs in relation to changing technologies.

At the job level, job analysis, work study and productivity assessment activities feed into the definition of the skills and experience requirements for particular jobs. At the individual level appraisal and performance assessment systems provide information on training needs and promotion potential.

Once training needs have been framed it is then necessary to assess how the needs can best be met and objectives set for the training activity. The selection of particular training techniques, methods and strategies must be considered in terms of the resources available, the suitability of different options, and the applicability of different approaches. Any training that is done should be evaluated in order to assess its effects in terms of objectives set.

PERFORMANCE APPRAISAL

Appraisal is an important way of assessing individual performance and identifying training needs and career development possibilities. Appraisal is a necessary part of all situations in which people are managed; supervisors or managers assess the performance and abilities of those they manage on an informal basis. These judgements may be important in terms of the allocation of work, recommendations for promotion, etc. More and more organizations see the need to put such processes on a formal basis through performance appraisal systems (Knueppel, 1991).

Performance appraisal and review has been a typical part of managerial and professional work for a long time. Appraisal systems are also a significant element of most approaches to management development. Surveys in Britain have suggested that other white collar workers and some manual employees are increasingly being included in formal appraisal procedures (Long, 1986).

Appraisal schemes can have a number of different objectives: to assess training and development needs; to assist career planning processes; for promotion purposes; to motivate employees to achieve desired performance; to link pay to performance; and to set performance objectives. Schemes may combine a number of different objectives – for example, to identify training needs and assess individuals with regard to pay levels. The focus of appraisal activity can be both positive and negative, that is, designed to develop performance or control it. This may present problems in systems where a number of different objectives are combined.

As Figure P4.1 suggests, an appraisal scheme which tries to combine development and control objectives may put the appraiser in the difficult role of being both a judge and a helper. The appraisee in such a situation is unlikely to view the appraisal situation as an opportunity for free and fair discussion of his or her work performance and development needs. A good appraisal system – that is, one that managers consider to be useful

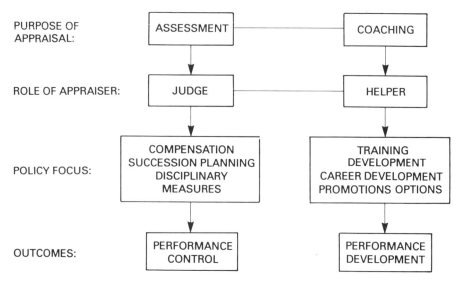

Fig. P4.1   Different approaches to staff appraisal.

to them and in which staff have confidence – can be an invaluable part of a training and development system.

MANAGEMENT DEVELOPMENT AND CAREER PLANNING

The development of an organization's managers concerns not only issues of training needs but the wider context of career structures, promotion policies and succession planning. In short, developing the managerial tier concerns the whole issue of organizational development and change. Case 13 indicates this link clearly in showing that determining the skills needs of managers in the post-communist economy of Czechoslovakia inevitably involves consideration of organizational restructuring and redesign.

Around Europe the typical routes into managerial employment and the career expectations of managers differ widely (Roomkin, 1991, pp. 222–3). In the increasingly international labour markets of the 1990s, organizations will have to develop their skills in recruiting, training, retaining and developing their managerial resources. Organizations in eastern Europe face particular challenges in developing a managerial cadre with the skills to manage new market-driven companies.

There are typically seen to be a number of interrelated components to a systematic approach to management development, as expressed in Figure P4.2. Organization development is linked to human resource planning in terms of posing the questions about where the organization is going and what kind of managerial talent will be needed; for example, the balance between technical, professional and general managers. The next part

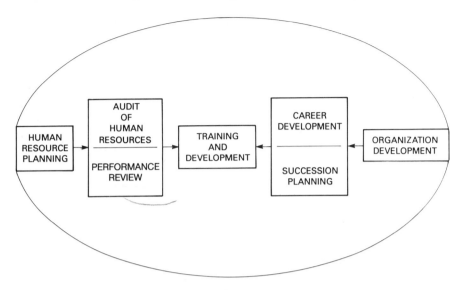

Fig. P4.2   The management development cycle.

of the cycle is consideration of current managerial stocks in terms of abilities, numbers, age patterns and skills mix. This links into assessments of career paths, succession planning and individual career development needs. The training and development activities required flow from these previous parts of the cycle. For smaller companies the level of sophistication needed in these analyses may be slight; however, manual replacement and succession planning can help to focus the management development effort to where it is needed.

Many commentators are arguing that in the 1990s the development of managerial talent will be a key factor for organizational success. Roomkin, reporting on a comparative study of managerial employment in a number of countries, has identified three key issues in managerial deployment: an interest in utilizing managers more effectively and efficiently; the increasing diversity in patterns of managerial employment and mobility and, thirdly, the widespread interest in women's increasing representation in managerial employment (Roomkin, 1991, pp. 220–1). Some of the trends identified are potentially contradictory; for example, increasing interest in foreign assignments and secondments for managers may conflict with equal opportunities policies which argue that mobility requirements for management promotions disproportionately disadvantage female managers (Beck and Steel, 1989).

It is also clear that attitudes to international and intranational mobility among managers and professionals vary from country to country and from person to person. Bournois and Metcalfe (1991, p. 243) report that Belgians and Danes are more geographically mobile than the Swedes or British. The development of dual-career families and changing male attitudes towards involvement in domestic activities will inevitably affect individuals' willingness to go wherever the company may want them to.

The cases in the rest of this section explore a wide range of training and development issues. Text 5, on accountancy training, gives the reader an opportunity to consider the problems of harmonizing qualifications and training standards within Europe and the attendant problems for training and managing an international workforce. Case 11, on determining skill needs in a leisure organization setting, provides a practical example of how to do a training needs analysis and provide appropriate training in a resource constrained environment. Case 12 looks at language training needs in multinational companies. It suggests that organizations may need to consider not only which languages their staff should be able to speak but also how to improve awareness of how business is done in other countries. The final case in this section, Case 13, involves the practical issue of how to determine and provide appropriate training for Czechoslovakian managers in the context of the change from state-owned to market-driven organizations. This clearly indicates that management development questions cannot be separated from the larger issues of organizational development.

SUGGESTED READING FOR PART FOUR

Beck, J. and Steel, M. (1989) *Beyond the Great Divide: Introducing Equality for Women in the Company*, Pitman, London.

Bournois, F. and Metcalfe, P. (1991) HR management of executives in Europe, in *International Comparisons in Human Resource Management* (eds C. Brewster and S. Tyson), Pitman, London. pp. 240–56.

Drake, K. (1991) Interventions in market financing of training in the European Community, in *International Comparisons of Vocational Education and Training for Intermediate Skills* (ed. P. Ryan), Falmer Press, London, pp. 207–30.

Finegold, D. and Soskice, D. (1988) The failure of training in Britain; Analysis and prescription *Oxford Review of Economic Policy* **4**(3) pp. 21–53.

Handy, C. (1987) *The Making of Managers: A Report on Management Education, Training and Development in the United States, West Germany, France, Japan and the UK*, National Economic Development Office, London.

Holden, L. (1991) European trends in training and development. *International Journal of Human Resource Management*, **2**(2), pp. 113–32.

Keep, E. (1992) Corporate training strategies: the vital component, in *Human Resource Strategies* (ed. G. Salaman) Sage, London, pp. 320–36.

Knueppel, K.-D. (1991) Staff appraisal as a management tool: practice and current trends. *Journal of European Business Education*, **1** (No. 1), 26–46.

Long, P. (1986) *Performance Appraisal Revisited*, IPM, London.

Mayo, A. (1991) *Managing Careers: Strategies for Organizations*, IPM, London.

Nordhaug, O. (1990) Human resource provision and transformation: the role of training and development. *Human Resource Management Journal*, **1** (No. 2). pp. 17–26.

Roomkin, M. J. (1991) The changing characteristics of managers and managerial employment in the 1980s, in *International Comparisons in Human Resource Management* (eds. C. Brewster and S. Tyson), Pitman, London. pp. 217–26.

Scase, R. and Goffee, R. (1989) *Reluctant Managers*, Chapter 4, Unwin Hyman, London, pp. 78–105.

Torrington, D. and Hall, L. (1991) *Personnel Management*, Chapter, 23, pp. 25–7. Prentice Hall, Hemel Hempstead.

TEXT 5

Training accountants in Europe

GERARD REILLY

This text presents an article reproduced, with permission, from the *European Accountant* July/August 1991, which indicates the different traditions in accountancy education throughout Europe. This profession provides one example of the problems faced in the attempt to harmonize qualifications across Europe in order to facilitate the job mobility of professionals.

Varied approaches to training for accounting students

As 1992 draws closer, EA loks at the different ways to qualify as an accountant in Europe

The UK remains the bastion of accounting profession, according to EA's Students Survey. With 161 160 students between the country's five institutes, the profession in the UK seems set to retain its numeric strength.

Elsewhere in Europe, numbers are lower with 3300 'experts-comptables' students in France and 5600 at the Dutch Institute. On the other hand, the Kammer Der Wirtschaftstreuhänder in Austria has 119 students.

The survey also shows the different approaches taken to the training of accountants. While in the UK, Ireland and some other countries these matters are handled by the institutes, in some European countries it is the responsibility of government and the universities. For example, in Germany, the institutes do not train students. Members are only admitted having passed their final examination, which is organised by the state.

There are different professional levels across Europe. In Austria, the profession is divided between Steuerberater (tax consultants) and Wirtschaftsprüfer und Steuerberater (auditors and tax consultants). 'Everybody must first become a steuerberater and work professioanally as

This article has been reproduced from EUROPEAN ACCOUNTANT, courtesy of Lafferty Publications Ltd, IDA Tower, Pearse Street, Dublin 2, Ireland. Tel. 353-1-718022, Fax. 353-1-718240.

Human Resources Management in Europe
Edited by Sarah Vickerstaff
Published in 1992 by Chapman & Hall, London. ISBN 0 412 45380 0

STUDENTS SURVEY

Country	Body	Number of students	Number sitting final exam	Number of members	Number admitted in past year	Average age of students	Number of women students (%)	Is a university degree necessary?	Experience required after college	Does degree have to be in a relevant subject?	How long does it take to qualify as a member of the institute?
Austria	Kammer Der Wirtschaftstreuhänder	119	41	514***	34	35	20	Yes	6 years	Yes	—
Belgium	Institut Des Experts-Comptables	—	582	734	159	—	—	No	—	—	—
Belgium	Institut Des Reviseurs D'Entreprises	374	70	782	63	25	29	No	—	—	3 years
Cyprus	The Institute of Certified Public Accountants of Cyprus	—	—	500ᶠ	80	—	—	—	—	—	—
Denmark	Foreningen Af Statsautoriserde	8	165	2435	60	32	30	Yes	3 years	Yes	8–12 year
France	Compagnie Nationale Des Commissaires Aux Comples	—	14	12246†	1132†	—	—	Yes	3 years	No	7 years
France	Conseil Superior De L'Ordre Des Experts-Comptables	3300ᶠ	1287	12300	975	22	50	Yes	3 years	Yes	7 years
Germany	Institut Der Wirtschaftsprüfer	—	—	6995	408	30	—	Yes	5 years	Yes	Degree + 5 years exp + exam
Germany	Wirtschaftsprüferkammer	—	—	12444	975	30	—	Yes	5 years	Yes	Degree + 5 years exp + exam
Greece*	SOL Institute of Certified Public Accountants of Greece	185	56	593	56	32	28	Yes	None	Yes	11 years
Iceland	Felag loggiltra endurskodenda**	50ᶠ	40	184	4	28	20	Yes	3 years	Yes	Uni + 3 years exp + exam
Ireland	The Institute of Certified Public Accountants in Ireland	1340	407	850	81	23	35	No	3 years	No	3–5 years
Ireland	The Institute of Chartered Accountants in Ireland	2500	716	7300	433	20	33	No	$3\frac{1}{2}$ years	No	$3\frac{1}{2}$ years

Luxembourg‡	Ordre des Experts-Comptables Luxembourgeois	13	—	95	4	25	15	Yes	3 years	Yes	3 years
The Netherlands	Nederlands Instituut Van Registeraccountants	5600	318	7436	590	26	20	Yes††	$2\frac{1}{2}$	Yes	$7\frac{1}{2}$ years
Norway	Norges Statsautoriserte Revisorers Forening	—	—	1250	71	—	—	Yes	2 years	Yes	6 years
Portugal	Camara Dos Revisores Oficialis De Contas	250ᵉ	160	680	45	40	$12\frac{1}{2}$	Yes	3 years	Yes	3–5 years
Spain	Consejo Superior De colegios Oficiales De Titulados Mercantiles y Empresariales De España	8	8	14000	1000ᵉ	8	20ᵉ	Yes	3 years	Yes	3–5 years
Spain	Instituto de Censores Jurados de Cuentas de España	—	1067	6200	—	—	—	Yes	3 years	No	6–8 years
Sweden	Foreningen Auktoriserade Revisorer	8	8	1827	223	27	29	Yes	5 years	Yes	$8\frac{1}{2}$ years
Switzerland	Treuhand Kammer	1200	330	2550	300	32	5	Yes	7 years	Yes	7–12 years
	The Chartered Association of Certified Accountants	82988	9643	35663	2075	—	35	No	—	—	3 years
	The Chartered Institute of Public Finance and Accountancy	3108	821	11193	451	18†	—	No	—	—	3 years
	The Chartered Institute of Management Accountants	50740	7169	30677	1637	29	28	No	3 years after college	No	3–4 years
United Kingdom	The Institute Of Chartered Accountants in England and Wales	22624	8790	96756	3922	23	35	No	3 years	No	3–4 years
	The Institute of Chartered Accountants and Scotland	1700	585	12500	432	23	40	Yes	3 years	No	3 years

ᵉ = Estimate, † = Including firms, †† = or a NIVRA education, ‡ = Institut des Reviseurs d'Entreprises did not respond, § = Registro de Economistas Auditores did not respond, * = The Association of Certified Accountants and Auditors of Greece did not respond to the survey, ** = Exams are organized by the University of Iceland, *** = Wirtschaftsprüfer only. NOTE: Neither of the Italian Institutes nor the Finnish Institute responded to the survey

European Accountant July/August 1991

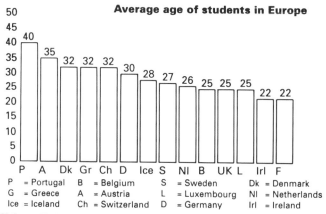

Average age of students in Europe

P   = Portugal   B   = Belgium   S   = Sweden   Dk = Denmark
G   = Greece   A   = Austria   L   = Luxembourg   NI = Netherlands
Ice = Iceland   Ch = Switzerland D   = Germany   Irl = Ireland

NOTE: Cyprus, Gibraltar, Norway and Spain - no figures supplied. Italy and Finland did not reply.

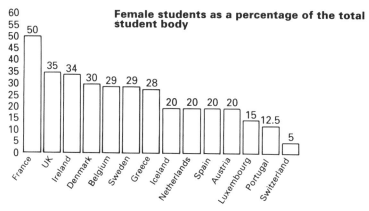

Female students as a percentage of the total student body

NOTE: Norway, Germany, Cyprus and Gibraltar - no figures supplied. Italy and Finland did not reply

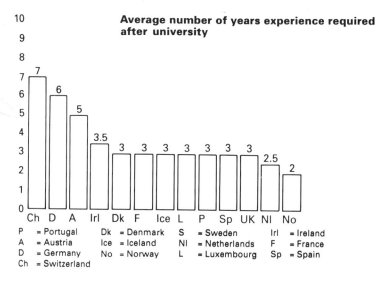

Average number of years experience required after university

P   = Portugal   Dk = Denmark   S   = Sweden   Irl = Ireland
A   = Austria   Ice = Iceland   NI = Netherlands F   = France
D   = Germany   No = Norway   L   = Luxembourg   Sp = Spain
Ch = Switzerland

such for three years before being admitted to the professional examination of Wirtschaftsprüfer,' said Dr Ernst Traar of the Kammer Der Wirtschaftsprüfer.

The age range of students reflects the varied approach to training. The UK, France, Ireland, Luxembourg and Belgium are the lowest with students in their low or mid-twenties, while in the Germanic countries they tend to be much older. In Portugal, the average is 40 years – the highest in the survey – while Greece and Austria are not far behind.

This is also the case in Iceland, Norway and Sweden. According to Stefan Svavarsson, Associate Professor of Accounting at the University of Iceland, 'students must have graduated from the University of Iceland in business administration with a major in accounting.' However, some of the students do not sit the professional exams, going instead to work in industry. In Norway, prospective accountants study at the Norwegian School of Economics and Business Administration and then follow this with advanced auditing studies and final accounting exams.

Women make up significant proportions of the student body of accountants throughout Europe. The figure is as high as 50 percent for 'experts-comptables' in France with the UK next highest at 35 percent followed closely by Ireland at 34 percent. The figure is significantly lower in Switzerland at 5 percent, although 10 percent of students were women in 1988. On average, 24 percent of students are women.

A university degree ia a necessity throughout most of Europe for entry into the profession. The UK and Ireland are the main exceptions to this.

In line with the Eighth Directive, three years experience is becoming the standard throughout the EC although all countries have not yet implemened this. Elsewhere, this period varies from two years in Norway to seven in Switzerland depending on a number of factors, including whether the applicant has attended university.

Gerard Reilly

DISCUSSION QUESTION

In the light of the above article consider the following task. You are the personnel manager responsible for the annual intake of junior accountants in a large management and accounting consultancy that operates throughout Europe. The company has major branches in Athens, Vienna, Lisbon and Stockholm with small satellites in many other major European cities. In the past you have always recruited home country graduates for each particular branch because of the difficulties in convincing other managers that qualifications from another European country are as good as their own. Also, because of the variations in the time it takes for individuals to qualify as accountants from one country to another there are always difficult issues over what the starting salary should be.

Headquarters has asked you to consider amending the policy as it is increasingly felt that tomorrow's senior managers will need to have international experience and a truly 'European' approach to clients' work. You have to put a report before the senior management team at HQ as to how you are going to set about introducing a new approach. In particular, you are concerned about the following issues: if you do start recruiting Portuguese accountants to work in the Vienna office, for example, what kinds of training and development will the individuals need, and what degree of resistance are you likely to face from the home nationals in that office?

Put forward plans for a pilot project to test out the benefits and disadvantages of more international movements and devise a training plan for both the individual junior accountants to be recruited and an attitude change programme for existing staff in the country offices.

SUGGESTED READING

Johnson, R. (1990) Are the British qualified to join Europe? *Personnel Management* (May). pp. 50–53.

Neale, R. and Mindel, R. (1992) Rigging up multicultural teamworking. *Personnel Management* (January). pp. 36–9.

Dowling, P. J. and Schuler, R. S. (1990) Training and development, in *International Dimensions of Human Resource Management*, Chapter 5, PWS-Kent Publishing Group, Boston. pp. 93–115.

Determining training needs in the leisure industries: the case of a local authority sports and leisure centre

LINDA KEEN

CONTEXT OF THE CASE

This case is derived from an MSC-funded project, undertaken in 1988 to examine training requirements in the leisure industry. The material presented here refers to the identification of training needs in a large local authority sports and recreation centre. Leisure was one of Britain's fastest growing industries in the 1980s – employment in local authority leisure departments alone increased by 9% between 1982 and 1987. Reports from bodies such as the MSC and the Local Government Training Board indicated that relatively low priority was given to training provision in local authority leisure departments and centres.

BACKGROUND TO THE CASE

The Centre, purpose built by the district council in 1978, was situated in an attractive landscaped site on the edge of a market town (population 65 000) with a rural 'catchment area' of round 25 000 people. The facilities included: outdoor pitches for tennis and netball; two multipurpose halls, accommodating a variety of sports, and also suitable for dances, exhibitions, etc.; squash courts; indoor bowls room; weight-training room; main swimming pool, plus a small learner pool; solarium; a suite suitable for weddings, dinner dances; bar and cafe; creche facilities. The 1987/88 budget allocation for the Centre was £1 148 619; £643 501 was generated through income – from charges, equipment hire, room bookings etc. – and the council funded the remaining £505 118 from the general rate fund; loan charges of £282 519 were also funded by the council.

Human Resources Management in Europe
Edited by Sarah Vickerstaff
Published in 1992 by Chapman & Hall, London. ISBN 0 412 45380 0

THE CASE PROBLEM

Significant changes were taking place in the Centre's operating environment in 1988. The Centre faced increased competition from expanding local private sector leisure facilities. Informal feedback and complaints from Centre users indicated a growing public demand for more attractive surroundings and accommodation in the Centre, and for a wider and more sophisticated range of services and activities. The local authority required greater operating efficiency from the Centre to meet national restrictions on local authority spending, and also to enable the Centre to prepare for compulsory *competitive tendering*; in 1991 the Centre workforce would have to compete with private sector contractors to run the Centre. The local labour market was tight, with extremely low unemployment levels, a buoyant local economy with an expanding private sector, and declining numbers of young people.

In response to these developments, significant changes were required in the Centre's management and service delivery systems. The key changes, some of which were already underway, can be summarized as follows:

Service objectives

Although there was no written statement of aims and objectives, the Centre had tended historically to see its role basically as the provider of an essential social or community service, with low point-of-entry costs for users. In the absence of any formal marketing strategy, the range of sports and services provided by the Centre had tended to be directed towards the 'serious' sportsman and woman, and had developed incrementally over the years. Pricing policies – deciding on the charges to be levied for the use of Centre facilities – and promotion activities had also developed in the same piecemeal fashion.

The Centre manager planned to introduce a formal marketing strategy in 1988–89. He wanted to develop more imaginative recreation programmes, with a leisure/entertainments orientation, to supplement the traditional 'serious' sports programmes. New activities were to be offered, such as tennis and netball, the martial arts, a health and beauty suite, aerobics, etc. These programmes, together with more flexible pricing policies, would be targeted towards specific user groups – such as the disabled, parents and toddlers, women, the elderly, etc. – to ensure maximum usage during new extended opening hours, and to fill spare capacity at off-peak times. To enhance the new 'entertainment' focus of the Centre, the existing range of basic pre-packed bar and cafe snacks were to be expanded to include more sophisticated fast food, more freshly cooked meals, using fresh ingredients, together with cocktails, cut-price 'happy hours' and the introduction of children's parties as part of combined sports/party packages. Underpinning these developments was the introduction of a new customer care culture throughout the organization.

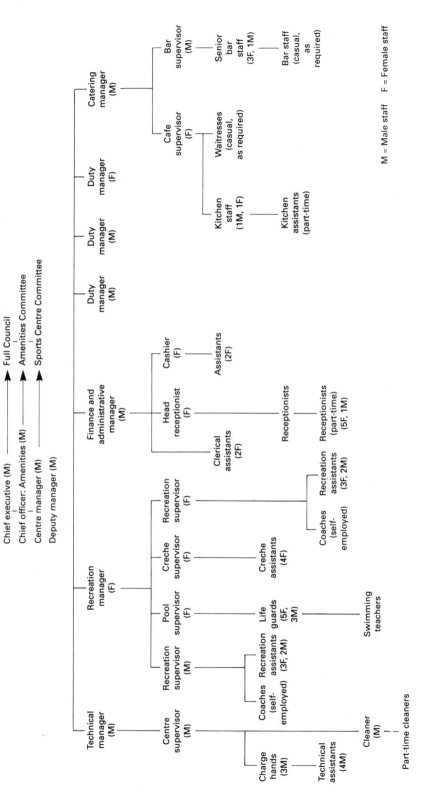

Fig. C11.1 Centre organization and structure.

Officers (Appointed)

Chief executive (M)
Chief officer: Amenities (M)
Centre manager (M)
Deputy manager (M)

Councillors (elected)

Full Council
Amenities Committee
Sports Centre Committee

M = Male staff   F = Female staff

Technical manager (M)

Recreation manager (F)

Finance and administrative manager (M)

Duty manager (M)

Duty manager (M)

Duty manager (F)

Catering manager (M)

Centre supervisor (M)

Charge hands (3M)

Technical assistants (4M)

Cleaner (M)

Part-time cleaners

Recreation supervisor (M)

Coaches (self-employed)

Recreation assistants (3F, 2M)

Pool supervisor (F)

Life guards (5F, 3M)

Swimming teachers

Creche supervisor (F)

Creche assistants (4F)

Recreation supervisor (F)

Coaches (self-employed)

Recreation assistants (3F, 2M)

Clerical assistants (2F)

Head receptionist (F)

Receptionists

Receptionists (part-time) (5F, 1M)

Cashier (F)

Assistants (2F)

Cafe supervisor (F)

Kitchen staff (1M, 1F)

Kitchen assistants (part-time)

Waitresses (casual, as required)

Bar supervisor (M)

Senior bar staff (3F, 1M)

Bar staff (casual, as required)

Management systems

Located within the Amenities Department, Centre management was fully integrated within the council's overall management systems. Centre policies, and many operational decisions, required approval by Amenity Department senior management, and then by the elected councillors on various committees and on the full council (illustrated in Figure C11.1) However, to meet the 1991 competitive tendering requirements, the council would need to adopt a 'client' role, which would concentrate on specifying the service required and monitoring performance against stringent quality standards. To prepare for its 'contractor' role, the Centre needed to develop its own independent managerial and operational systems, operating essentially as an autonomous strategic business unit within the council. The Centre manager had already identified the need for a Centre business plan, including marketing, public relations, financial and personnel strategies. Centre managers would acquire almost complete responsibility for all central services, such as personnel, from the council's central services departments.

Personnel management systems

Staffing levels, pay and conditions (performance-related pay system to be introduced in 1989) and training requirements (apart from informal on-the-job training) were all determined centrally by the Personnel Department for the whole council workforce, including that of the Centre. (See Figure C11.1 for details of the Centre's workforce and organization structure.) The Centre had no formal written training policy, nor did any formal systems exist for updating job descriptions, for staff induction, staff appraisal or development, or the determination of training needs. Training was provided (funded from central budget allocations) on an *ad hoc* basis arising from requests made by individual staff members, or from the introduction of new equipment, new sports activities, etc. On-the-job training was organized informally by Centre line managers. The deputy manager, who was to become the Centre's personnel officer, would be taking over almost complete responsibility for all personnel functions from the council's central Personnel Department.

Health and safety

The health and safety of employees and customers is a very important issue in the leisure industry. The Centre management had an excellent health and safety record, with very low accident/injuries rates; new, more stringent national regulations would require the introduction of more rigorous safety standards and procedures.

These changes in operational and management systems would have a significant impact on the duties of all Centre staff, many of whom would

Table C11.1 Key changes in staff roles

Although these roles are clearly distinguished here, some changes were already underway – for example, the new computerized booking system was already running alongside the existing manual systems.

Staff	Existing roles	New roles
Manager	Centre administrator: emphasis on control of inputs	Entrepreneurial management style: strategic planning, rigorous service and financial targets
Deputy manager	Implementing council personnel policies	Designing and monitoring Centre personnel policies, including new Centre culture
Recreation manager	Organizing existing and developing new activities, programmes, etc.	Strategic marketing, including pricing and promotion policies, new computerized MIS
Finance/ administration officer	Cost centre: cost control within the budget allocation	Profit centre: pricing relative to costs, new computerized cost control systems
Duty managers (on a rota basis)	Overall operational control of Centre, events scheduling and programming	As before, but increased levels of, and more diversified events require tighter, more efficient scheduling
Technical manager	Responsible for building and equipment maintenance, health and safety officer	Increased range of equipment, higher standards of building maintenance, more rigorous health and safety procedures, new emphasis on staff training
Technical staff	Undertaking building and equipment maintenance to high safety standards	As above, plus faster changeovers between increased numbers of events, increased functional flexibility among staff
Supervisors	Coordinating and overseeing safe service delivery, organizing shifts/rotas	Ensuring adherence to stringent service standards, new emphasis on staff training and development and staff appraisal
Recreation assistants; lifeguards	Setting up equipment, monitoring safety Some coaching	As before plus adoption of 'Butlin Redcoat' role with provision of new sports clubs, entertainments, etc.
Clerical/ reception	Operating booking systems, balancing till and cash receipts	New computerized booking and work scheduling systems, more emphasis on 'hotel receptionist' role
Catering supervisor	Organizing bar and cafe as cost centre	Profit centre, new computerized stock control, wider range of catering services, new emphasis on staff training/development
Bar/catering staff	Balancing till/cash receipts, usual bar/waiting, cooking duties	Wider range of food and drink provision, new 'host' role for integrated sports/catering functions, children's parties, etc.

have to take on new and unfamiliar roles. (These are outlined briefly in Table C11.1.) While generally welcoming and fully appreciating the need for these changes, staff in all categories felt that they needed training to equip them with the additional knowledge and skills required to carry out their new duties effectively. For example, the introduction of the new 'customer care' culture was already underway, with name badges and corporate uniforms for the staff, but many staff, although eager to adopt more 'user-friendly' attitudes and behaviour, were not sure exactly what this entailed, or what changes in operating procedures should be made. In addition, most staff felt ill-equipped to meet the more rigorous safety requirements; neither the first aid certificates (mandatory for recreation assistants) nor training in the safe erection and use of equipment had been regularly updated as required.

Of the nine Centre managers, one was halfway through a public sector management diploma course, and three held management qualifications, but all felt that their skills and knowledge required updating. The Centre manager and the recreation manager were particularly concerned about their ability to introduce effective marketing procedures; their problems ranged from making the most effective use of the new computer – for generating appropriate statistical information for planning purposes – to designing suitable promotion literature for the Centre. The technical manager and the duty managers were dissatisfied with delays and in-accuracies in the newly computerized booking and work-scheduling systems, which caused problems for the duty managers in accurately programming each day's events (requiring the use of complex spread-sheets) and for the technical supervisor in planning the allocation of work to the technical assistants. The supervisors (one of whom held a certificate in management) were also particularly concerned about their abilities to carry out effective staff appraisal and more rigorous on-the-job training. Two senior managers and several supervisors wanted the opportunity to gain management qualifications.

Unlike the rest of the Centre staff, the recreation assistants and life-guards experienced relatively low levels of job satisfaction; absenteeism and sickness rates were higher than any other staff group. As one life guard explained: 'Being a pool attendant with just a bronze medallion is the most boring dead-end job in the world. To get on, I need experience on the dry side and teaching and coaching experience, and then I want some management training so I can go on to supervision.' The most satisfying part of their work involved occasional help with coaching and instruction, but there was insufficient time available for them to develop the skills properly – and, in any case, they needed to acquire the appro-priate coaching/instructor certification. Many assistants wanted the introduction of bonus or incentive schemes, and more contact with management to discuss operational problems and suggest solutions and for regular staff development interviews.

Some of the staff in the technical section also expressed dissatisfaction with their career prospects; they wanted the chance to gain qualifications from the local college, rather than simply receiving casual on-the-job training from senior staff. These staff also lacked the skills to function adequately across the occupational boundaries of carpentry, painting, plastering work, etc.; they had tended to develop specialisms in just one of these areas, rather than developing more general 'handyman' type skills.

As the main operators of the new computer system, the receptionists, clerical assistants and cashier suffered most from the difficulties of using the system. The cashier also had to deal with recurring problems of incorrect returns from the booking till at reception, and incorrect stock control information (not yet computerized) from the catering section. While welcoming the opportunity to become more customer oriented (more like a hotel receptionist, instead of just taking money, as one staff member put it), the receptionists were sceptical of their abilities to deliver the required level of service to the public, without extra staff to cope with the queues at peak times.

The Centre deputy manager, allocated responsibility for personnel management, was aware that training was required to achieve a smooth transition to the new culture, and was planning the introduction of a coherent training policy for the Centre. However, his training budget would be severely limited, and there were particular problems in providing off-the-job training for many Centre staff.

He was aware of the low morale existing among the recreation assistants, most of whom were young people with one or two 'O' levels, and various life-saving and/or coaching/instructor certificates in particular sports. The senior managers were unable to reach a consensus on the job content, or the qualifications and experience required by these staff members. Two managers felt that recruitment should be targeted towards graduates with sports degrees, while others were dubious about the value of over-qualified assistants who might become bored, and who might lack basic practical skills. Provision of courses at local colleges, leading to qualifications for these assistants tended to require one full-day attendance each week for two years, resulting in prohibitive training costs, as cover always had to be provided for absent staff to meet the stringent health and safety regulations operated by the Centre.

This problem of funding replacements for staff undergoing training also occurred with the clerical/reception and catering staff. In addition there was a lack of local provision – by local colleges – of courses suitable for some Centre staff. The nearest college offering qualifying courses for management/supervisory staff, specifically geared towards recreation management, was nearly 50 miles away, and would require attendance for one full day every week for two years – a heavy drain on resources. The technical manager had complained about a lack of qualifying courses for his assistants which provided basic training in a combination of electrical, plumbing, bricklaying, decorating, carpentry skills, rather than specializing in just one of them. Moreover, there was the problem of finding or designing short courses, which covered precisely the new skills and knowledge required by Centre staff – for example, fast food prep-aration courses for the catering staff.

DISCUSSION QUESTIONS

For sessions of 1–1½ hours:

1. What managerial and operational changes are taking place in the Centre? What impact will these changes have on management and staff job responsibilities and activities?
2. What training do the Centre staff need to enable them to perform effectively in their new roles?
3. Bearing in mind the operational problems of providing and funding training for the Centre staff, what methods of training provision would you recommend for each category of staff? How would you determine priorities?
4. How would you attempt to evaluate the effectiveness of the training provision?

For longer sessions:

5. How would you resolve any potential conflict between the career development needs of staff and organizational requirements?
6. Suggest a training policy and management development policy for the Centre? How would you integrate it within an overall personnel management strategy for the Centre.
7. What other methods, in addition to training provision, should the Centre manager adopt for ensuring effective management of change in the Centre?

SUGGESTED READING

Livy, B. (ed.) (1989) *Corporate Personnel Management*, Part 3, Pitman, London, pp. 137–217.
Local Government Training Board (1988) *Personnel: the Agenda for Change.*
Sisson, K. (1989) *Personnel Management in Britain*, Part 4, Blackwell, Oxford.

CASE 12

Determining and training for language needs in the multi-national firm

GLORIA MOSS

WHY LANGUAGES ARE NEEDED

An increasing number of European companies are likely to need a range of foreign language skills in the years to come. This is due to a number of changing economic factors in Europe. Let us begin by looking at these. There are three main factors:

1. The European legislative framework. The Treaty of Rome established the common market in 1957 and the Single European Act (1987) should complete the process of the single market by 1992. The Commission, the policy-making body of the EC, and the lawmakers are based in French and Flemish-speaking Brussels and the European Parliament is based in French-speaking Strasbourg. Companies who want to be able to lobby effectively, and have an influence on this, need to be able to speak the languages of Brussels and Strasbourg.

2. The legislative framework is encouraging the liberalization and opening of a number of markets. The market for financial products, for example, will be opened up and financial products sold throughout Europe. In a separate area, that of public procurement, the European Commission is trying to ensure that monopoly organizations operate competitive tendering on a Europe-wide basis. At the moment, they hold significant powers: in 1990, purchasing by governments and other public bodies accounted for as much as 15% of the Community's gross domestic product. New proposals mean that this will now also affect organizations in the so-called WET sector (i.e. companies in the fields of Water, Energy and Transport) who will be exposed to competitive tenders from all over Europe.

3. The tendency to European mergers and takeovers. The present British government adopts a *laissez-faire* attitude to foreign takeovers and is unlikely to intervene in the event of a bid from a foreign company for an ailing British one. Ford was allowed to take over Jaguar cars in

Human Resources Management in Europe
Edited by Sarah Vickerstaff
Published in 1992 by Chapman & Hall, London. ISBN 0 412 45380 0

1991 and there were recent rumours of a takeover of Rolls Royce by BMW. For as long as we have a free market, British companies will be extremely vulnerable to takeovers, and we are likely to see more and more merged companies.

We do not need to look further than the examples of British water companies and financial institutions to see this tendency in operation. In the field of insurance, for example, Regency Life, Equity Law and Sun Life were all taken over recently by Dutch and French companies; and Unit Trust and Fund Managers Gartmore and Touche Remnant were both taken over by French banks. The British staff in these companies will need to have foreign language skills in order to survive.

It could be said that French and German companies are equally vulnerable to takeover. In fact, in practice this is not the case since the banks in these countries hold a very large proportion of shares in national industries. It is very difficult for anybody to take these industries over. The takeover business seems distinctly one-sided.

Some mergers do not arise through predatory activity but through a joint decision by national governments to collaborate in projects too large for one country's industry to resource alone. The Tornado fighter, Concorde, Airbus Industrie, and Superphenix are all examples of this.

OBTAINING FOREIGN LANGUAGE SKILLS

There are two ways in which companies can obtain foreign language skills:

1. Through recruitment of native or foreign language speakers.
2. Through training of existing staff.

Which one is Britain adopting? The evidence seems to suggest a bit of both.

Table C12.1 Adults (18+) who speak a European foreign language as % of total population (Gallup Survey, 1986)

Adults who speak	Belguim	Denmark	France	Germany	Ireland	Italy	N'th	Spain	UK
English	26	51	26	43	99	13	50	13	100
French	71	5	100	18	12	27	16	15	16
German	22	48	11	100	2	6	61	3	9
Italian	4	1	8	3	11	100	2	4	2
Spanish	3	1	13	1	1	5	2	100	3
Dutch	68	1	1	3	-	-	100	-	1

As far as the first option is concerned, an increasing numb·
seem to be 'buying in' the foreign skills. According to a sur
Association of Graduate Recruiters (*Personnel Today*, July 19‹
the firms surveyed were already recruiting graduates in Euro₁
20% said that they were about to start. This suggests that t'
50% of graduates would all be British.

As far as language training is concerned, it is difficult to obtain raw data on how much is going on. We do know how much it is needed, however, judging by the statistics on British abilities given in Table C12.1, there would certainly seem to be a need to learn foreign languages.

In the rest of this chapter, we shall dwell on the option of language learning and begin by lookng at the tradition of language learning in Britain and Europe. We will then consider the case of three companies who decided to increase their language skills, and will look at the issues of how to go about the training. In doing this, we will consider issues such as deciding the language objectives, deciding language content, method of delivery, timing of training and also methods of testing.

LANGUAGES IN BRITAIN

The issue of foreign language learning in Britain has for a long time been a source of humour, the delight of cartoonists and writers alike. This tradition is still going strong. Journalists on the *Daily Mail* recently telephoned, in French, the top ten British exporters to ask about placing an order. Responses ranged from switchboard operators collapsing into fits of nervous giggling to the caller just being left hanging on the line or having the calls disconnected. A foreign language induces instant apoplexy or strange distorted sounds. The words 'pedigree', 'puny', and 'Rotten Row' (in Hyde Park), derived from the French words '*pied de grue*', '*puis ne*' and '*route du roi*', all bear witness to this lively talent for mutations.

FOREIGN LANGUAGE LEARNING OUTSIDE BRITAIN

As we can see from the figures in Table C12.1, France and Germany do justify their reputaion as good Europeans. We can take comfort from the fact that it was not always thus. In fact, in Shakespeare's *Henry V* we see the new Queen, the French Katherine, struggling with English lessons from her maid Alice:

Katherine: Alice, tu as été en Angleterre, et tu parles bien le language.
Alice: Un peu, madame.
Kath: Je te prie, m'enseignez: il faut que j'apprenne à parler. Comment appelez-vous la main en anglais?
Alice: La main? Elle est appelé de hand.
Kath: De hand. Et les doigts?
Alice: Les doigts? Ma foi, j'oublie les doigts; mais je me

souviendrai. Les doigts? Je pense qu'ils sont appelés de fingres; oui, de fingres. . . .

Kath: Et le coude?

Alice: D'elbow.

Kath: Je m'en fais la répétition de tous les mots que vous m'avez apris des à present . . . écoutez; d'hand, de fingre, de nails, d'arma, de bilbow.

Alice: D'elbow, madame.

Kath: O Seigneur Dieu, je m'en oublie! D'elbow. Comment appelez-vous le col?

Alice: De nick, madame.

Kath: De nick. Et le menton?

Alice: De chin.

Kath: De sin. Le col, de nick; le menton, de sin.

And so it goes on. The moral is that perseverance will win in the end.

THREE CASE STUDIES

We mentioned above, some of the reasons why British companies would need to gain greater language skills. These were:

1. Increase in European legislation and the need to influence or respond to this.
2. Deregulation of European markets.
3. Creation of merged or bi-national companies.

In this section, we will take one example of each type of need, and show how this influenced the decision to train staff in languages.

Example 1

This case study concerns an organization that found its focus of activity shifting increasingly to Brussels as a result of the increased regulation of the industry from Europe. Many of the government standards which now exist in this industry (water) are the result of European Community Directives.

The Water Services Association   The Water Services Association (WSA) of England and Wales was established in 1989 and is an association of water and sewerage undertakers. Currently its members are the ten water service companies which are the successor companies to the water authorities and are licensed to provide both water and sewerage services. One of the main functions of the WSA is to promote and protect the common interests of the members of the association.

The two principal products with which the WSA deals – water production and sewage – are regulated from Brussels in the form of EC Directives. The WSA is able to take a proactive role and influence the legislation that Europe produces by organizing meetings of other European water associations and discussing policy issues with them. By forming alliances, it can take a European consensus to the Commission, and influence the form that future legislation takes. It can also, in the same way, help amend existing legislation.

An increasing amount of legislation is being produced in Brussels. Some of the major Directives which already exist are:

- Directive relating to the quality of water intended for human consumption.
- Directive concerning urban waste-water treatment.
- Directive concerning the quality required of surface water intended for the abstraction of drinking water in member states.
- Directive concerning the quality of bathing water.
- Directive concerning the protection of fresh, coastal and marine waters against pollution caused by nitrates from diffuse sources.
- Directive on pollution caused by certain dangerous substances discharged into the aquatic environment of the Community.
- Directive on hazardous waste.
- Directive on urban waste-water treatment.

A number of important Directives are proposed. These include a Directive on the dumping of waste at sea and a Directive on landfill. To influence the latter two, the WSA recently organized a workshop on sewage sludge in Brussels. The draft EC legislation seemed to be closing off or limiting disposal routes and the WSA felt that a more positive approach needed to be taken.

In all of its dealings with Europe, the WSA was finding that it was spending increasing amounts of time in Europe, outside the UK, and that it needed to improve the French-speaking skills of key members of staff. It therefore organized individual French tuition for the head of policy administration and for the members of the policy secretariat. The emphasis in the training was on listening skills and relevant areas of vocabulary.

The training took place early in the day when the staff would not be encumbered by conflicting priorities and continued for four hours a week for six months. The staff were highly motivated and covered the ground needed in six months. They observed that this was sufficient time given that the main requirement in meetings was to have a passive, and not active, understanding of the language. In international meetings, it is normal practice to speak one's own mother tongue, but to be called upon to listen to and understand the other person's language.

Example 2

This case study concerns a company that decided to take advantage of the new deregulated market for financial products arising from the single European market and train its staff in language skills in preparation for the launch of new products.

The Prudential Corporation   The Prudential Corporation is Britain's largest insurance company, and a very large provider of a range of other financial services. These include corporate pension schemes, personal pensions and unit trusts.

During the past five years, Directives have been drafted to permit a free export of all sorts of insurance and pension services. These concern grouped life insurance, individual life insurances and pension fund investment services. Only one of these Directives is now law, the so-called UCITS (Undertakings for Collective Investment in Transferable Securities) Directive, and this allows investment funds which comply with the UCITS criteria to be marketed throughout the EC. Thought has been given for some time to creating a new umbrella fund in 1992 from which investors throughout Europe could gain experience of the Prudential's investment expertise.

In order to provide the staff with the language skills they would need, the Prudential decided in 1989 to embark on a programme of language training for its headquarters staff. At that time, there was relatively little language competence within the group in French and German but a clear awareness that very considerable language skills needed to be built within the management team. Buying in the skills was not an option since the staff needed to be extremely expert in the field of investments. The staff needed to be trained well in advance of the date at which the skills were needed.

Key staff (about 40) were therefore allowed to attend two two-hour French and German lessons a week during work time in the course of a year. Many of the students had never studied a second language before, or at least had not studied since school. The programme therefore targeted a certain level of attainment (Threshhold and Intermediate level in the London Chamber of Commerce exams) and endeavoured to ensure that a wide range of business vocabulary (especially finance related) was covered.

In the event, because the groups were highly motivated, and introduced to relevant materials from the beginning, the target levels were reached in half the time estimated by the London Chamber of Commerce (LCCI). Thus the Preliminary level was reached after 60 hours' tuition and not after 120 as estimated by the LCCI. This meant that certain groups were able to progress further in the time given than had originally been supposed.

This example showed the importance of planning ahead and starting language training well in advance of the date at which the skills were needed. It also showed that the speed at which people learn languages varies, and some groups will learn faster than others.

Example 3

This case study concerns a large bi-national operation, focused on the construction, commissioning and commercialization of a large transportation facility.

Anglo-French company   This company is currently employing 500 staff but has plans to employ up to 2500 by the year 1993. The workforce is divided roughly equally between French and English speakers, with the two working closely together throughout the organization. The workforce is such that a group of French employees could have a British manager and vice versa.

The company has locations in both France and Britain and it clearly needed to recruit people of both nationalities. Language training was needed throughout the organization to ensure that the two nationalities could communicate with each other at whichever level was appropriate. This could be a basic or very advanced level. The training needed to be fitted into a period of intensive work, and suitable for a number of specialist groups of people.

The training also needed to teach people about cultural differences between the two nations since the two nationalities were meeting on a daily basis. People were noticing that the two nations worked in different ways and that the French would, for example, spend longer in meetings and making formal presentations and that the British tended to work much more on paper. Attitudes to authority and notions of job responsibility/achievement also varied between the two nationalities. One Frenchman, for example, remarked that in France performance was judged more by how one behaved than by what one did, than was the case in Britain.

A number of steps had to be taken to get the training on the road:

1. A detailed language training needs analysis was carried out (see Appendix A for results of a sample of managers for the management group training).
2. It was agreed that the training would take place in bursts of a week in order to:
   (a) speed up the training – it is estimated that intensive training like this accelerates the learning process by 50%;
   (b) ensure that people were trained away from their jobs and not liable to interruptions – this is very important since most people find it very difficult to combine language training with a working day on a regular basis, and a lot of training is wasted if done in this way.
3. An estimate had to be made, given the number of people involved, of how long the training would take (see Appendix B). The estimates made were based on the assumption that the training would take place in intensive but non-consecutive weeks. During the weeks when the courses were not taking place, the students would be expected to supplement their training with coursework and practice on the job.

At all stages, standards were linked to external assessable levels to provide a common language of achievement.

As regards the cultural training, this compared French and British cultures under a number of different headings:

- Use of time
- Social framework

- Family and school
- Management
- Performance evaluation.

One was amazed to discover how different the two nations were, even though a small band of sea separated them. This shows the importance of teaching not just the language but also the culture of the target foreign country.

DISCUSSION QUESTIONS

You are a personnel manager for a British manufacturing company that is going to sell into continental Europe for the first time next year. You commissioned the above report from a consultant in order to discover what other companies are doing about meeting their language skills needs. You must now develop your own training response.

1. How would you assess your company's language needs?
2. How would you evaluate the different options of buying in the skills as opposed to training existing staff?
3. How will you assess the need for wider cultural awareness training?
4. What affect will your chosen strategy of Europeanization have on the ways things are done in your company?

SUGGESTED READING

Reeves, N. (1989) 1992 Languages: The barrier that no EC Directive can eliminate. *The Linguist*, **28** (No. 1).

Pinder, M. (1990) *Personnel Management for the Single European Market*, Pitman, London.

Barsoux, J.-L. and Lawrence, P. (1990) *Management in France*, Cassell, London.

Smith, P. B. (1992) Organizational behaviour and national cultures, *British Journal of Management*, **3**, 39–51.

APPENDIX A

LANGUAGE TRAINING NEEDS

	Do you need the skill? (%) Yes
1. GLOSSARY LEVEL	
(A) *Listening/Speaking*	
Greeting somebody	91
Inquiring about the visitor's/customer's/colleague's/etc.	
– needs	58
– job	41
– health	25
– other (please specify)	8
Giving information about oneself on the above	100
Asking the way and giving answers	91
Describing where things are and different parts of a *machine*/computer, etc.	58
To talk/ask about the time, dates and be able to spell names	100
Responding to emergencies	50
Technical:	
– how to use a machine	58
– how to describe machine breakdown:	
– office equipment	33
– cars	41
– train	
– others?	
To talk about what has happened	100
To talk about what will happen	100
To deal with matters outside work:	
– order food in restaurant	41
– book a room in hotel	58
– go to a doctor's	25
Receiving and making short telephone calls	100
(B) *Reading*	
Reading basic notices and signs	100

	Do you need the skill? (%) Yes
Understanding simple articles from press on ET	58

(C) *Writing*
Writing a simple business letter   50

2. INTERMEDIATE LEVEL

(A) *Listening/Speaking*

General:

Formal and informal greetings	100
Making social inquires about the visitor and their job: giving similar information	78
Describing breakdowns in detail	42
To understand the basic language of:	
– marketing	28
– finance	21
– technical	28
– management	42
– economics	14
Making detailed explanations	85
More complex telephone conversations	85
Complaining about:	
– a late delivery	21
– lateness	20
– absenteeism	20
Responding to such complaints (including apologizing)	42

Working with people:

Giving instructions and asking people to do things	85
Asking about lateness or failure to do things	66
Explaining the Health and Safety procedures	35
Basic interviewing	35
Basic disciplining	28

(B) *Reading*

Reading matters regarding:

– personnel policy	20
– training policy	20
– safety policy	35
– schedule planning	28
– technical matters	50

	Do you need the skill? (%) Yes
– payment terms	28
– transport	28
To summarize articles in newspapers, magazines and work-related journals (particularly Tp related)	35
Minutes of meetings	71
Reports	35

(C) *Writing*

Complaining in writing about a late delivery, poor quality work, etc.	28
Writing a simple business letter:	
– ordering supplies	66
– confirming a meeting	35

3. FLUENT LEVEL

(A) *Listening/Speaking*

Desribing the state of one's company	64
Giving a presentation (technical and general)	71
Training and instructing	21
To understand the language of:	
– marketing	42
– finance	28
– technical and transport	57
– management	64
– economics	21
To be able to actively participate in business meetings and negotiations:	
– giving your own opinions	
– clarification	
– attack and response	
– suggesting courses of action	
– interrupting	
– changing the subject	
– reinforcement	
– balancing arguments	
– overcoming opposition	92
Employment matters:	21
– appointing/interviewing	21
– offering advice	7
– carrying out appraisal and discipline interviews	14

	Do you need the skill? (%) Yes
To understand a fluent conversation with colloquialisms	17

(B) *Reading*

Understanding all registers of French	52

(C) *Writing*

Writing regarding:

– personnel policy	21
– training matters	14
– safety matters	35
– schedule planning	35
– technical matters and Tp	42
– payment	14
Writing minutes	35
Writing sophisticated business letters	21

APPENDIX B

LANGUAGE COMPETENCE CHART

Language competence chart showing the levels to be attained, the exams to be passed, and the hours of formal training needed at each level.

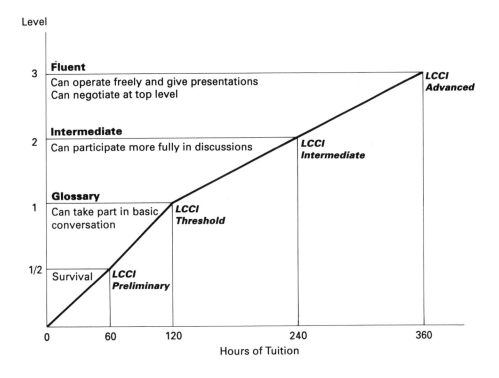

LANGUAGE DEVELOPMENT

Overview of the organization of training showing that a lot of the administrative work (e.g. pre-course assessment and organization of groups) is done prior to an employee joining the company

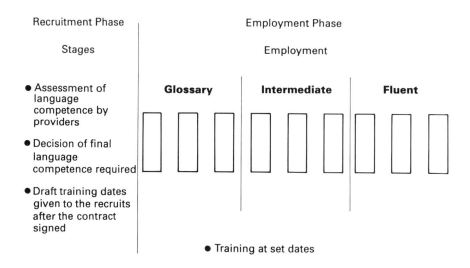

LANGUAGE PROGRAMME

A close-up view of the way training is organized for a particular level of competence (i.e. 'Glossary', 'Intermediate' or 'Fluent').

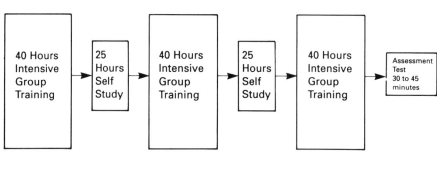

CASE 13

Developing management skills in post-communist countries: the case of Czechoslovakia

RICHARD SCASE

INTRODUCTION

In December 1989, Dr Brown was one of the first western specialists to lecture at the Institute of Management in Czechoslovakia, after the collapse of the Communist regime. His brief was to discuss the importance of effective corporate leadership in market economies and to describe the competences needed of managers in profit-making businesses. Over the following years, he has made frequent trips to Czechoslovakia, working with groups of managers selected from a variety of work settings. However, he has become pessimistic about developments in management training in Czechoslovakia and, hence, the extent to which the country is capable of making the successful transition to a profitable and internationally competitive market economy without a dominant role being played by joint ventures. This case highlights some of the key issues that emerge in management development programmes in post-Communist economies. It invites suggestions for the resolution of some of these through the development of more effective management training strategies.

MANAGEMENT DEVELOPMENT PROGRAMMES UNDER THE COMMUNIST REGIME

Delegates attending management development programmes at the Institute under the old regime held senior and middle management posts in various state-owned petrochemical companies. They were selected because of their 'leadership' positions and those that Dr Brown lectured to in December 1989 had been attending such a programme over a 12-month period. Delegates attended on a residential basis, with each

Human Resources Management in Europe
Edited by Sarah Vickerstaff
Published in 1992 by Chapman & Hall, London, ISBN 0 412 45380 0

course unit lasting one week every two months. As part of the programme, three short field trips were organized so that delegates could
study management techniques in different countries: Holland, Italy,
Poland and the USSR. In total, there were 24 course participants, all of
whom were graduates, were men, and were aged between 28 and 49.
Many were Communist Party members but by December 1989 this fact
was being greatly underplayed – certainly to such foreign lecturers as
Dr Brown.

Methods of teaching and learning were highly formalized with delegates *listening* to lectures. Each teaching session would be of half a day's
duration with 10-minute breaks after each hour. The Course director
encouraged lecturers to stimulate interaction dialogue but this proved
difficult to achieve. Dr Brown felt this was because of the 'mind set' of
Czechoslovakian managers, shaped as it was by the role requirements of
their jobs in their employing organizations. Dr Brown was particularly
surprised by the wide-ranging nature of any question-and-answer
sessions which would, almost inevitably, focus upon general *sociopolitical*
issues in Europe and the United States irrespective of the substance of the
management topic under discussion. The teaching inputs under the old
regime were primarily by Czechoslovakian management specialists but
there were also contributions from leading western and Soviet experts.
Dr Brown was the only lecturer invited from Britain. For the sessions
organized for these foreign speakers, simultaneous translation was used
with interpreters who had little knowledge of western management
terminology.

Under the Communist regime, the petrochemical industry was
organized on the basis of a number of large state-owned enterprises
whose production levels, product ranges and investment plans were
determined by the state ministry. The activities of the separate enterprises
were highly integrated through centralized planning directives. This
applied not only to product range and development but also to human
resource planning and management. The function of the Institute of
Management was to offer training programmes according to the specialist
needs of the separate enterprises as well as for the petrochemical industry
as a whole. It existed not only to meet the technical training requirements
of managers but also to 'develop' the 'correct' attitudes and values of
Leading Workers – as managers were described under the old regime –
so that these were compatible with the 'scientific' beliefs of Marxist–
Leninism. The roles of managers under the old regime were more
broadly defined than those of their colleagues in western countries.
As Leading Workers they were responsible for the management of
production within economic enterprises but also they were seen as
responsible for bringing about the realization of socialism within society
as a whole. This purpose was reflected in the content of management
development programmes in that many of the sessions were devoted to
sociology, social psychology, philosophy and Marxist economic theory.
Their social responsibilities were emphasized and, as Leading Workers in

state-owned enterprises, their roles were seen to have important social and political as well as economic functions. Accordingly, as managers it was their duty to maintain harmony and social consensus within their work settings as well as to achieve production targets. This was in sharp contrast to their interpretations of western corporations which they viewed as conflictual and antagonistic even though they recognized that, compared to their own enterprises, such corporations were usually more cost-effective and productive.

THE NATURE OF MANAGEMENT COMPETENCES UNDER THE 'OLD' REGIME

As middle and senior managers in state-owned petrochemical companies, they had little involvement in the formulation of corporate strategies. A feature of the management process under the Communist regime was that these were determined within the relevant ministries and then allocated to separate enterprises for implementation. This greatly affected the role of management – at all levels – since it determined that its function was to be entirely *responsive* to ministry orders. Production targets were allocated to enterprises and, accordingly, the management process was entirely associated with the achievement of these. Hence, the *key* management issue was to set up procedures so that the imposed targets could be achieved. Strategy implementation at the enterprise level, therefore, inevitably brought about a process of bureaucratization and the imposition of rules and procedures and it was the determination of these which constituted the management challenge. Once such procedures had been established, there was little for managers to do except to monitor output and quality of performance. More often than not, personal creativity and management initiative could only be exercised in those circumstances when goals had to be achieved by circumventing the rules rather than by operating through them. This would require 'bartering', 'bargaining' and negotiating 'trade-offs' with other managers within the same and other enterprises. Equally, machine breakdown, shortages of raw materials and components and other production-related uncertainties within highly bureaucratized work settings demanded the exercise of managerial resourcefulness that could often only be nurtured within the *informal* systems of enterprises rather than through their formalized structures. In this sense, in order to achieve pre-set targets, managers often became entwined within two separate but nevertheless interdependent and mutually reinforcing organizational processes and often managerial creativity was more likely to be exercised within the informal process rather than in the formalized structures. Indeed, the latter tended to foster managerial compliance and role conformity. The exercise of managerial competences within and according to bureaucratic procedures had further psychological effects because it encouraged individuals to *role play*, to undertake what was required of them *solely* in terms of their job descriptions, and to *satisfy* rather than to *optimize* in their task accomplishments. It also encouraged them to psychologically *distance* themselves from the management process and to abdicate *personal* responsibility for any shortcomings in quality control and the under-achievement of performance targets. Managers under the old regime, therefore, undertook their tasks according to the *demands* and *constraints* of their job descriptions and any *choices* or *decisions* which they were 'compelled' to exercise tended to occur, often illegitimately, within informal systems of barter, negotiation and exchange. The formal structures of state-owned enterprises encouraged managers to 'pass the buck', to abdicate personal responsibility, and to attribute blame elsewhere. Perhaps most importantly of all it led them to feel psychologically 'dis-empowered' and generally, alienated from the 'core' management decision-making process.

What, then, were the management competences required within such organizational settings and how did these affect the content and teaching of management development programmes? First and foremost, they required a detailed knowledge of the rules and procedures. Particularly since the petrochemical industry, in any country, is characterized by highly integrated technological systems according to which raw materials are sequentially processed and converted into user goods of one kind or another. Hence, there needs to be strict adherence to procedures by the workforce if quantity and quality standards are to be maintained as well as health and safety standards. Coupled with this, managers have to be *technically* competent in their knowledge of products, work processes and *operational* management techniques. They need firm grounding in the principles of work study, quality control and systems analysis. But most importantly of all under the old regime, it was necessary for them to be skilled in handling interpersonal relations. This was not only for the purposes of achieving their tasks – in order to get things done through negotiations within the informal systems – but also for their own career pursuit within formalized organisational structures.

In pre-1989 Czechoslovakia, managerial compliance to the goals of employee organizations as well as to the broader aims of socialism was expressed by personal conformity to the attitudes, values and opinions of immediate bosses. Indeed, it was through such interpersonal forms of 'control' that the ideological supremacy of the Communist Party was maintained. Failure to conform in this way could lead to demotion, job transfers, and the allocation of targets which, for one reason or another, would be difficult to achieve. In many ways, the management process of the state-owned enterprises constituted complex systems of patron–client relations similar to those often found within larger family-owned businesses in the west. In Czechoslovakia, however, these tended to be hidden behind what appeared to be bureaucratically rational and ideologically legitimate rules and procedures. But as industrial enterprises became increasingly inefficient in the 1980s, the dependency upon these informal patron–client relations of reciprocity for the purposes of achieving both individual and organizational goals became more apparent as the legitimacy of the formalized, bureaucratic methods of mangerial control declined.

Management development programmes until 1989 emphasized, therefore, the need for competences associated with operational management; performance measurement; the exercise of technical functional and specialist skills; interpersonal relations; and the theory and practices of Marxist–Leninism. The nurturing of these organizational-relevant skills was closely intertwined with the fostering of broader social attitudes associated with the responsibilities of management within a socialist society. There were heavy teaching inputs to do with the 'laws' of social change, personality development and, of course, Marxist–Leninist sociopolitical philosophy. The overall objective was for course participants to acquire personal competences compatible with their organizational and broader societal roles as *agents* of socio-economic change.

MANAGEMENT DEVELOPMENTS IN THE POST-COMMUNIST ERA

Since his first visit in 1989, Dr Brown has contributed to various development programmes at the Institute of Management. During this period there have been a number of changes affecting the role and purpose of the Institute, the composition of course delegates and the nature of teaching inputs. The Institute is no longer a provider of training geared solely to the needs of the petrochemical industry. It continues to be a state-funded institute but it has to break even financially on the training courses and development programmes which it offers. It has to market its courses in competition with other providers which have been established in recent years. This has forced it to reduce staff levels and to appraise the extent to which its various programmes generate revenue. Its profit-making goals are hampered by a lack of financial competences as well as a general inability to calculate costs, manage cash flow and to market its services to potential clients in a cost-effective and efficient manner. Many of its senior staff have left either to join other organizations or to set up their own management development and consultancy centres. Indeed, the director of management development programmes at the Institute until 1989 has established his own centre and being in competition, has been able to 'under-cut' the Institute in the provision of a number of teaching programmes. But alongside such changes, the most fundamental are those associated with the delivery of programmes which are being provided to meet the training needs of managers who are now responsible for reorganizing industrial enterprises so that they are profitable and can compete in international and national markets. They need a variety of new skills, the nature of which can only be appreciated by reference to the rapidly changing organizational settings within which they now work.

According to managers in Czechoslovakia, the major reason accounting for the inefficiencies and the poor productivity of state-owned enterprises under the Communist regime was poor organizational design which, in turn, enabled them to abdicate personal responsibility for shortcomings in the production process. Such structures were highly centralized and bureaucratic because of political rather than for economic and cost-effective reasons. Most managers worked in enterprises which produced a variety of products for a large number of customers. Often they would be uncertain as to the precise number of products which they produced, and for which customers. There was often lack of clarity as to what proportion of customers accounted for which particular values of output and product demand. But what was most significant was that the manufacture of these goods was undertaken according to management systems that were centralized and organized according to functional departments. Alongside personnel, transport and distribution, and administration, for example, the production department of an enterprise would be responsible for producing a range of finished products. From a managerial point of view, this constituted a nightmare since it was impossible to establish monitoring mechanisms for determining the costs associated with the manufacture of *specific* goods and products for *specific* user needs. Under the old regime this was not important because management performance was measured not in terms of profit-and-loss calculations but according to the achievement of ministry-determined plans.

One of the first reforms after 1989, therefore, was for senior managers in state enterprises to formulate policies for restructuring their enterprises. This, for many, is seen to be the panacea to their production problems and in their view, is all that is required to create highly efficient and cost-effective units that could compete in world markets. It is their opinion that the redesign of organizations should take the form of *decentralized* and *divisionalized* structures. Each division would then be responsible for the production of a specific or highly limited but related range of products which can then be developed, produced and marketed on a much more focused and customer-oriented basis. Alongside this, the traditionally centralized departments of such functions as personnel, administration and planning will be devolved to newly established product divisions so that these will be more effectively oriented to particular product and market needs. In essence, the general shift in organization design is shown in Figure C13.1.

Such a programme of restructuring makes sense to Dr Brown but even so, he is unhappy about both the lack of strategic and detailed analyses that have been undertaken before these changes are introduced. He is even more concerned about the procedures according to which these changes are being implemented which, he feels, will have serious consequences for worker productivity, morale and managerial authority. He is strongly of the opinion that such restructuring programmes could be counter-productive not because the end result of such changes is undesirable but rather because of the manner in which these are being prepared and implemented.

It is in relation to these organizational changes that Dr Brown con-

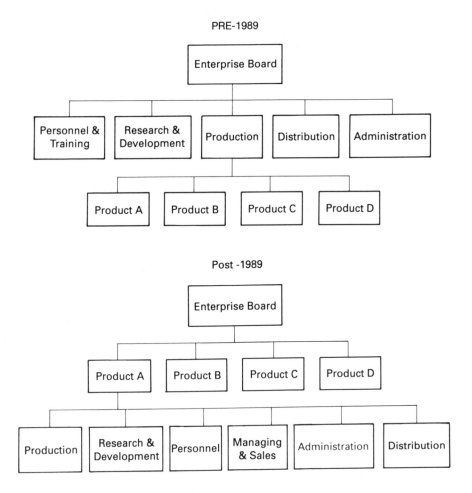

Fig. C13.1 Organization design of a typical petrochemical enterprise under pre-1989 Communist regime and post-1989

tinues to contribute to management development programmes at the Institute. As it is now more or less a self-financing unit which has to 'break even' through selling training to corporate customers, it is important that its programmes meet the specific needs of its clients. The Institute now has to offer courses which are relevant to managers in their newly restructured and soon to be privatized enterprises. Accordingly, it has redesigned its traditional programmes of training eliminating, of course, Marxist–Leninist theory and much of the earlier inputs of macro-economics and socialist-based sociopolitical philosophy and in their place, it focuses upon specific management skills. But although the *content* of programmes has changed, the method of delivery remains much the same. They continue to be organized on the basis of week-long residential units, drawing delegates from different organizations with many inputs from guest speakers normally on a half-day or daily basis. The teaching style continues to be 'formal' with delegates attempting to learn through listening to tightly structured presentations. Increasingly, course instructors are drawn from business schools and management consultancy groups in Europe and the United States. They fly to Czechoslovakia to make their half-day or one-day contributions to programmes and return home as soon as their teaching assignments are completed. Accordingly, their knowledge of course delegates is limited and the temptation to take advantage of teaching inputs to 'sell' consultancy services to delegates – and, through them, their employing organizations – is great.

The content of the redesigned programmes increasingly possesses the features of short-term management development programmes as they are offered to senior and middle managers in European business schools. On the basis of half-day, one-day and two-day modules, delegates are *taught* the principles of strategy formulation and implementation, marketing and selling, production and operational systems, finance and budgetary control, organizational design and human resource management. Often these ideas are illustrated by the use of case studies and increasingly, course participants are encouraged to work in groups in order to undertake case study analyses. However, instructors often find that case analyses that would require several hours' study and discussion in European business schools are undertaken within 20–40 minutes. Often course delegates will perceive key issues to be non-problematic and they readily offer 'quick-fix' solutions which instructors consider to be impractical and with ill thought-through implications.

Dr Brown is now becoming pessimistic about developments in Czechoslovakia. He is of the view that both the content and the method of delivery of management development programmes at the Institute are ill-conceived and, accordingly, that they are failing to meet the *real* training needs of corporate delegates. On his most recent return from working in Czechoslovakia he was of the opinion that the most effective strategy for transforming state-owned enterprises into high-performing, competitive and profit-making corporations would be through joint ventures with large American, European and Japanese companies. This, he feels, would be a more effective way of developing the appropriate management skills in Czechoslovakia.

DISCUSSION QUESTIONS

1. Why, do you think, is Dr Brown unhappy about how the redesign of state-owned enterprises in the petrochemical industry is being prepared and implemented? How should an effective strategy for organizational change be *formulated* and *implemented*?
2. Although it is adopting the teaching methods of European business schools, with inputs from leading experts, why does Dr Brown

feel that the content and delivery of management development programmes at the Institute are flawed and need fundamental revision?
3. What are the *real* issues of management development in post-
communist countries? How can these be effectively met?
4. Why does Dr Brown feel that joint ventures offer the most promising
route for the successful development of profit-making corporations in
Czechoslovakia?

SUGGESTED READING

Adair, J. (1985) *Management Decision Making*, Gower, Aldershot.
Drucker, D. (1954) *The Practice of Management*, Heinemann, London.
Hunt, J. (1986) *Managing People at Work* (2nd edn), McGraw-Hill, London.
Stewart, R. (1988) *Managers and their Roles* (2nd edn), Macmillan, London.

PART FIVE

Reward Management

Compensation policies have always been a high visibility area of human resource management policy. Pay has been a crucial issue in the effort bargain between management and employees. By using different payment systems, management have sought to encourage employees to behave in certain ways, for example, by linking pay directly to output to encourage high productivity. Since the early scientific management theories the impact of money on motivation, productivity and worker satisfaction has been hotly debated.

We should remember, however, that reward management is not confined to wage or salary policy but also includes fringe benefits or indirect compensation. The compensation package is typically made up of a number of different elements including basic pay or salary, performance or merit elements, bonuses, share options, pension entitlement, insurance policies, discounts on company products, paid holidays, etc. These last elements of indirect compensation are highly variable from company to company and country to country. The attractiveness of different benefits changes markedly from context to context: private medical insurance is unlikely to be a significant element of reward packages where the public health care system is extensive; the prevailing taxation system can encourage or discourage elements such as profit sharing or company cars; where living accommodation is scarce and expensive, company housing or assistance with mortgages may be very attractive.

Although the role of pay and other material aspects of reward cannot be neglected, we should also remember that people judge their jobs in terms of the context in which they work. Thus, when considering an employee's satisfaction with his or her job we also have to consider the working conditions; stress and boredom factors; hours and shift patterns and the opportunities for social interaction. There are also the rewards in doing the job, the intrinsic benefits of the activity; for example, the status derived from the occupation, the scope for career advancement, pride and satisfaction in being able to do the job well and a sense of involvement in making decisions about the tasks to be done.

All these factors make up the reward from employment that an individual experiences. Increasingly, human resource management approaches have argued for the need to see remuneration policies in the light of the total compensation package which comprises all the factors that affect motivation, satisfaction and commitment to the organization (Beer *et al.*, 1984, pp. 146–51).

PRESSURES ON REWARD SYSTEMS

Product market pressures and the need to remain competitive in the labour market are constant factors in an organization's reward policies. Any organization must tread the balance between keeping labour costs low while still being able to attract and retain the kinds of staff that it needs. These pressures have continued to increase in the last decade in Europe as competition in world markets has intensified.

Increasing labour mobility in Europe and disparities in standards of living and income between European countries are likely to exert an influence on reward strategies. Workers from eastern Europe will continue to drift westwards in search of a better standard of living; the 'Euromanager' of the 1990s will have an eye on the purchasing power and benefits that multinational organizations are offering in different countries; good graduates from southern Europe and Britain may move northwards. Conversely, companies may choose to locate new plants in the lower wage economies of the south. The reference point for market rate surveys of reward levels may become increasingly international. New technologies are also exerting considerable pressure on traditional compensation policies. Technology in manufacturing and in the office have challenged the old demarcations between jobs and thus serve to undermine the prevailing pay and grading structures. Linked to this are new forms of work organization with the accent on team working, flexibility and multi-skilling, which make rate-for-the-job systems of remuneration less applicable.

> Employees must possess the readiness and ability to perform a variety of functions, and to acquire new competences as techniques and products evolve. Hence the thesis that new technology serves to increase rather than reduce skills; and hence also the concern to manage workers in ways which will stimulate their active commitment to efficient and high-quality production.
>
> (Hyman, 1988, pp. 49–50)

Although there is debate as to how widespread such changes in work organization are (Hyman, 1988), the redesign of jobs necessarily impacts upon reward systems. Case 16 shows how a major change in organization and work design undermined the piece rate pay system that had existed.

In the context of these changes the individual contribution to production/service provision is increasingly being highlighted. Many of these pressures are seen to reinforce a trend towards individual-based and performance- or merit-based pay as opposed to job-based pay (Mahoney, 1992, p. 343). Where technology is stable – and where the product is standardized and it is possible to define clearly the division of labour and the individual jobs – traditional 'rate for the job' compensation based on job evaluation is both feasible and practical. It provides a means to analyse and describe the characteristics of given jobs and rank different jobs in a grading structure. However, in more technologically turbulent contexts, where there is a premium on product development, innovation and change and where employees are deployed flexibly across different tasks within a team, it makes more sense to determine pay on individual- or team-based performance criteria. Person-related pay reinforces flexible allocation of tasks among team members as individuals take their pay with them whichever particular tasks they may be doing. Individual pay may be made up of a number of different elements: a seniority factor, skill-based elements and performance assessment for example. The variable factors may be a considerable or relatively small proportion of total salary.

Another pressure on reward strategies has been the spread through Europe of legislation on equal pay for men and women doing the same jobs, and equal value assessments, which compare different jobs of equal skill, effort and responsibility. Some job evaluation schemes have been criticized for using discriminatory job factors that lead to traditionally female jobs being evaluated as less skilled than men's jobs (see, for example, Armstrong and Murlis, 1988, pp. 102–7).

Figure P5.1 summarizes the contemporary pressures on reward strategies. The most obvious managerial concern about reward strategies is how much to pay; however, there are a number of other issues about which the organization needs to have policies. These have been summarized in Figure P5.2.

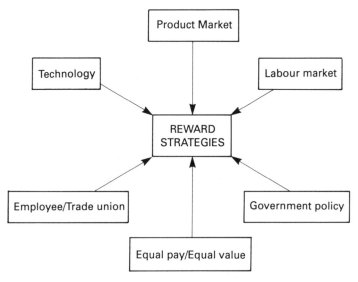

Fig. P5.1   Contemporary pressures on reward strategies.

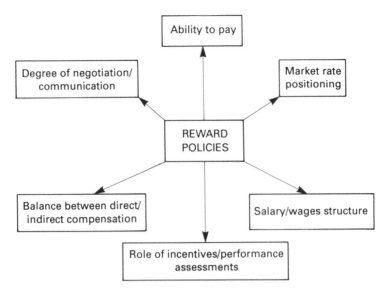

Fig. P5.2 Issues for reward policies.

We have already mentioned the necessity for the company to compete in product and labour markets and therefore the centrality of ability to pay and market rate positioning to any reward strategy. In addition, any organization has to decide how different jobs within the company will be remunerated and consider issues of pay relativities and internal equity; in other words, there has to be a means for determining the wage and salary structure.

Management also has to decide upon the role of financial incentives or performance measures in pay determination and the balance between direct salary or wage and indirect or fringe benefit elements. Lastly, the organization will have to respond to prevailing pressures for negotiation of reward issues, with trade unions or individuals, or even governments in the context of incomes policies. Cases 14 and 15 show that some managements take the decision to exclude certain groups from the prevailing negotiation machinery.

INDIRECT COMPENSATION

Traditionally, the terms and conditions of employment of blue-collar and white-collar employees were clearly differentiated. Hours of work, working conditions, holiday entitlement, pension entitlement, the disciplinary regime all tended to vary markedly between the two groups. Equally, access to fringe benefits reflected and reinforced differences in income, with managers and professionals having considerably better indirect compensation than routine non-manual or manual employees.

In the last two decades more organizations have moved to single status terms and conditions of employment, or harmonization between blue-collar and white-collar groups. In a number of European countries governments have supported these moves through legislation (for example, Sweden and France); in Italy and Germany the centralized multi-employer collective bargaining systems have encouraged the spread of single status, where agreements can be reached for whole industries (Price, 1989, p. 281). In Britain, moves towards harmonization have been slower and the influence of Japanese and American companies has been significant.

There are a number of arguments behind the trend towards single status systems. Changing patterns of work, diminishing the boundaries between manual and mental labour, have been seen as a form of impetus. Technological changes are once again seen as significant, as Price (1989, pp. 284–5) comments:

> New technology has also frequently had the effect of underlining the importance of winning workers' commitment to the objectives of the enterprise in a far more wholehearted way than has traditionally been the case; a willingness to be flexible and to exercise discretion and initiative in the enterprise have been seen to depend crucially on the development of a more 'unitary' relationship between workers and company – in short, to seek to put manual workers onto the same footing as was traditionally assumed to be the case with non-manual workers.

Harmonization is seen as having a particular message to transmit; it should reinforce an organizational culture that seeks to minimize differences between groups of employees. By stressing common status, harmonization intends to diminish 'them and us' attitudes (Wickens, 1987, pp. 7–21).

In the competitive environment referred to above, companies may seek other ways of using financial incentives to encourage employee commitment to the organization. In France and Britain profit-sharing schemes of varying sorts have become increasingly popular (Uvalic, 1990). Profit sharing may take the form of profit-related cash bonuses, share option schemes or savings schemes (Armstrong and Murlis, 1988, pp. 247–56). The rationale for such financial participation is to give employees a better sense of belonging to the organization, to increase commitment, and to improve cooperation and efficiency.

Indirect compensation is typically used to reinforce the objectives of wage and salary policies; however, as we see from the examples above, fringe benefits may be designed to support commitment strategies and organizational culture.

In the following cases we have the opportunity to consider some of these trends in compensation. In Case 14 we explore the introduction of a performance-related pay scheme for managers in British Rail. Readers are asked to assess a major change in the traditional reward strategies of the organization and to evaluate the appropriateness and effectiveness of the new system.

Case 15 looks at the establishment of a new grading system in a bank. Facing product market pressures and the legacy of grade drift resulting in high labour costs, the bank is forced to modify its traditional grading and career structure. This case shows how decisions about rewards are necessarily embedded in the wider human resource management context; policies on pay inevitably affect recruitment and selection, human resource planning and career planning.

Case 16 investigates the impact of changing technology, organizational design and job redesign on traditional pay structures. It links back to the cases in Part Two on job redesign and again shows how the different policy areas of human resource management must be integrated if people are to be managed effectively. The final text gives comparative information on the popularity of profit-sharing schemes in different European countries, inviting the reader to explain why such schemes should be more common in some places than others.

SUGGESTED READING FOR PART FIVE

Armstrong, M. and Murlis, H. (1988) *Reward Management*, Kogan Page, London.

Beer, M., Spector, B. and Lawrence, P. *et al.* (1984) Reward Systems, in *Managing Human Assets*, The Free Press, New York, pp. 113–151.

Hyman, R. (1988) Flexible specialisation: miracle or myth?, in *New Technology and Industrial Relations* (eds R. Hyman and W. Streeck), Blackwell, Oxford, pp. 48–60.

Mahoney, T. A. (1992) Multiple pay contingencies: strategic design of compensation, in *Human Resource Strategies* (ed. G. Salaman), Sage, London, pp. 337–346.

Price, R. (1989) The decline and fall of the status divide?, in *Personnel Management in Britain* (ed. K. Sisson), Blackwell, Oxford, pp. 271–295.

Uvalic, M. (1990) *The PEPPER Report*, Commission of the European Communities and the European University Institute, Brussels and Florence.

Wickens, P. (1987) *The Road to Nissan*, Macmillan, London, Chapters 1 and 8, pp. 7–21 and 111–26.

CASE 14

Performance-related pay in British Rail

ANDREW PENDLETON

INTRODUCTION

This case[1] is concerned with the introduction of performance-related pay (PRP) for managers in British Rail (BR). BR is the main provider of railway passenger and freight services in Great Britain. In 1991 it was one of the few remaining nationalized industries in Britain, the majority of state-owned industries having been privatized in the 1980s. It currently employs around 130 000 people, of whom nearly 10 000 are management staff. Trade union membership is high: approximately 75% of managers are members of the transport industry white collar union, the Transport Salaried Staffs Association (TSSA). Until PRP was introduced in 1988 managerial pay rates (like those of manual and clerical staff) were negotiated annually in collective bargaining between the railway trade unions and BR.

Railway employment is characterized by long service and well-developed internal labour markets for all grades of employees. It is common for managers to begin their railway careers in clerical or manual jobs and work their way up through the hierarchy. For much of its existence BR has adopted the policies associated with the 'good employer' model (commonly found in the British public sector). Formal grievance and disciplinary procedures are well established. There is an engrained tradition of equity on the railways: the principle is that individuals doing the same job should be treated equally (except where they have different seniority, i.e. length of service). Until recently the railways have been managed by and large in a consensual way. All these factors have engendered a distinctive railway 'culture', of which a strong commitment to the railway is one facet. This has enabled BR to make major reductions in its workforce since 1960 with very little conflict. Critics argue, however,

[1] The material for this case was obtained from archival sources, the *TSSA Journal*, BR's Annual Report and Accounts, and interviews with key personnel. Ian Kessler of Templeton College, Oxford, provided invaluable comments on an earlier version.

Human Resources Management in Europe
Edited by Sarah Vickerstaff
Published in 1992 by Chapman & Hall, London. ISBN 0 412 45380 0

that this culture has prevented the adoption of ideas generated outside the railway and stifled innovation.

BACKGROUND TO THE CASE: WHY BRITISH RAIL ADOPTED PERFORMANCE-RELATED PAY

British Rail announced 'out of the blue' during the 1988 pay negotiations that it intended to end collective bargaining for management pay and replace it with a performance-based system. From 1989 annual increases in managers' pay were to be determined entirely by their performance in the preceding year. BR's objectives were:

(1) to provide a reward system which recognizes individual contributions and places the emphasis squarely on performance;
(2) to adjust salary ranges so that they provide the necessary incentive to individuals to make a full contribution to business objectives;
(3) to devolve responsibility for individual salary reviews to the lowest practicable level of the organization within well-defined budget criteria.

Behind these reasons for introducing PRP are a number of broader objectives and contextual factors which derive from the Thatcher and Major governments' beliefs about public sector organizations. Conservative Ministers in the 1980s and 1990s wanted to force public sector organizations to adopt similar aims and methods of operation to those said to be found in private sector organizations. In BR's case they were concerned to improve financial performance and to reduce the railway's call on public funds. In their view these two objectives were intimately related: reductions in public subsidy would force BR managers to improve efficiency which, in turn, would lead to healthier finances. Accordingly, government grants to BR were steadily reduced during the 1980s (they have subsequently risen) so that their contribution to turnover decreased from just 27% in 1980 to 17% in 1989/90. Despite some claims to the contrary, this has caused acute financial difficulties for BR. Performance pay can be seen as an attempt to improve individual managerial performance in order to cope with this situation, even though, in the short term, it could add to the salary bill.

One by-product of the difficult financial situation recently has been a deterioration in service quality. For instance, the percentage of trains cancelled in Network SouthEast (the web of commuter services around London) rose from 1.6% in 1986/87 to 4.0% in 1989/90. Consumer organizations have become increasingly vocal about train cancellations, punctuality and overcrowding. Fears have also been expressed in some quarters about a possible deterioration in safety standards. These concerns have increasingly taken on a political dimension and it has become imperative for BR to improve the standard of services offered to the passenger. Once again PRP may be seen as a way of encouraging managers to improve their performance in order to secure collective benefits.

Some critics argue that one of the barriers to high-quality performance is BR's culture. BR is said to be inflexible, bureaucratic and hierarchical. This is expressed in a management style which is risk averse rather than innovative and entrepreneurial. In this view this culture must be fragmented if sustainable improvements in railway performance are to be achieved. One way of doing this is to provide incentives for individual managers to maximize their own performance. Collective bargaining over managerial pay is believed to be inappropriate on the grounds that it encourages uniformity by rewarding all managers in a similar way, regardless of their actual performance. It also embodies a centralized approach to pay determination which is inconsistent with recent moves to devolve management authority and responsibility in BR. One of the benefits of performance-related pay is that it decentralizes pay determination from national level to individual performance review groups.

The railway managers' trade union, TSSA, decided to ballot its management staff members over whether this new payment system should be accepted. However, in the meantime BR issued new individual contracts incorporating the PRP system to all management staff. All managers except one signed the new contract within the time specified by BR. Thus the union was effectively by-passed and, unlike most human resource management innovations on the railways, PRP was introduced without formal agreement with the unions.

HOW PERFORMANCE-RELATED PAY OPERATES IN BRITISH RAIL

All but about 200 very senior management jobs in British Rail are grouped into five management grades with MS1 being the lowest and MS5 the highest. At the end of the 1980s there were approximately 9500 jobs in this grading structure. The grading of each management job was determined by job evaluation techniques, taking into account levels of responsibility, decision making, etc. Until the PRP scheme was introduced, each grade contained a salary scale: each year managers would receive an increment and hence move one point up the scale. The pay associated with the scales was revised each year as a result of collective bargaining between BR and the TSSA. There was also provision for a modest merit element with managers being able to secure an extra 3% approximately for good performance. By 1988 BR believed that this had degenerated and that many managers were receiving 'automatic' merit increases regardless of their actual performance.

The main feature of the PRP scheme introduced from 1988 is that managers' annual pay increases are based entirely on merit. The five grades have been retained but the salary scales within them have been replaced by salary ranges with a minimum and maximum point. Movement within these ranges is now determined solely by performance. Full collective bargaining over salary rates has ceased but the minimum and maximum points of each salary range are settled after negotiation with the TSSA each year.

Evaluation of performance is achieved through a performance appraisal scheme. In May of each year (when budget targets for the new financial year have been released to managers) each manager meets an appraiser to set objectives for the coming year. BR guidelines indicate that six core objectives are an appropriate number and require that there must be at least one quality of service and at least one staff communication objective. Progress is reviewed in November with a view to refining the objectives (if necessary) and to identifying whether any training and development needs have emerged. The latter requires that managers honestly identify weaknesses in their performance during their discussion with their appraiser. A final meeting is then held in May (when the money available for PRP increases has been decided) to assess the individual's performance over the year and to award a rating. The possible ratings are:

1. A performance which substantially exceeds all objectives and job requirements, reflecting all-round excellence and outstanding attainments.
2. A performance which meets all objectives and job requirements and exceeds many, reflecting high quality and attainment.
3. A performance which meets all objectives and job requirements.
4. A performance where overall attainment falls short of the full job requirement.
5. A low level of attainment reflecting a lack of ability and/or commitment.

There are between 200 and 300 review groups of staff for appraisal purposes ('cells' in BR parlance) with between 15 and 70 staff in each.

The appraisal rating is used as a basis for giving the manager a percentage increase in salary from July. However, there is no automatic link between the rating and the salary increase. Another key factor that determines an individual's salary award is the total money available to the appraisal group for pay increases. The increase paid to each manager will depend in part on that paid to others in the same review group. Each group is allocated the same pot of money pro-rata according to the number of managers within it.

THE EFFECTS OF THE PRP SCHEME

The role of the union in pay determination has been substantially reduced. BR will not reveal to the union how much money is set aside each year for performance pay increases, nor what the maximum percentage increase for each performance level is. Since BR has been reluctant to provide details about salary awards made under the new scheme, the TSSA has conducted annual surveys of its management staff members to collect basic information on salary increases. The following findings are taken from the 1990 survey:

1. Sixty-eight per cent of respondents were placed in the middle category, i.e. their performance met all objectives; 31% received a 2

rating, i.e. their performance met all objectives and exceeded some; 0.35% received a 1 rating; 0.79% received on adverse evaluation.

2. The average award was 12.2%, with most managers receiving between 10 and 14%. The union calculated that, if the previous pay system was still in operation, most managers would have received a salary increase of 12.1%.

3. The higher the grade the more likely a manager was to get a good (i.e. 2 rating) evaluation. Fifty-five percent of MS5 managers received a good evaluation compared with 22.5% of MS1 managers. The higher the grade the more likely a manager was to get an increase in excess of the average award.

4. However, *within* each grade those at the bottom of the salary range tended to secure larger percentage increases than those at the top.

5. A number of anomalies have been reported. Some people with satisfactory evaluations have been awarded higher percentage increases than people in the same grade with a better rating. For instance, the lowest increase reported by a MS2 manager with a good rating was 9%, while some with a satisfactory rating achieved over 20%.

6. Thirty-six per cent of managers thought their individual salary review was unfair.

7. Most BR managers would prefer a pay system with a cost-of-living increase coupled with a performance pay component.

A number of other points should be borne in mind.

1. Some union representatives report an increase in the number of managers approaching them with grievances about their pay.

2. The PRP system was modified by BR for some groups of staff to respond to labour market difficulties. In some offices of the civil engineering department, BR introduced interim salary increases to individuals who were deemed likely to leave and whose departure would have adverse effects for the railways.

3. In 1991 financial stringency forced top BR management to restrict the pay increase of nearly half of all managers to between 7.7 and 7.8% (comparable to the 7.75% awarded to manual employees as a result of negotiation and arbitration). The average overall increase was 8.1%.

4. In 1991–92, BR made major changes to its organization structure. This has caused major upheavals within management: many managers have been shifted to new jobs in new locations. Morale is said to be low.

5. In the 1991 review, 66% of managers thought their salary award was unfair.

6. The TSSA has lodged a complaint under the Employment Protection Act that BR has failed to disclose information required for collective bargaining, which would be in accordance with good industrial relations practice to disclose.

DISCUSSION QUESTIONS

1. What are your observations of BR's PRP system?
2. What are the strengths and weaknesses of the pay system from the perspective of
   (a) a line manager?
   (b) a personnel specialist?
   (c) a trade union representative?
   How could any weaknesses be remedied?
3. What are the consequences of including the Training and Development Review in the pay review process?
4. Do you think PRP is the most appropriate pay system for BR in the current context?

SUGGESTED READING

Bowey, A. and Lupton, T. (eds) (1989) *Managing Salary and Wage Systems* (3rd edn), Gower, Aldershot.

Brindle, D. (1987) Will performance pay work in Whitehall. *Personnel Management* (August), pp. 35–9.

Fowler, A. (1988) New directions in performance pay. *Personnel Management* (November), pp. 30–4.

Bank of Ireland: introduction of new bank assistant grade under a plan to improve competitiveness

BILL ROCHE and TOM MURPHY

INTRODUCTION

Until recently, Ireland's retail banking sector was dominated by a small number of associated banks of which the Bank of Ireland was one of the largest. It had the largest market share with 277 full service branches. With increasing competition from outside the traditional banking system, and in anticipation of additional competitive pressure from European banks and other financial institutions under the arrangements for the Internal Market from 1992, the bank sought to strengthen its competitive position. Costs were a particular cause of concern as these had been rising at a considerably faster rate than income.

On 25 March 1987 the managing director of the bank outlined to the Irish Bank Officials Association (IBOA), which represented all grades of staff up to and including manager level, its Plan to Improve Competitiveness (PIC). Among the details of the plan was the proposed introduction of a new 'bank assistant' grade, which would eventually account for 35% of total staff.

MARKET CHANGES AND LABOUR COSTS

Up to the 1970s the Associated Banks, including the Bank of Ireland had dominated the Irish savings market. Since then, in spite of an overall increase in the savings/deposits market, the Associated Banks' share of new savings fell alarmingly in both percentage and absolute terms – see Table C15.1. In the case of personal sector savings, the trend was even more worrying for the Associated Banks. Between 1975 and 1985 their share of this market had dropped from 47.8% to 11.4%. In the case of the Bank of Ireland the loss of market share was especially severe, as this

Human Resources Management in Europe
Edited by Sarah Vickerstaff
Published in 1992 by Chapman & Hall, London. ISBN 0 412 45380 0

Table C15.1   Market share – savings and lending

	Savings (%)		Lending (%)	
	1972	1987	1972	1987
Republic of Ireland:				
Associated Banks	48.1	38.2	51.5	40.0
Non-associated Banks	14.4	24.1	29.7	34.6
Building Societies	9.9	19.7	10.3	18.3
Others	27.6	18.0	6.7	7.1
	100.0	100.0	100.0	100.0
Bank of Ireland:				
Bank	23.1	18.8	24.4	17.6
Subsidiaries	3.1	5.4	3.7	6.8
Bank of Ireland Group	26.2	24.2	28.1	24.4

Sources: Central Bank reports; Bank of Ireland.

sector alone accounted for 56% of the bank's total deposits/savings base. On the international front, the pending completion of the Internal Market by 1992 posed further competitive pressures from European competitors with substantial economies of scale and more advantageous cost structures.

The fundamental problem which gave rise to the bank's initiative was its concern that its costs had been rising considerably faster than its income. In the five-year period between 1982 and 1987 operating costs rose by 91% and income by 64%. Staff costs were the single biggest element of costs and represented two-thirds of total operating costs. This was a considerably higher figure than that pertaining in the nearest comparable market, Britain, where in 1987 the comparable rates ranged from 53.3% in the case of Standard Chartered, to 60.4% in the case of Barclay's, with an overall average rate for all banks in Britain of 57.3%. Staff costs were the principal influence in the Bank of Ireland's adverse cost trends. The bank had indicated that these costs could be reduced by cutting back business, but this would involve large-scale branch closures with a consequent significant reduction in staff numbers. The bank believed, however, that an extensive network, retailing competitively priced products, was the correct strategy and so large-scale closure was not a preferred option. Productivity levels were high, and although further minimal reductions in numbers could be achieved through systems changes, there was no scope for a substantial drop in staff numbers while retaining a major branch network.

PLAN FOR IMPROVED COMPETITIVENESS

It had been said of the Bank of Ireland, in a banking review of 1988, that:

Staff costs make up two-thirds of operating costs and offer the greatest potential for significant savings. Most employees are on pay scales so the Bank is facing a situation where payroll expenses will continue to grow faster than inflation unless corrective action is taken. In an environment where it faces low-cost competition its market share will be particularly vulnerable. The Bank can compete effectively only if it has a cost structure in line with the other players.

The Bank of Ireland had operated on the basis of the 'life-time' human resource flow system typical of the industry from its beginnings. A job in the bank was a job for life. Staff were recruited out of second-level education and rose through the career system along a clear career path. Promotion to senior positions was from within the bank, and seniority was a major criterion of promotion.

A substantial part of the bank's problem with its staff costs lay in the fact that over the previous decade a low turnover of staff, coupled with an automatic system of promotion, had produced a serious imbalance in its staff-grading profile. A major problem of 'grade drift' had arisen.

Between 1975 and 1988 the proportion of staff on the senior bank official grade trebled from 19% to 58.5%. In the same period the proportion of staff on junior grades fell from 62% to 10%. By 1988, whereas there were about 600 staff occupying the junior grades, there were almost 3500 staff enjoying the higher bank official salary scale, with many of them carrying out only routine junior-level tasks. Table C15.2 contains the full breakdown of staff from bank official to manager grade.

The bank regarded this mismatch between staff grading and the level of job content as the very root of its problem, and believed that the only way it could be tackled effectively was through the introduction of a new lower paid entry grade to accommodate the more routine jobs in the organization. Recruitment to this new grade would be counter-balanced by a corresponding reduction in the number of senior-graded staff. This was to be achieved by an attractive package of schemes for voluntary severance, early retirement and career breaks.

Table C15.2   Bank of Ireland staff breakdown by grade

	No.	%
Manager	580	9.9
Assistant manager/officer	1269	21.6
Senior bank official	3446	58.5
Bank official	585	10.0
Total	5880	100.0

Sources: Central Bank reports; Bank of Ireland.

Recruitment to the proposed new bank assistant grade would be greatly facilitated by the plentiful supply of willing school and college leavers. As a result of Irish demographic trends, the supply of young people onto the labour market was at an unprecedented level. The Irish economy was in deep recession and emigration was in the order of 30000 per year; many migrants were young, educated school and university leavers, who were likely to be particularly attracted to the prospects of a job at home, even at a low salary.

BANK PROPOSALS AND FAILURE TO AGREE

In December 1986 the bank informed both staff and IBOA that it had commenced a review of staff costs as a means of producing savings and making the bank more competitive. Through the early months of 1987 the bank continued to communicate to the staff its concerns about staff costs, so that they were, at least to some extent, mentally prepared for the scale of the proposals when they were eventually announced to the IBOA on 25 March 1987. The plan (PIC) outlined by the bank was an integrated package with a three-year time frame. The plan incorporated:

1. An Early Retirement/Voluntary Severance Package, with the aim of an overall reduction of 2000 senior-graded staff over the three years of the plan. In the first year it was expected that 700 or 800 would leave.
2. The introduction of a new recruitment grade (bank assistant) in addition to the existing bank official recruitment grade, with a starting salary of £6500 p.a. rising to a maximum after ten years of £10 200 (this is based on the original proposal *plus* a general increase of 7% which was subsequently awarded to all staff). The scale of pay proposed by the bank was based on rates paid to staff in comparable employments for similar duties. The scale compared with the bank official scale of £8340 to £9987, but in this case, there was provision for progression after five years to the senior bank official scale, which stood at £10 059 to £18 201. There would be no automatic progression out of the bank assistant grade but in any one year 10% of recruitment onto the bank official grade would be reserved for serving bank assistants. Recruits to the new grade would perform such tasks as keyboard, cash, customer service, filing, sorting, routine enquiries, general assistance. They would not undertake such duties as taking or perfecting of securities, lending decisions, balance sheet analysis, opening of non-personal accounts.

The essential element of the bank's plan to improve its labour cost competitiveness was, therefore, the new low-cost entry grade with a salary maximum after ten years' service which would still be considerably below the average industrial wage, and with access to the bank's career grade proper severely restricted. Additionally, although not proffered by the bank in its documentation and public statements, it was clear that a high turnover of staff in the new grade was an important assumption on which the viability of the plan depended in the longer term. Only on the basis of a high level of staff turnover could the bank hope to avoid 'scale drift', with its attendant problems.

In the course of meetings which followed the bank's announcement of its plan, the IBOA indicated that while they were not opposed to the early retirement and voluntary severance proposals, they could not agree to the introduction of a new recruitment grade. They suggested that the bank adopt a similar approach to its problem as had been used by one of the other banks, i.e. a voluntary parting scheme. The bank turned down the suggestion on the grounds that the aim was not to reduce numbers but to improve competitiveness. Even if those parting were to be replaced by recruits onto existing scales, this would give only temporary respite because as new staff moved up through the scales the same problem would be recreated in a few short years. Neither was the bank attracted to the suggestion of an across-the-board cut in salaries. The bank was determined that there should be no adverse consequences for conditions or prospects of existing staff. While the bank was willing to alter some of the details of the plan, it was not prepared to change the plan's underlying structure; the bank was strongly committed to the implementation of the new grade at the salary stated.

Between May and November 1987 negotiations on PIC were interrupted because of a major dispute between IBOA and the Associated Banks over pay and new technology. When talks were resumed in December it was clear that no progress would be made in further direct talks and it was decided to continue discussions under a neutral chairman. Little progress was made, however. When asked if it was prepared to recompence the staff remaining after the plan was introduced, the bank responded that any ongoing payment to existing staff would be incompatible with the aims of the plan. The matter was then referred to a tribunal for consideration and recommendation.

UNION RESPONSE AND NEGOTIATIONS

During IBOA's annual conference in April, the bank was accused of attempting to marginalize the union. Fears were expressed that the bank would implement the plan unilaterally. Managers, in a secret ballot, voted to retain their membership of the union. This had become an issue within the Association when managers had accepted individual contracts on performance-related pay and conditions separate to those previously negotiated on their behalf by IBOA. The revised arrangement, known as the 'Enhanced Overscale System' (EOS), effectively removed managerial pay from collective bargaining. Disquiet had also been caused by the inclusion of managers' handling of industrial relations at branch level as a criterion of performance to be appraised under the new performance-based payment system. It was pointed out that this might include a manager's ability to 'deliver' his or her branch's assent to management proposals, or, indeed, his or her support for management's position in an industrial dispute such as the one that threatened under PIC. Members of the union were also concerned that these developments would ultimately set managers against IBOA, with the eventual result that their member-ship of the union might become untenable. IBOA had not been consulted about EOS. Agreement on the scheme had been achieved with almost all managers within four weeks. The number of managers consulted at any one time had been carefully controlled by head office, as had the individual order in which managers were approached. The bank first approached those to whom the scheme was likely to appear particularly attractive, or who had shown themselves to be supportive towards the bank in the past.

On raising the issue with the bank, IBOA was informed that it was a private package between managers and the bank. In dealing with PIC, the IBOA Conference directed the Executive to ballot all members to secure their support, 'for industrial action up to and including all-out strike in the event of the bank implementing change without agreement'. In a letter to all its members, the union explained that this 'was a defensive measure but will be used to the full in the difficult months ahead if it is found necessary'. The bank took this mandate for strike very seriously but had already formulated a strike contingency plan. Managers had been advised that in the event of a strike their support was expected.

The tribunal established to consider the dispute over PIC comprised an independent chairman, a member nominated by the union and a member nominated by the bank. It met on 30 May 1988 and issued its recom-mendation on 3 June. It recommended unanimously in favour of the bank and accepted that the bank was entitled to introduce the new grade by September 1988. It also recommended some improvements to the severance and early retirement packages, and a lump-sum pay-ment of 4% of pensionable salary to remaining staff for facilitating the implementation of PIC.

The bank accepted the tribunal's recommendation. Surprisingly, perhaps, in view of the unanimity of the tribunal's decision, IBOA rejected the recommendation. The Association's decision was issued by way of a circular to its members in all banks. In the circular IBOA also affirmed its opposition to negotiating basic pay on an individual bank basis. This was a reference to recent trends in the industry towards company-level bargaining over pay and conditions, in place of the long-established practice of industry-level bargaining between IBOA and the Irish Banks' Standing Committee, the bank's employer association.

The IBOA warned the bank against unilateral action on implementing PIC and a confrontation seemed imminent. Behind the scenes, however, talks were taking place to avoid confrontation, and these led to the parties agreeing to attend a conciliation meeting on the issues at the Labour Court. At that time the Labour Court was Ireland's principal agency for the settlement of industrial relations disputes. It provided two main services, conciliation and formal investigation followed by the issuing of a non-binding recommendation. Conciliation conferences continued at the Labour Court between 24 June and 28 August but failed to resolve the dispute. Again a work stoppage appeared likely. Both sides agreed, however, to refer the dispute back to the Labour Court, this time to permit a formal investigation by the Court. In its recommendation of 21 October, the Court found the bank's proposal for the introduction of the new grade of bank assistant to be reasonable. It recommended an eleven-point salary scale:

$$£6700 \times £400 \text{ to } £10\,750$$

It further recommended in favour of the improvements which had been recommended by the tribunal. Finally, it recommended that the bank should accept the recommendation and indicate its acceptance to IBOA at an early date. IBOA should then ballot its membership before taking any decision on its acceptance or otherwise.

Although totally opposed to the concept of two-tier recruitment, the Executive Committee of IBOA decided to ballot its members in the bank on PIC. The result of the ballot was in favour of the bank's plan by a majority of 700 votes (for, 3300; against, 2600). The result was not altogether unexpected. According to the bank, 1200 staff had already opted for the early severance package, and 400 stood to obtain promotion directly as a result of the plan. If we add the managers who had entered into personal contracts with the bank, the combined total accounts for two-thirds of those voting in favour of the plan. The bank, seemingly, had skilfully done its homework. On 2 November 1988 IBOA advised the bank of its acceptance of the PIC.

THE RECRUITMENT PROCESS AND ITS AFTERMATH

While the plan to introduce the new grade of bank assistant at a salary below average industrial earnings aroused considerable public controversy, the bank was inundated with thousands of unsolicited applications before the posts were advertised in the press. Eventually about 23 000 applications were received for some 800 new bank assistant positions.

The selection process was based on a detailed personal history inventory (biodata), followed up by structured interviews. The biodata questionnaire contained 41 questions, ranging over biographical details, education, leisure pursuits and personal values and attributes. Question 3, for example, asked applicants 'how much freedom and independence' their parents had allowed them up to the age of 16. They could reply in scaled categories ranging from 'personal freedom generally constrained by parents' wishes' to 'free to do as I wished'. Question 34 sought information on the importance to applicants of a set of factors reflecting personal priorities. These included such things as 'having an easy life', 'having a nice house', 'always being courteous' and 'having enough money to live well'. Applicants were invited to score such attributes on a scale ranging from 'not important', through 'important', to 'very important'.

The personal attributes included in the inventory were based on an analysis of the attributes of those existing employees who were viewed as exemplary in their performance of the types of tasks to be undertaken by the new bank assistants. Some existing bank officials criticized the exercise as one designed to preclude recruitment of the types of person whom the bank might traditionally have desired to attract to a career in banking. In particular, it was suggested by critics and sceptics that the exercise was designed to identify and deselect young people of ambition and dynamism, as such people would sooner or later become unsatisfied with the conditions and prospects attached to the new grade. The bank itself refused to be drawn on the precise rationale for the biodata instrument. Some union members nonetheless referred to the new bank assistants as the 'yellow packs', after the proprietary brand of one of Ireland's leading supermarket chains. There was speculation as to whether the new staff would join the union in strength.

The integration of bank assistants into the general work of the bank's branches proceeded smoothly. Management have expressed satisfaction with the performance of staff in the new grade; indeed, there are indications that branch managers consider many bank assistants to be capable of more demanding work that that which was originally mapped out for those working in the new grade. The viability of the division originally identified between the duties of bank assistants and bank officers has thus come into question. Bank assistants often appear to work shoulder to shoulder with higher paid bank officers. This has become a focus point of attempts by IBOA to increase its membership among bank assistants.

One key assumption involved in the initiative to introduce the new grade has not been borne out. The turnover of staff in the new grade has been significantly lower than predicted due to Ireland's continuing high level of unemployment.

The IBOA has continued its efforts to recruit bank assistants and has declared its intention to press a claim for a significant improvement in pay and conditions for the grade. A prominent union officer has predicted that bank assistants might yet become the most militant section of IBOA membership.

DISCUSSION QUESTIONS

1. In the light of the lower than predicted turnover of staff in the bank assistant grade, discuss the human resource problems for management to which scale drift might give rise.
2. Discuss the possible implications of the bank assistant grade and of the Enhanced Overscale System (EOS) scheme for the IBOA.
3. Discuss the rationale for the use of the personal history inventory in the bank's recruitment strategy. Does the case illustrate any limitations

on the capacity of such instruments to predetermine the attitudes and behaviour of employees?

4. In terms of Beer *et al.*'s typology of human resource flow systems, how would you describe the flow system of the Bank of Ireland, following the introduction of the new grade?

5. Discuss the bearing of the bank assistants case on Atkinson's theory of the flexible firm. Does the case illustrate any theoretical weaknesses or lacunae in Atkinson's model?

SUGGESTED READING

Atkinson, J. (1984) Manpower strategies for flexible organisations. *Personnel Management* (August), 28–31.

Beer, M., Spector, B. and Lawrence, P. *et al.* (1984) Human resource flow, in *Managing Human Assets*, The Free Press, New York, pp. 66–112.

Legge, K. (1989) Human resource management: a critical analysis in *New Perspectives on Human Resource Management* (ed. J. Storey), Chapter 2, Routledge and Kegan Paul, London, pp. 19–40.

Townley, B. (1989) Selection and appraisal: reconstituting social relations, in *New Perspectives on Human Resource Management* (ed. J. Storey), Chapter 6, Routledge and Kegan Paul, London, pp. 92–108.

CASE 16

Perceived reward incongruencies as a result of an organizational renewal process

HENK VAN DEN HONDEL and SANDRA SCHRUIJER

BACKGROUND

The engineering works called 'The Future' is part of a large international concern. The plants belonging to this concern were for strategic reasons until recently obliged to have their production means manufactured by 'The Future'. 'The Future' manufactures machines used in production and components thereof for internal clients. The factory is known for the excellent quality of its products. The plant employs approximately 575 people: 400 craftsmen and 175 individuals in managerial functions and in support and staff departments. The product mix is very varied, and ranges from large machines to different kinds of components.

In recent years 'The Future' has undergone a major organizational renewal process. Below we shall describe how 'The Future' was organized in the past and its associated problems which were the impetus for change. Then we shall focus on the new organization and its consequences in terms of structure, promotion and reward.

'THE FUTURE': PAST HISTORY

Structure

In the past, 'The Future' was a functional organization. It was designed in accordance with the kind of activities which had to be executed. That is, pieces of work were transported from one workplace to the other according to the type of activity that had still to be performed. This is the traditional design of an engineering works. The craftsmen were grouped per specialism and each specialism had its own fixed location. The structure of the organization is shown in Figure C16.1.

Human Resources Management in Europe
Edited by Sarah Vickerstaff
Published in 1992 by Chapman & Hall, London. ISBN 0 412 45380 0

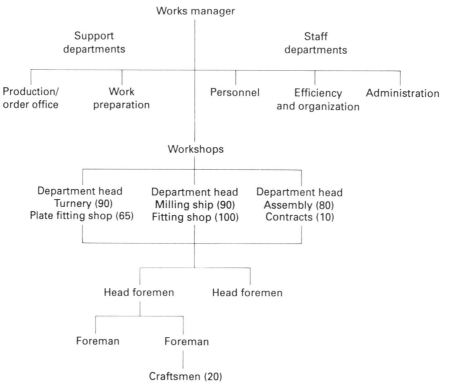

Fig. C16.1　The organization structure before the organizational renewal.

As can be seen, five hierarchical layers existed: craftsman, foreman, head foreman, department head, and works manager. Ultimate responsibility for the factory and its strategy resided with the works manager. The latter plus his department heads were responsible for the operational day-to-day management.

Problems

Before discussions about organizational change emerged, 'The Future' was very successful. The factory had a good image and the craftsmen were widely respected. Modern machines and tools were used. Product quality was high.

However, several problems arose. Pay differences between skilled and unskilled employees decreased due to a levelling of financial rewards. The status of and social esteem for the craftsman and his education diminished. Career perspectives were limited as a result of a stagnated growth of the factory.

Due to the advances in technology more and more sophisticated machines were introduced. Although this was generally appreciated by the craftsmen it also meant that a different type of craftmanship was called for: manual skills were replaced by programming skills.

The change from piece rates to a fixed wage system had indirect consequences for the craftsman's attitude towards his work. Performance-related pay stimulated him to produce a large quantity of units. All regulating, controlling and supporting tasks were left to others so that as little time as possible was lost. A fixed wage made job enlargement and enrichment possible but the existing Tayloristic separation between deciding, executing and regulating prevented this.

The consequences of these developments were a widespread dissatisfaction among the craftsmen, increased turnover and increased absenteeism. Moreover, the competitive position of 'The Future' eroded due to a growing number of complaints concerning delivery time and price.

An investigation revealed that the organizational structure was too rigid and promoted inflexibility. No distinctions were made between simple and complex orders. Another conclusion was that job commitment was low, both among management and craftsmen. One became acutely aware that in a large functional organization price, quality and delivery time are outside management's and especially outside the craftsmen's field of vision. Work preparation, production management and quality control were separate departments yet despite these regulating bodies complaints about delivery time and price were received continuously. It was decided to redesign the functionally organized factory into a product-oriented one.

HOW 'THE FUTURE' CHANGED

After a time-consuming and intensive process people and machines were grouped according to types of similar products. Four product-oriented groups emerged which resulted in a considerable simplification in production management. Under the new system each group produced its own products and was to a certain extent autonomous. Group members could jointly execute all the necessary activities in the manufacturing of a certain product, and could simultaneously regulate the group's actions. Regulating tasks which before were executed by support and staff departments were now decentralized and carried out by the independent product groups. Thus the jobs of the craftsmen were enlarged and enriched. Consequently, the layout of the factory changed: different activities were grouped together per product group.

The transition from a vertical and hierarchical organization to a more horizontal and flat organization was an enormous cultural change, both for management and craftsmen. Via work groups employees were involved in the decision making so as to create sufficient support for the changes.

Although the number of people remained the same, the organizational structure differed, as can be seen in Figure C16.2.

The positions department head (work preparation), and department

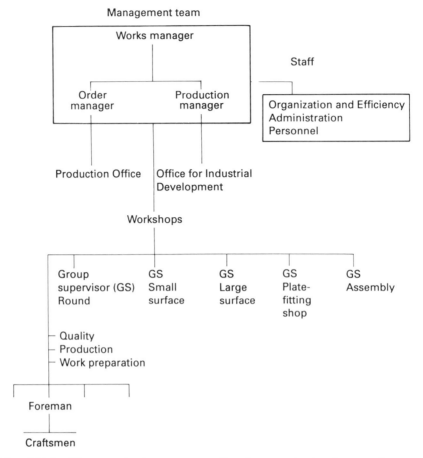

Fig. C16.2 The organization structure after the organizational renewal.

head production/order office became extinct. Overall the organization kept four hierarchical levels as compared to five before: craftsman, foreman, group supervisor (the leader of the autonomous group) and management team. The management team in the new organization had the final responsibility for 'The Future' and strategic management. The management team, the five group supervisors and the three staff departments formed a management body which was responsible for the day-to-day functioning of the organization. The restructuring meant a promotion for all functions except for the craftsmen. The works manager became chairman of the management team. The department heads were part of the management team and were also promoted. The head foremen of the old organization now occupied staff positions, which implied a considerable increase in responsibility and hence promotion. Provisions were also made for foremen to be promoted: they now were responsible for more complete products. All these promotions implied that the employees in question moved upwards in the job classification scheme and thus received higher pay.

The craftsmen, however, were not promoted. As stated above, it was already difficult to motivate them. In the new organization the craftsmen were given greater responsibility: they were expected to be multi-skilled, were responsible for simple work preparations and drawings, responsible for leadtime, for simple machine maintenance, and for product quality. But . . . no promotion. This was formally explained by the job specialists by stating that the extra responsibility given to the craftsmen already formed part of their original job description. Moreover, granting a higher pay scale to craftsmen working for 'The Future' could have serious consequences for other workshops belonging to such a large concern. Subsequently, the works management and the Works Council exerted such strong pressure on group management that the craftsmen were also given some promotion. The final result was that the craftsmen were rewarded with half a function: a specially created position ensured that they were promoted to a position half-way between their former position and the next higher one. A very strenuous and difficult process preceded this outcome.

CONCLUSION

The instruments of personnel management were grafted upon a traditional Tayloristic organization and hence prevented an increase in flexibility and innovation in and of the organization.

DISCUSSION QUESTIONS

For sessions of 1–1½ hours:

1. Piece-rate motivated the craftsmen in making many units. Performance was directly linked to rewards. Evaluate performance-related pay as a strategy to motivate.
2. Does a functionally designed organization prescribe a specific way of rewarding? If so, what are the advantages and disadvantages?
3. Which of 'this engineering works' problems are directly related to the functional organization design?
4. Compare the cultures of the old and the new organization.

For longer sessions:

5. What does the transition to the new form of organization mean for employees working in the staff and support departments? Which measures would be suitable? (Think, for example, of job content, guidance and support, training.)
6. Which instruments of personnel management need to be revised in order for the new organization to be successful?
7. Will absenteeism and turnover drop in the new organization? If so, why?

8. Evaluate the chosen solution for the situation of the craftsmen. Does it solve all problems? May it create new ones? Which?

SUGGESTED READING

Cherns, A. (1987) The principles of sociotechnical design revisited. *Human Relations*, **40**, 153–62.

Kapalan, R. S. (1984) Yesterday's accounting undermines production. *Harvard Business Review*, 95–101.

Mahoney, T. A. (1989) Multiple pay contingencies: strategic design of compensation. *Human Resource Management*, **28**, 337–47.

Thierry, H. (1992) Pay and payment systems, in *Employment Relations* (eds J. F. Hartley and G. M. Stephenson), Blackwell, Oxford, pp. 136–60.

TEXT 6

Profit sharing: different perspectives in Europe

INTRODUCTION

Table T6.1, which compares the different attitudes and practice with regard to profit sharing in Europe, is taken from M. Uvalic (1991), *The PEPPER Report*. The acronym PEPPER stands for 'Promotion of Employee Participation in Profits and Enterprise Results'. The report is a comprehensive consideration of the traditions, legal and fiscal frameworks and practice of profit sharing in the 12 member states of the EC, and was prepared for the Commission of the European Communities, Brussels.

DISCUSSION QUESTIONS

1. What are the main trends in profit sharing in Europe?
2. Why do you think profit sharing is more significant in France and Britain than in many other European countries?
3. Would you expect profit sharing to continue to increase in Europe in the 1990s? What factors are likely to encourage and to hinder its further development?

SUGGESTED READING

Armstrong, M. and Murlis, H. (1988) *Reward Management*, Kogan Page, London, pp. 247–56.

Pendleton, A. (1992) Employee share ownership schemes in the UK: *Human Resource Management Journal*, **2**, (No. 2), 83–8.

Uvalic, M. (1991) *The PEPPER Report*, Commission of the European Communities/European University Institute, Brussels and Florence.

Human Resources Management in Europe
Edited by Sarah Vickerstaff
Published in 1992 by Chapman & Hall, London. ISBN 0 412 45380 0

Table T6.1 PEPPER schemes in member states of the European Community in the late 1980s: summary of principal findings. The PEPPER Report for the Commission of the EC. © 1991 Dr Milica Uvalic

Country	General attitude	Legislation		Diffusion of PEPPER schemes			
		Specific laws and year of introduction	Tax benefits	Prevalent types	No. of schemes/firms involved	Employees involved	Employee benefits or profit share/employee
Belgium	Mainly unfavourable, but now discussed	Various, but only on ESO (since 1982), including SO (1984)	Rather limited, especially for SO	ESO	Around 30 quoted companies	On average 5% (varying from 1–28%)	Shares reserved for employees: 4% on average of total shares issued
				CPS	Multinationals Insurance Banks Distribution		Around 5% of distributable profits; 8–15% of performance-related pay
Denmark	Mainly favourable and discussed	On SPS and ESO (since 1958)	Some for SPS (shares or bonds) and ESO	CPS	Min. 50 schemes		
				SPS BPS	20 schemes 27 schemes		2% of share capital DKR 3400 per employee
				ESO	32 schemes		Less than 2% of total share capital
				Total	200 or more		
France	Very favourable and intensively discussed	Various: CPS (1959) DPS (1967) SO (1970) ESO (since 1973)	Substantial for both firms and employees	DPS	12 000 firms and 10 000 agreements	4 500 000 (3 000 000 benefiting)	Profit shares on average 3.4% of the wage bill
				CPS	4600 agreements	1 000 000	Profit shares on average 4.1% of the wage bill

			Employee invest. funds (1973) EBO (1984) Unique legisl. on all forms (1986)	ESO*	350 firms (2/3 quoted)	600 000*	Free distrib, of shares: 3% of the wage bill
				SO	A total of 40 schemes in 1971–84		
				EBO	10–20 per year in 1980–90		
Germany	Mainly favourable except for CPS: intensively discussed	Minor until 1984, only for DPS and ESO	Some: on DPS (since 1961) and ESO (primarily since 1984)	ESO and DPS	1600 firms (0.1% of total)	1 300 000 80% usually participate	Employee capital: DM 15 bln (only 5% of firms' annual balance)
				PS in general	Max. 5000 firms, mainly small scale	5.4% of individuals	6.8% of wages
Greece	Not clearly defined; discussions only starting	No	Non-existent	CPS	Very limited; in banking, insurance, clothing, food		Lump sum of GD 30 000–50 000
Ireland	Favourable and discussed	Modest	SPS (1982) SO (1986)	SO	139 schemes	Executives	Probably high
				SPS	87 schemes	35 000	
					All in the private sector		
Italy	Not clearly defined, but some forms discussed	No	Non-existent, except general provisions (1942 Civil Code)	CPS	25% of all large firms; 60 private firms in 1988	400 000; applied to 80% of all employees	3% of average earnings (but can be as high as 10% or more)
				ESO	30 quoted companies		Less than 5% of total share capital
Luxem-bourg	Not clearly defined	No	Non-existent	CPS ESO	22% of firms Mainly in banking		Usually not more than 0.5–2 months' salary

Table 6.1 *Continued*

Country	General attitude	Legislation		Diffusion of PEPPER schemes			
		Specific laws and year of introduction	Tax benefits	Prevalent types	No. of schemes/firms involved	Employees involved	Employee benefits or profit share/employee
Netherlands	Favourable and intensively discussed	Some incentives offered only to CPS	Minor, conditional on freezing of CPS	CPS	6–30% of firms	350 000 in 1975	4.5–6.5% of average earnings
				SPS, BPS & SO	Very limited (3% of all schemes)		
Portugal	Not clearly defined and mainly not discussed	Only general provisions in other laws (favourable)	Minor	CPS	Limited, but most diffused form		
				SPS	Large firms in finance	Restricted to executives	
Spain	Not clearly defined, but discussed	Only general provisions in Statute of Workers; and EBO (1986)	Minor, except for EBO	CPS	44% of medium and large firms but only in 6% directly linked to profits	2% of salaried employees (often restricted to executives)	Profit-linked payments: 5% of labour costs; in some cases as high as 10–25% of total pay
UK	Very favourable and discussed	SPS (1978) SO (1980) DSO (1984) CPS (1987) ESOPs (1988–) ESO (1978–)	Substantial for both firms and employees	DSO	4326 schemes		Substantial
				CPS	1175 "	293 000	7% of employee pay
				SPS	890 "	757 000	2–4% of total wages
				SO	891 "	623 000	
				ESOPs	20 "		
				Total:	7282 schemes 30% of firms	2 000 000 employees benefiting	

* Refers only to free distribution of enterprise shares to employees.
Abbreviations: SPS: share-based profit-sharing; BSP: bond-based profit-sharing; CPS: cash-based profit-sharing; DPS: deferred profit-sharing (investment funds); ESO: employee share-ownership; SO: stock options; DSO: discretionary share options; ESOP: employee share ownership plans; EBO: employee buy-outs.
Source: Uvalic (1991).

PART SIX

Industrial Relations and Employee Involvement

Throughout this volume we have seen how a variety of approaches to personnel management problems are adopted in different European settings. This diversity is perhaps nowhere more apparent than in the field of industrial relations processes, practices and procedures. The industrial relations systems of the different countries have developed and matured over a long historical trajectory; the particular pattern of industrialization and economic development in each situation has been crucial in setting the context in which the industrial relations actors meet.

In the study of comparative industrial relations the question of convergence, the extent to which industrialized countries' systems are developing towards a single model, is an old one. In recent years the persistence of national differences have led theorists to realize that the impact of industrialization and technological advance are moulded and conditioned by country-specific circumstances and the strategic choices of industrial relations actors. (See for example, Bean, 1985, pp. 9–12; Sorge and Streeck, 1988). Grahl and Teague (1991) have summarized the key areas of differentiation in contemporary Europe as follows: the level of trade union density; the extent of centralization in the industrial relations arena; the role of law and the ideological and political context of industrial relations (pp. 68–9).

To take the first factor, the table below indicates that throughout western Europe trade union density varies considerably:

In the last decade levels of trade union membership in many western European countries have declined. In France, the Netherlands and Britain the reduction has been marked. In countries such as Sweden, where trade unions have traditionally been strong, membership levels appear to have been maintained (Hyman, 1991, pp. 627–30).

Despite the persistence of such differences, a number of developments in the last decade have urged a qualified reconsideration of the notion of convergence. On the one hand the increasing internationalization of markets and the dominance of multi-national companies have raised questions about the transfer of human resource management practices from one national context to another. In particular, the considerable

Table P6.1 Union membership and union density in OECD countries, 1970–1989

	Type of data[a]	Union membership (thousands)			Change in membership (%)		Union density (%)					Rank order		Change in density (%)	
		1970	1980	1989	1970–79	1980–89	1970	1975	1980	1985	1988	1970	1988	1970–80	1980–88
Canada	R	2231.0^c	3487.2	4030.8	56.3	15.6	31.1^c	34.4	35.1	35.9	34.6	(16)	(14)	12.9	−1.4
United States	R	21248.0	22377.0	"	5.3	"	30.0	29.1	24.7	"	"	(18)	"	−17.7	"
	E	19335.0^g	20095.0	16960.0	3.9	−15.6	"	22.8	23.0	18.0	16.4^q	"	(22)	"	−28.7
Japan	R	11604.8	12369.3	12230.0	6.6	−1.1	35.1	34.4	31.1	28.9	26.8	(14)	(17)	−11.4	−13.8
Australia	R	2331.0	2955.9	3410.3	26.8	15.4	50.2	56.0	56.4	56.5	53.4	(7)	(11)	12.3	−5.3
	E	2512.7^f	2567.6^k	2535.9^p	"	−1.2^s	"	51.0^f	49.0^k	46.0^m	42.0	"	"	"	−14.3^s
New Zealand	T	"	678.0^l	611.3^r	"	−9.8^t	"	"	"	54.1	50.5^r	"	(8)	"	−6.7^t
	M	378.5	516.3	437.1^r	36.4	−15.3	46.2	50.1	55.0	47.3	42.1^r	(9)	"	19.0	−23.5
Austria	R	1520.3	1661.0	1644.4	9.3	−1.0	70.4	67.0	65.3	60.8	58.2	"	"	−7.2	−10.9
	E	1292.2	1370.1	1290.8	6.0	−5.8	59.8	56.1	53.8	48.6	45.7	(3)	(10)	−10.0	−15.1
Belgium	R	1606.0	2310.0	2291.4^r	43.8	−0.8	54.9	69.0	75.7	80.9	77.5	"	"	37.9	2.4
	E	1345.0	1723.3	1567.3^r	28.1	−9.1	46.0	55.3	56.5	54.3	53.0	(10)	(6)	22.8	−6.2
Denmark	R	1143.4	1795.8	2033.6^r	57.1	13.2	62.2	74.2	91.4	90.8	86.0	"	"	46.9	−5.9
	E	1101.8	1584.8	1730.9^r	43.4	9.2	60.0	67.4	76.5	78.3	73.2	(2)	(3)	27.5	−4.3
Finland	R	950.3	1646.4	1895.0	73.3	15.1	58.8	78.3	85.8	86.6	90.0^q	"	"	45.9	4.9
	E	830.5	1339.6	1587.5	61.3	18.5	51.4	67.4	69.8	68.6	71.3^q	(5)	(4)	35.8	2.1
France	E	3549.0	3374.0	1970.0	−4.9	−41.6	22.3	22.8	19.0	16.3	12.0	(19)	(24)	−14.8	−36.8
Germany	R	8251.2	9645.5	9637.0	16.9	0.0	37.9	41.7	42.9	44.0	40.1	"	"	13.2	−6.5
	E	7167.6	8327.6	8081.5	16.2	−3.0	33.0	36.6	37.0	37.4	33.8	(15)	(15)	12.1	−8.6

Greece	R	"	556.6[g]	650.0[l]	"	"	"	35.8[g]	"	36.7	(25.0)	"	(19)	"	"
Iceland	R	"	60.6[h]	103.1	"	70.1	"	"	68.1[h]	"	78.3[q]	"	(2)	"	15.0
Ireland	R	422.9	544.5	474.0[o]	28.7	−12.9	59.0	61.3	63.4	62.2	58.4[o]			7.5	−8.2
	E	380.6	490.0	426.6[o]	28.7	−12.9	53.1	55.2	57.0	56.0	52.4[o]	(4)	(7)	7.3	−8.1
Italy	R	5 224.5	8 772.0	9 568.2	67.9	9.1	40.8	54.2	60.5	59.6	62.7	"	"	48.3	3.6
	E	4 646.1	7 142.3	5 816.7	53.7	−18.6	36.3	47.2	49.3	42.0	39.6	(13)	(13)	35.8	−19.7
Luxembourg	R	52.4	72.0[j]	75.0[q]	37.5	4.2	46.8	45.8	52.2[f]	"	49.7[q]	(8)	(9)	11.5	−4.8
Netherlands	R	1 585.4	1 740.8	1 635.9	9.8	−6.0	40.5	42.7	39.9	34.1	30.2	"	"	−1.5	−24.3
	E	1 450.6	1 538.7	1 351.4	6.1	−12.2	37.0	38.4	35.3	28.7	25.0	(12)	(19)	−4.5	−29.2
Norway	R	759.2	1 049.1	1 203.5	38.2	14.7	58.1	60.4	65.3	65.4	67.7[q]	"	"	12.4	3.7
	E	660.1	913.6	1 013.9	38.4	11.0	50.6	52.7	56.9	55.7	57.1[q]	(6)	(5)	12.5	0.4
Portugal	R	730.9[b]	1 669.7[i]	1 463.0[n]	128.4	−12.4	59.0[b]	52.4	58.8[i]	51.6[n]	(30.0)		(16)	0.3	−12.2
Spain	R	"	1 703.0[j]	1 163.0[l]	"	−31.7	"	30.4[d]	22.0[j]	16.0	"	"	(23)	"	−27.3
Sweden	R	2 546.4	3 486.4	3 855.1	36.9	10.6	74.2	82.1	89.5	94.2	96.1	"	"	20.6	7.4
	E	2 325.3	3 114.5	3 415.1	33.9	9.7	67.7	74.5	80.0	84.0	85.3	(1)	(1)	18.2	6.6
Switzerland	R	842.9	954.3	899.9[m]	13.2	−5.7	34.2	36.6	34.5	32.6	30.0[o]	"	"	0.9	−13.0
	E	758.1	849.1	781.7[m]	12.0	−7.9	30.7	32.9	30.7	28.8	26.0[o]	(17)	(18)	0.0	−15.3
Turkey	R	973.4[e]	"	1 492.1	"	"	"	18.1	"	"	19.2[u]	(20)	(21)	"	"
United Kingdom	R	11 178.0	12 947.0	10 238.0[p]	15.8	−20.9	49.7	53.6	56.3	50.5	46.1	"	"	13.3	−18.1
	E	10 060.2	11 652.3	9 214.2[p]	15.8	−20.9	44.8	48.3	50.7	45.5	41.5	(11)	(12)	13.2	−18.1

[a] R = recorded membership; E = employed; T = total membership; M = membership in market sector.
[b] 1969.
[c] 1971.
[d] Average 1974–79.
[e] 1975.
[f] 1976.
[g] 1977.
[h] 1979.
[i] Average 1979–84.
[j] 1981.
[k] 1982.
[l] 1985.
[m] 1986.
[n] Average 1985–86.
[o] 1987.
[p] 1988.
[q] 1989.
[r] March 1990.
[s] 1982–88.
[t] 1985–90.
[u] Density rate for 1989 calculated on the basis of extrapolated employment data.
Sources: See Annex 4.A.

interest in Japanese management techniques and their transfer into the European context have, at least, raised questions about the potential for overriding national industrial relations patterns and assumptions (see for example, Garrahan and Stewart, 1991). On the other hand the development of the European Community has raised awareness of the impact of different industrial relations systems on economic growth. The Social Charter has also created a debate about the desirability of trying to harmonize basic employment rights and conditions across member states (Teague, 1991). Another factor which will be of increasing significance is the extent to which models of industrial relations and patterns of trade union organization from western European countries can, and should, act as guidelines for eastern European development. If systems of industrial relations appear to sustain considerable national divergence in terms of the degree of legal regulation and the extent of centralized bargaining between government, employers and trade unions, at the level of the individual enterprise in western Europe there do seem to be common themes emerging:

> . . . a number of common trends and developments in European industrial relations have emerged in recent years. Among the most discernible trends are new forms and new areas of work, decentralization, the adoption of labour market flexibility strategies and the growth of human resource management (Grahl and Teague, 1991, pp. 69–70).

A number of writers have suggested that one of the defining characteristics of human resource management, as opposed to personnel management, is a focus on employee involvement or commitment strategies. (e.g. Guest, 1991, pp. 151–2) This is framed by some commentators as an attempt to move away from a reliance upon worker compliance with managerial authority towards employee commitment to corporate goals (Walton, 1985; Beer *et al.* 1984).

This suggests a renewed focus upon the individual employee and has been seen as an explicitly anti-union approach in some contexts. (Guest, 1989; Beaumont, 1992) In other accounts, the individualistic focus of human resource management ideas are seen as the logical outcome of changing technology and work organization.

Management needs to both motivate and control their employees towards the pursuit of organizational goals. The most obvious form of managerial control is direct and unilateral. Typically this kind of regime elicits a compliance response; employees do just enough to avoid sanctions. Progressively this kind of managerial control has been challenged. Firstly, by employees who have resisted arbitrary managerial power and have demanded a right to some say in how work is organized and remunerated, and rights to negotiation and consultation. In addition through the formation of trade unions and the development of social and political programmes for industrial democracy managements' right to manage has been tempered.

In the 1970s within western Europe, but also in the 1980s in eastern Europe, industrial democracy and workers control were key aspects of national debates about industrial relations. Many European countries in the post second world war period institutionalized systems of industrial democracy, through works councils and arrangements for the co-determination of managerial decisions by management and employee representatives. For example, there are works councils in Germany, Belgium, France, the Netherlands and Portugal, and employee representatives or directors on company boards in Germany, Denmark and Spain (Bean, 1985, pp. 158–83).

In many parts of Europe the role of the social partners, that is employers' organizations and trade unions, in economic, social and political life are taken for granted. Liberal corporatist patterns of industrial relations have been the bedrock of political and economic management in countries as diverse as Austria and Sweden. This is one model which governments in a number of Eastern European countries are currently flirting with. Unilateral forms of management control have also been contested from within management. Increasingly, management theorists have argued that people work better when they are involved, consulted and allowed to participate in decisions about their working situation. This suggests that management should seek a commitment rather than a compliance response, by more participative management styles and systems.

In the 1970s the initiative on industrial democracy was on the employees or trade union side, in the 1980s developments have been more employer led. The arguments are less about the social and political desirability of extending democracy to the workplace and more about the efficiency benefits of employee involvement. For example:

> The Federation is strongly committed to the promotion of management-led employee involvement. Companies benefit from enlisting the constructive participation of employees in promoting the productivity, competitiveness and prosperity of the undertaking in which they work. Employee involvement promotes industrial efficiency and good industrial relations. (Engineering Employers Federation, undated, p. 1)

From the management side the 1980s have witnessed the growth of new employee involvement strategies. There has been a trend, more pronounced in some countries than others, for collective bargaining to be decentralized, and for the growth of other consultation and communication arrangements at plant level. We have already looked at some of these ideas in previous parts of the book. In part 2 we considered how work is organized and the impact of job design on motivation, job satisfaction and organizational culture. In part 5 we considered the growth of profit sharing schemes as a major development in the financial participation of employees in their enterprises. Thus, commitment strategies as part of human resource management are not confined to the industrial relations arena, but may be part of a strategic attempt to develop high trust cultures and work systems through changes in a broad range of personnel policy areas.

In reviewing the whole area of employee involvement and participation, it is useful to make a distinction between individual or direct and representative or indirect forms of involvement. (Brewster and Connock, 1985 p. 123) Further it is instructive to ask which issues or topics are subjects for participation; following Brewster and Connock again we can distinguish between policy issues or task related issues. Policy issues refer to the business and market strategies of the organization, for example: decisions on investment, wages, redundancy and relocation etc. Task related issues refer to the implementation of policies and work related questions, such as, allocation of work, shifts etc. (1985, p. 123). By cross referencing these dimensions we can develop a typology of forms of employee involvement:

CONTENT OF
INVOLVEMENT

	Policy	Task-related
Individual		
Representative		

FORM OF
INVOLVEMENT

Current trends in employee involvement have tended to focus upon individual, direct involvement over task related issues. One of the most well known examples of these developments are Quality Circles and their many derivatives. Other direct forms of involvement that appear to have become increasingly prevalent are team briefings, newssheets, attitude surveys, suggestion schemes, company videos and financial participation (Townley, 1989). Indirect involvement through representative structures remains very significant, especially in those countries mentioned above where joint consultation is formalized by legal regulation. In Britain there is some evidence to suggest that company advisory boards, company councils and other forms of joint consultation have been on the increase in the 1980s (ACAS, 1991).

Collective bargaining through trade union and management negotiations still accounts for a large proportion of the means by which employees have voice in decisions affecting their working lives. Trends in collective bargaining are difficult to summarize, but there seems to be something of a general move, more pronounced in some countries such as Britain and Italy, towards decentralized, company or plant level bargaining; a development mirrored to a lesser extent in some of the more traditionally centralized systems such as Sweden and Denmark.

Interest in a wide range of employee involvement and communication

programmes and ideas seems set to continue. So far the evidence suggests
that these new forms of participation co-exist with, rather than replace,
trade union channels of negotiation, at least where trade unions are
already established. They may however combine with other developments that have tested unions ability to build and sustain membership.
In broad terms most western European economies have witnessed a
progressive decline in manual employment in manufacturing and heavy
industry and a commensurate increase in the numbers of people working
in white collar jobs in service industries. Although the strength and
effects of these trends have varied considerably from country to country,
we saw in earlier sections of the book the related effects of an increase in
the number of women working outside the home and the growth in part
time and self employed forms of work. Trade unions have traditionally
found it more difficult to organize outside the male, manual manufacturing sector. In the 1990s trade unions are likely to continue to face
the challenge of responding to a different kind of workforce, doing
different kinds of jobs, as well as needing to orientate themselves to new
managerial strategies for employee involvement which are at least in part,
a response to these same trends.

In the rest of this book readers have the opportunity to look at three
very different cases illustrating various aspects of industrial relations and
employee involvement. Case 17 looks at the closure of a steel factory in
France and how the social partners responded to the threatened loss of
jobs. Case 18 involves an example of workplace conflict that arises from
poor communication and involvement processes and invites the reader to
assess various alternatives for resolving the dispute. The final case looks
at the development of 'progress teams', akin to quality circles, in a
Spanish manufacturing context. The case questions involve implementation issues of how to introduce and sustain new forms of involvement
in a relatively low trust context, where rationalization has already led to a
considerable reduction in the labour force.

SUGGESTED READING FOR PART SIX

Advisory, Conciliation and Arbitration Service, (1991) *Consultation and Communication*, Occasional paper 49, ACAS, London.

Bamber, G. J. and Lansbury, R. D. (1987) *International and Comparative Industrial
Relations*, George Allen and Unwin, London.

Bean, R. (1985) *Comparative Industrial Relations*, Croom Helm, London.

Beaumont, P. B. (1990) *Change in Industrial Relations*, Routledge, London,
chapter 3, Free Press, New York, pp. 39–65.

Brewster, C. and Connock, S. (1985) *Industrial Relations: Cost-effective Strategies*
chapter 3, Fress Press, New York, pp. 39–65.

Brewster, C. and Connock, S. (1985) *Industrial Relations: Costeffective Strategies*
Hutchinson, London.

Collard, R. and Dale, B. (1989) Quality Circles in *Personnel Management in Britain*
(ed. K. Sisson) Basil Blackwell, London, pp. 356–77.

Engineering Employers Federation (undated) *Employee Involvement*, EEF,
London.

Garrahan, P. and Stewart, P. (1991) Work organizations in transition: The human resource management implications of the 'Nissan Way', in *Human Resource Management Journal*, **2**(2) Winter 1991/1992, pp. 46–62.

Grahl, J. and Teague, P. (1991) Industrial relations trajectories and European human resource management, in *International Comparisons in Human Resource Management* (eds C. Brewster and S. Tyson) Pitman, London, pp. 67–91.

Guest, D. (1989) Human resource management: its implications for industrial relations and trade unions in *New Perspectives on Human Resource Management* (ed. J. Storey) Routledge, London, pp. 41–55.

Guest, D. (1991) Personnel management: the end of orthodoxy in *British Journal of Industrial Relations*, **29**, (No.2), pp. 149–75.

Hyman, R. (1991) European unions: towards 2000 in *Work, Employment and Society*, **5** (No.4), pp. 621–39.

Sorge, A. and Streeck, W. (1988) Industrial relations and technical change: the case for an extended perspective, in *New Technology and Industrial Relations*, (eds R. Hyman and W. Streeck) Basil Blackwell, Oxford, pp. 19–47.

Teague, P. (1991) Human resource management, labour market institutions and European integration, in *Human Resource Management Journal*, **2**, (No.1), pp. 1–21.

Townley, B. (1989) Employee communication programmes, in *Personnel Management in Britain* (ed. K. Sisson) Basil Blackwell, Oxford, pp. 329–55.

Walton, R. E. (1985) From control to commitment in the workplace in *Harvard Business Review*, **63**, pp. 76–84.

Société des Forges de Froncles: managing redundancies

MICHEL FERON

INTRODUCTION

One morning, in the assembly room of a metallurgy plant, the President, a union representative, a Human Resource Management consultant, another union representative, a trainer, etc. follow one another to the rostrum. Inside the room the workers are assembled, waiting with anticipation. People are talking about the coming together of the social actors, trust in mankind, mobilization of the whole company: in short, about the future they have to build together.

Why is this meeting of personnel taking place?

The reason is simple: 150 posts out of the 400 in the company are to be lost. Odd? Not really. Let's go back to the beginning.

PRESENTATION OF THE COMPANY

S.F.F. (Societe des Forges de Froncles) is a unit of the Belgian iron and steel group: COCKERILL-SAMBER (fifth largest European iron and steel producer, with a turnover of 28 billion francs). It is situated in Froncles, a small township of 2500 inhabitants, where it is the main employer. Froncles is located in the department of Haute-Marne, a region in which companies, heir to a long metallurgic tradition, are based but where, overall, the economic situation is difficult. S.F.F. manufactures spare parts for the group PSA (Peugeot-Citroën).

It specializes in two distinct activities:

- cold laminating of large plates, employing 150 people;
- cold beating of steel wire (special screws and bolts), employing 250 people.

These two sectors developed in different ways:

Cold beating has always been maintained with 'state of the art' technology and has therefore remained quite competitive. On the other hand, the rolling mill technology, which was established in the 1950s, has become progressively obsolete. The plates produced are not treated which has made them progressively less marketable. For that matter, closing down the rolling mill was contemplated in 1983 by Citroën, which was SFF's owner at the time.

Cockerill finally took SFF over, because of an interest in its laminating activity. As a matter of fact, as it was facing a depression in the iron and steel industry, the group opted for a strategy of specializing and wished to take advantage of production quotas, which were allowed in the context of the European plan for the steel and iron industry restructuring. At that time, the plant numbered 620 people.

There has been a succession of market losses in laminating, with an initial crisis in 1988 (94 job losses), followed by the 1990 announcement that the rolling mill would close down as a consequence of lost quotas.

THE SOCIAL ACTORS

The main protagonists are:

- the plant President, M. Leuven, who was previously Production Manager. Being heavily involved in the future of the plant, he enjoys considerable autonomy and is determined to fight the closure.
- The Confédération Generale du Travail (CGT)[1] section and its shop steward, M. Rojot. The CGT has been established in the company for a long time. Its constituency has progressively decreased, but it has retained a great deal of power with regard to mobilisation.
- The section of the Confédération Française Democratique du Travail (CFDT) and its leader, M. Pelissier, who is acting secretary to the Comité d'Entreprise, (Works Committee)[2]. In contrast to the CGT, the CFDT has, more recently, developed an image as a union that has tempered its militancy with a good dose of realism.
- The association 'Strategie et Avenir' and its chairman, M. Pouthas. This association was created on the initiative of the CFDT and is marked by its chairman's strong personality. It defines itself as a meeting point for social partners from many sides, M. Pelissier and M. Pouthas met before, during the 1988 job losses. M. Pouthas is also CFDT Metallurgy Federation General Secretary in Champagne Ardennes.
- 'Development et Emploi', a Consultancy specializing in the articulation between social and economic strategies, and its consultant, M. Babinet.

[1] The CGT is the oldest French trade union confederation which has traditionally had links with the Communist Party.
[2] All firms employing at least 50 employees are supposed to establish a Comité d'Entre-prise. Management is required to give information to the Comité about the general financial position of the company.

THE ANNOUNCEMENT OF THE CLOSURE
OF THE ROLLING MILL

At the end of September 1990, the plant President presents the restructuring plan before the Comité d'Entreprise

- The rolling mill will be closed and 136 posts will be lost, with a social plan including early retirement departures, voluntary departures with financial incentives; and dismissals.
- Screwing and bolting activities will be taken over by the French iron and steel group: USINOR SACILOR, which supplies the steel wire needed for this manufacture.

Reactions are quick to come.

CGT rapidly distributes leaflets. Here are a few significant extracts:

STOP THE ROW!

The way management made decisions about the economic activity of our company, especially about the plate sector, does not leave us much hope about the near future, if we offer no resistance.

ACTUALLY, DO THEY REALLY WANT TO LOSE THIS ACTIVITY WHICH INVOLVES ABOUT A HUNDRED JOBS?

In no case will the CGT allow this because it would mean mutilating our national and local economy. All these plans correspond to class choices:

- To accelerate restructuring industrial activities such as steel plate works on a European and world wide scale, in order to increase mergers, specialization, and, at the end of the day, rationalizing the production capacities of men and sites, notably against France (Europe of 1993).
- To answer profit demands from multinational companies.

It means that without your intervention and a power struggle, a hundred jobs and the company's future will be threatened.

AND YET, IT IS POSSIBLE TO SET ABOUT IT IN ANOTHER WAY!

- COCKERILL'S financial means should be used primarily to invest in modern machinery and satisfying grievances, such as improved conditions of work. It is possible to modernize and invest in plate laminating, especially with an electric zincing production line, etc. . . .

We want to produce French goods, keep our company alive at Froncles.

The CFDT's leaflet has another approach:

We are standing at the crossroads:
– COCKERILL gives us up on 31 December.
– USINOR-SACILOR takes us over on 1 January.
The CFDT was able to obtain three things from COCKERILL:
– Job creations at Froncles and its surrounding area (the downtown plant could be given life again).
– a social plan that answers all problems
– maintenance of the forge at Froncles.
The CFDT's action looks towards EMPLOYMENT.
WITHOUT THIS ACTION ALL THE JOBS WOULD HAVE BEEN LOST.

Because the CFDT chose to support an industrial plan, together we will get from USINOR SACILOR the investments which are necessary to develop Froncles in the future.

The CFDT does not intend to make concessions on vested interests: we asked for a social bargaining commission to be set up without delay.

THE DEADLOCK

M. Leuven, the plant President, rapidly states that no solution will be found if there is no external help. He appeals to M. Pouthas, 'Strategies et Development' chairperson, whom he had already contacted at the end of 1989.

The latter agrees to serve as mediator and progressively integrates himself into the process. The stages are as follows:

First of all, M. Pouthas's intervention is made official by the president.

Afterwards, the dossier is investigated and a plan of action is worked out with M. Pelissier, Comité d'Entreprise secretary.

Then, a delicate negotiation is held with the CGT shop steward, M. Rojot. In exchange for CFDT support to put pressure on COCKERILL, he agrees to take part in the multipartner piloting committee that will serve as a contact point with the economic environment.

This participation will lead him to be harshly criticised by some CGT leaders, who will try to put him back in the ranks.

Finally, all the workers will be informed about M. Pouthas's ideas during a collective meeting.

First deadlock at this stage: the person in charge of COCKERILL's French subsidiary, to which SFF belongs, disapproves of the President's initiative and threatens to simply make people redundant.

Thanks to a network of contacts, M. Pouthas succeeds in informing M. Gandois, General Manager of COCKERILL, of the situation. The latter considers that M. Pouthas's plan of action represents a constructive outcome, even if it constrains the President to go beyond his traditional social role.

M. Pouthas then begins the second phase of his action, which consists of relying on some people from outside the company, expertise that is not available internally:

– A consultant, because of her experience in restructuring.
– A trainer, because of his practice of learning pedagogy (action/analysis/ conceptualization/experimentation).
– A communication agency, because of its ability to draw up internal and external communication systems.
– ANPE (Agence Nationale Pour l'Emploi), because of its knowledge of the labour market.
– Local authorities (municipality, department, Regional Council), because of their knowledge of the local political and economic environment.

Second deadlock as far as employers' associations are concerned: M. Leuven is strongly advised to give up this venture and come back to more traditional practices and procedures. Actually, the point is to separate clearly the different roles: the body of employers should deal with economic decisions whereas the redeployment group piloted by trade unionists should restrict itself to offering some help to those workers who have lost their jobs.

Finally, after much bargaining, M. Leuven wins the employers' approval, the latter agreeing to take part in the piloting committee.

THE 'REBOUND' OPERATION

A strategy integrating economic as well as social matters is progressively worked out and finally presented to the personnel by the piloting committee.

This presentation constitutes a moment of intense emotion: one needs to be aware that the die is cast (the rolling mill will close down), but that there is still a future, which everyone has now to build.

Finally, the message must be: since everybody has to find a project for him/herself, let's get to work!

The general scheme of action can be summarized in a table listed in the booklet that was created by the communication agency.

A DOUBLE APPROACH: ECONOMIC AND SOCIAL

	ECONOMIC
Reflection started at the end of 1989	
LEADERSHIP AND COORDINATION: SFF management; Comité d'Entreprise; CFDT; CGT;	Contribution to the local economic development Small businesses existing or to be created

'Stratégie et Avenir';
'Dévélopment et Emploi'

ENVIRONMENT'S
INVOLVEMENT:
Piloting committee

Reflection ON SKILLS

SOCIAL: 2 STAGES

1. INDIVIDUAL
REFLECTION ON ONE'S
FUTURE: each his/her own
project!
2. CONTRIBUTION TO THE
ACHIEVEMENTS OF
THESE PROJECTS:
'ORECA'

End 89 → Summer 90 → November 90 → March 91

The process of skill analysis that has been adopted focuses on 'at risk' jobs (those which are bound to disappear or to change). It enables one to identify the fundamental abilities which are likely to be used in the redeployment programmes.

The social partners' definite positions are as follows:

The president

'Preparing the future. This is the nature of the process that we are now undertaking. It relies entirely on mutual trust. The company's adjustment to market changes is an unavoidable necessity. Ensuring this adjustment: this is the aim of the Economic Plan decided by the group. My mission is to lead it. This plan has consequences for everyone's future. Stopping laminating and changes in cold beating imply that some of us will leave the company and those who stay will have to move towards more responsibilities and new competencies. Facing these issues, two ways of action were possible: to impose or to involve. The first one was the simplest. I chose the second one, with the whole range of drawbacks it brings but also with all its advantages.

I invite you to seize the opportunity that occurs in your professional life to determine your own future.

CGT shop steward

We express real doubts and reservations because:

1. Closing the rolling mill corresponds to an industrial policy aimed purely at profit.
2. We think that a market does exist for plates and that it remains profitable. Furthermore, COCKERILL group did not make much effort to improve the plate sector and propose new activities. This results in a bad situation for the town and its environment (trades, school . . .).

Moreover, the group had encouraged personnel to get apartments; if these people are made redundant, they will find themselves with heavy mortgages, which will block their mobility. As COCKERILL took the decision without worrying about the physical and moral consequences for the personnel concerned, we thought it necessary and consistent with our vocation to help our redundant comrades. We do so while enrolling in the different projects for accompanying and reclassing workers.

As CGT representative (first national trade union) and supporter of legislation, I answer for social laws to be respected.

CFDT shop steward

For the CFDT, employment is the priority.

The CFDT believes that employment can last only if it is offered by profitable companies, with a job for everyone.

As soon as we began to fear for the future of Froncles forges, the CFDT – the majority association inside the company –, analysed the viability of the site, assisted by experts. The latter said unambiguously that if the rolling mill is not stopped, the whole company is condemned.

Facing this reality and COCKERILL'S determination, we strived to obtain:

- Maintenance of forging at Froncles.
- Redeployment of the employees deprived of work.
- The creation of new jobs in the environment.
- Implementation of a project aimed at helping redeployment, so that people are not left all alone with their employment problem.

This process is carried out with the unity and support of all the actors, which is a token of its success.

CASE STUDY QUESTIONS

1. What are the main differences between the CGT and the CFDT positions with regard to the problems posed by giving up one of the company's main activities?
2. What were the main characteristics of the restructuring plan that was finally set up?
3. What factors, in your view, favoured the success of the restructuring activity?
4. To what extent can the process that was used in this case be generalized to other close-down situations?

SUGGESTED READING

Bean, R. (1985) *Comparative Industrial Relations*, Chapters 2, 3 and 4, Croom Helm, London, pp. 20–99.

Erbes-Sequin, S. (1988) Industrial relations and workers' representation at the workplace level in France, in *New Technology and Industrial Relations* (eds. R. Hyman and W. Streeck), Basil Blackwell, Oxford, pp. 272–83.

Goetschy, J. and Rojot, J. (1987) French industrial relations, in *International and Comparative Industrial Relations* (ed. G. J. Bamber and R. D. Lansbury) Allen and Unwin, London, pp. 142–164.

The trouble with technical services at Midsize University

THARSI TAILLIEU

Midsize University is located somewhere in Benelux. It is a university which originated from a School of Economics around 1920. Gradually it developed into a medium sized university (6000 students) offering a wide range of degrees in the Humanities: Economics, Business Administration, Law, Social Sciences, Literature and Philosophy. The University is relatively prosperous and quite progressive in its undertakings.

MR CORNU'S HEADACHE

On Friday 20 December 1985 late in the afternoon, Mr Pierre Cornu, the Administrator of the Department of Psychology, closed his office and slowly drove home. He was very much aware that he would need the weekend to find a way out of his problems.

As usual at this time of the year, he was involved in budget planning for the next year. In his position as Administrator of the faculty he has an advisory role in the research budget review procedure controlled by the Scientific Council. As head of non-scientific staff personnel he is responsible for approving and consolidating the budget proposals for the technical staff and secretarial pools.

That afternoon, during the reviews of the budget proposals of the technical staff, a row broke out between several members of the technical staff. Failing to reconcile their differences he had to suspend the meeting. Afterwards he spoke to each of the parties individually. The whole Saturday and Sunday, Pierre Cornu analysed the incident and the context in which it could develop and pondered what action to take in order to remedy the problem situation.

THE PSYCHOLOGY DEPARTMENT AT MIDSIZE UNIVERSITY

Over the last decade the Psychology Department has evolved into the following structure. The department has about 600 regular students and

Human Resources Management in Europe
Edited by Sarah Vickerstaff
Published in 1992 by Chapman & Hall, London. ISBN 0 412 45380 0

250 part-time students (mostly older and working), some of whom follow a special programme. The academic staff consists of 50 full-time and 20 part time members, including junior members in the process of finishing their PhD project. The department is headed by the Dean, a position which is taken in turns among the full professors for a period of three years. The Dean is assisted by the Administrator of the Department, who acts as managing director and is also responsible for the pools of secretaries and a technical staff of about 15 people.

The department consists of nine basic units, responsible for teaching and research: Social Psychology, Work and Organizational Psychology, Developmental Psychology, Educational Psychology, Statistics and Methodology, Personality Psychology, Clinical Psychology, General and Experimental Psychology, Neurological Psychology – commonly Neuro-Psychology – (See Figure C18.1). About twelve secretaries located in four physical offices serve the basic sections (mail, telephone, student administration etc).

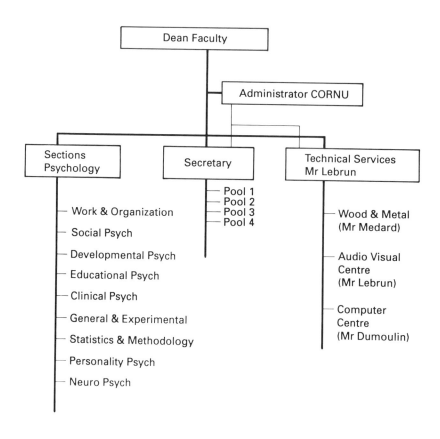

Fig. C18.1

Technical services of the department

The technical staff consists of a variety people, serving and maintaining facilities such as projectors, video-equipment, laboratories and computers. Initially a few people worked on them all together, gradually several specialized clusters have formed. In line with University practices Mr Lebrun, the most senior member of the technical staff, has served as head for more than a decade. Close to 53 years old, Lebrun who has a technical degree in Sound Engineering, was initially recruited for setting up the Audio Visual Centre, later he began coordinating the other services and eventually he was appointed Head of Technical Services. Most people still refer to him as Head of Audio Visual Services, the more visible part of his function. Given this double role, he was expected to and acted as *primus inter pares* with regard to his colleagues in technical services. His job officially entails the supervision of a diversity of technicians.

One of the oldest services is the Wood and Metal section. In the earlier days, almost all experimental and laboratory equipment was home-made by craftsmen. Nowadays specialized firms provide all instruments. The Wood and Metal section, once counting five full-timers, has shrunk to one person, providing a general purpose repair and maintenance service.

The Audio-Visual Centre (AVC), currently consisting of five full timers, for many years provided the bulk of technical support to the academic staff. The section provides audio-visual equipment and support for teaching and research. The section also staffs and runs the studio, a fully equipped almost professional TV studio. The studio was built during the seventies, at a time when great expectations were placed upon audio-vidual technologies as means for active involvement in learning and teaching. A quite impressive amount of educational films and videos have been produced by this team. Apart from their production activities, they also keep the studio operational for classes, seminars and training sessions. Generations of students have spent many hours of observation and skill training in the studio. Since the beginning of the eighties, the general drive towards cost-effectiveness in college education has severely reduced the amount of class time available for practice and work sessions. The decline of interest in studio work is reflected to some extent in the time lag of repair and renewal of equipment. For two or three years the AVC submitted budget proposals for modern cameras and a full electronic mixing and composition table. Thus far their demands have not been met.

Another primary task of the audio-visual section consists of running and maintaining the Social Psychology Laboratory. This laboratory contains a general control room and twelve separate cubicles which are used for experimental work on interaction and communication, occasionally for training purposes as well. The cubicles are equipped with audio- and video equipment enabling the control room to manipulate sound and pictures in any combination. Although the laboratory is called the Social Psychology Laboratory, after its founder, it is commonly used by different disciplines. Social, Clinical, Developmental and Organizational Psychologists are the most frequent users. Currently the lab is being equipped with keyboards, which could well overtake cameras and microphones as the basic instrumentation for experimental work.

The area in the building occupied by staff members of General and Experimental Psychology and the researchers around the Professor of Neuro-Psychology has become known as the Neuro-lab. This space contains several rooms for experimental work. Up until 1983 an annex to the building housed pigeons which were used for experimental research and course illustrations on learning and conditioning. Changed national laws with regard to animal testing led to closure of these facilities. Some of the laboratory rooms have quasi-permanent instrumental settings which are used in undergraduate teaching and practice sessions. The settings permit experimentation and computer registration of elements of the basic human functions such as vision, sensations, motor functions, reflexes etc. Two rooms in particular can be properly designated as the Neuro-lab. They are rooms which are equipped to study the voluntary and involuntary effects of stimulus materials on the origination and development of nerve signals in the brain and the spinal column. To do so, human subjects are completely wired with electrodes and a battery of powerful 16-channel analog signal recorders collects brain, spine, skin potentials and resistances. The set-up and service to the Neuro-lab is provided by the Computer Section.

What is commonly referred to as the Computer Section, in fact constitutes a variety of machines and technicians. The first general purpose mainframe computer appeared in 1968. The latest version now provides the calculating capacity and the administrative support to the faculty. This machine is served by two technicians, who entered as programmer and system analyst around 1970. Today, little programming takes place, as virtually all the computational needs of the social sciences are being met by canned statistical packages. This evolution in turn brought a small soft-ware oriented group into existence, consisting of one full and three part-timers. The group takes care of data acquisition and data management for the staff, and serves as help-desk for the students. These people quite often assist in the field and strongly promote the advent of personal computers, a new issue in the faculty.

A major part of the work and the effort of the Computer Section goes to the Neuro-lab. The output of the Neuro-lab is prepared for the mainframe by two smaller special minicomputers, able to deal with analogous data. The research of the Neuro-Psychological section generates massive amounts of data, which have to be condensed and digitalized for further treatment. The work is so specialized that collaboration has been sought with a technical university in the area. On several occasions the computer section was unable to handle the computer suppliers, or to arrive at the necessary specifications. Lebrun took the initiative to set up a collaborative network with a technical university. For a couple of years a specialist (Engineer with a degree in Electronics and Computer Science) and two technical engineers, have been attracted to assist in the methodological and operational aspects of the research of the Neuro-Psychological Section. Currently about four students of the engineering school are completing their apprenticeships on projects of that group.

The evolution of research and service needs of the department

As Mr Cornu has an advisory role to the Scientific Council of the faculty, he is able to discern the profile and the trends in the research of the different sections of the faculty. As far as related to the use of Technical Services he considers the following observations to be relevant.

The Developmental and the Clinical Psychologists are and remain the main users of AVC support, extensively using video materials and studio support. Given the high rate of unemployment among clinical psychologists, one might expect a decline of enrolment and there is even debate about the abolition of that field as a major at this university.

Social and Organizational Psychologists are changing their patterns of research. It would seem that the emphasis on process studies is fading away. The amount of effort put into studies of interaction, communication, group-decision making, is declining. The trimming of the staff and research assistance which has taken place over the last few years, almost makes it impossible to maintain these time-expensive methods of recording and analysing human processes by that particular technology. The demands for computer facilities and keyboards in addition to the microphones and video recorders in the lab prove the point.

The research of the Educational Psychology section most clearly reflects the fashions in modern computer technology. Computer assisted learning, instructional and feedback systems are the main focus of research. All varieties of electronic communication systems have already been used in experimental classroom settings, and as soon as the price for the latest innovation, Personal Computers, starts dropping somewhat, a budget claim for 20 or more of those can be expected, totalling at least 80% of the annual research budget.

The General Experimental Psychology section is in disarray. The chairholder, a very much respected professor, suffered a stroke and died. The appointed successor proves to be a transitional figure. The recent national legislation with regard to animal research has not only necessitated compliance with the law, but the overzealous University Council decided to abolish animal research altogether. Whatever was needed for teaching purposes has been video-taped and recorded. A large part of the competence of that section suddenly became irrelevant. Some members left, others sought association with the Neuro-Psychology section.

The Neuro-Psychological section is an exceptional group. Its teaching is restricted to one of the basic introductory courses and some seminars on Human Physiology. Officially this calls for one teaching position. Free from involvement and responsibilities in student projects, in fact totally outside of the main stream of student interest, and led by an ambitious professor who happens to be a first class researcher, the section has developed into a real research imperium. During the abundant years before 1980, the Neuro-lab has taken up 75% of the instrumentation budgets. Pierre Cornu can remember having signed multiple authorization to buy registration equipment. First two-channel recorders, followed by four-, eight-, and sixteen channel recorders. An even bigger replacement is on the budget for this year.

This evolution has not been without criticism. Gradually most people have realized that besides the investment in expensive and exclusive hardware, the complicated nature of the research has necessitated a group of specialists as well, currently a full time engineer, two technicians and some engineering students as apprentices. Either on a project basis or as part-timers, a number of outsiders are constantly at work to analyse and to interpret these research data.

The budget squeeze of the last years has raised tensions between the Neuro section and especially the applied psychology sections. The clash originated last year with a letter of protest by the Organizational Psychology Section when they found out that the Technical Services Committee approved almost all of the claims of the Neuro section and none of theirs, arguing that they should use income from contract work outside. Not only the applied disciplines, but also the other theoretical sections started having second thoughts on the position of the Neuro section in the department. Some staff members have openly voiced their resentment about the fact that a group with little contribution to the primary educational objectives of the institute and a research program that seldom attracts a student, can persistently spend almost three quarters of the institutional resources.

Mr Cornu realizes very well that any further budget cuts in the financial means of the Psychology Department will increase the competition and the antagonism between the different sections. One can expect that the nature of activities, their essentialness in relation to the mission of the institute, and the efficiency in realizing these goals will be subject to much debate. It is not unthinkable therefore that the Neuro section, in the not too distant future, could be forced into a secondary role, being allowed to do research only insofar as it supports its teaching purposes.

The conflict during the budget meeting of the technical services

Each year during the autumn the different sections of the department submit their research proposals to the Research Committee. This committee reviews and sets priorities for the proposals. The advice of the Research Committee is presented to the Faculty Council which, in general, endorses the work of the committee and allocates the funds.

Parallel to the work of the Research Committee, the technical services employees have assisted the academics with their proposals as far as instrumentation and technical assistance is concerned. Upon receiving the total collection of research proposals and the first screening by the Research Committee (not necessarily the final list of priorities), the Technical Services Committee discusses the claims for instruments and equipment; the choice of what to buy and where, in order to remain flexible; the implications in terms of manpower for installment and service; and a couple of final scenarios to be presented to the Faculty Council for final decision. The Faculty Council seldom ignores the advice of the technical staff, and sometimes even slightly changes some project priorities on the basis of their recommendations.

The Technical Services Committee is chaired by Lebrun, and is composed of three other members of technical services. Mr Medard from the Wood and Metal section brings in a general maintenance budget and scans the proposals for anything relating to rooms and infra-structure. The chairman, Lebrun, as head of the Audio Visual Section also represents his own group in the budget discussions. The computer section is represented by two members. Until now, Engineer Dumoulin, the specialist of the labs represents the whole computer section. From this year on Mr Bonami, more or less supervising the software group with its three part-timers, asked to be included in the budget preparations. Pierre Cornu, as the head of all technical personnel and as liaison to the Research Committee attends those meetings as well.

During the week of that memorable Friday, the committee has been together three times for reviewing the research proposals and the associated technical desiderata. Cornu was aware that the preparations for these meetings had already been full of incidents. This year the AVC section was determined to get its share of the funding to renew the studio and its labs. Instead of the usual moderating role played with regard to the claims of the researchers, they enthusiastically endorsed all equipment demands. From his part, being deeply involved in the content of the research of the Neuro section, Dumoulin was aware of a new type of 16 channel recorder, which if properly adapted, could decisively solve major measurement problems which hindered the research of the section. Nobody thus far was known to have come up with a solution for that problem. Although criticized at least twice by Lebrun, Dumoulin has independently sought contact with new computer suppliers and has collected a number of offers. He has stopped Lebrun by saying that Lebrun did not understand what was going on in the field of brain-recording, or for that matter about computers in general. Finally, Bonami who leaned more closely towards the applied scientists, had been propagating the possibilities of personal computers and needed his share of the budget to get a start in the new direction.

What in the past was an example of rational allocation of resources and a sharing of responsibility in setting priorities serving the department became a bar brawl. Three consecutive meetings could not resolve agreements on budget portions. Instead of converging, priorities diverged even more by the minute. The Friday meeting which was the deadline for advice to the Research Committee turned into name calling. Lebrun wanted his share of the budget to renew his facilities, Dumoulin was pushing for the latest in computer instrumentation, Bonami agreed with Lebrun that this was only serving a fraction of the institutional needs. On the other hand he would side with Dumoulin in that renovating the old technology was a waste of money. None of the others supported his point of view that personal computers were the only things worth investing in. The brawl ended with declarations of incompetence for Lebrun, repugnance at Dumoulin's ego-tripping, and derision for the ignorance of Bonami. Dumoulin and Lebrun declared that they were not willing to work together anymore.

Pierre Cornu took control over the discussion. He could not get them to finish their work constructively. He broke the meeting up and spoke to each participant individually. A lot of what they talked about was related to the situational context given above. Lebrun was disillusioned and felt lost. At his age he had hoped to get early retirement at 55, or possibly a move to a larger university where he could stick to his specialism: audio-visual work. Dumoulin could not hide his ambition in any way. The computer era is here, his qualifications are the best and he is to be the boss. Lebrun should go, all he does is put up red tape and confusion. In private, Bonami conceded some ambitions too. He clearly saw that the department could not go on like this, the cost of the Neuro section and people such as Dumoulin is too high. It would be better if they moved to a university which had a Medicine Department or an Academic Hospital. Anyway, he quite firmly stated that he was not willing to work under Dumoulin as head. He believes that service in a small department like this should focus on applications, data support and software for staff and students, exactly the kind of visibility he is striving for.

THE OPTIONS OF ADMINISTRATOR PIERRE CORNU

Pierre Cornu realizes that more than a single action will be necessary to bring things back to normal, and that normal might be different from before.

On Monday morning he has to bring the advice of the Technical Services Commission to the Research Committee. All he can do is to present the different budget proposals. They are not integrated and no priorities are given this time. Through the Research Committee he can enforce a priority and budgetary limits. This almost reverses the roles played in the past. He is really not sure he should do it that way.

No question, he has to go to the Dean and perhaps to the Faculty Council as well. The rivalry and the discontent among the sections of the faculty is reflected among his technical staff. Unless the strategic issues of research priorities and resource allocation are dealt with at that level, he feels he cannot manage his technical services units very well. Looking into that matter, Cornu realizes that it will not be easy.

The current Dean, with one more year to go, is the Professor of Educational Psychology. It is far from certain that he will be considered an objective judge in a discussion about institutional priorities. Anyhow the discussion has to be held in a lot of decision making bodies, and here lies the difficulty. The Neuro section has been aware of these feelings. At least, they have always carefully positioned their representatives in strategic places on the Budget Council, the Research Committee, and the Faculty Council, the ultimate decision-making body. Lacking outside obligations, and not being burdened with heavy teaching loads and student projects, the Neuro section members have been among the most diligent council members of the faculty.

On a shorter term basis, Cornu has to do something about the structure of Technical Services, the responsibilities of the sections and the relationships among the members. Ambiguity in the pecking order is difficult. But how to tackle the problem, in the light of the evolution of the Department?

It might be possible to reinstate Lebrun's position, while indicating that this is a temporary situation, awaiting his departure and a more general reorientation of Technical Services. Provided he is given some assistance and help, Lebrun could find another place or early retirement.

It is possible for Cornu to (temporarily) change the structure of Technical Services, given the development of quite divergent technologies, and to act directly as Head of Technical Services. This would mean that Wood and Metal, Audio Visual Centre, and the Computer Group (eventually divided up) would report directly to the Administrator.

A similar situation could be worked out in which the Technical Services were linked directly to the Secretary of the Department, an economist who is in charge of the pools of secretaries.

In terms of technical competence, it is clear however that Engineer Dumoulin is the best available person to become head of Technical Services, perhaps only for a period of three to four years. But how could he be made to identify with the interests of the institute? And how could such a solution be sold to Bonami? Perhaps the personnel manager has an answer to this question.

Of course in a university it would always be possible to put an advertisement for a redefined and enhanced job of Head of Technical Services, assess the applicants and then decide among insiders and outsiders.

CASE TASKS

In small groups of three or four discuss the following issues:

1. How would you characterize the policy of education and research in this department?
2. In what ways are the problems of technical services linked to the development of the total department?
3. In what ways could the Administrator approach the Dean and the Research Council in order to deal with the priority issues in a lasting way?

4. What immediate action could the Administrator take with regard to the structure and the relations within Technical Services? Discuss the pros and cons of the options given in the text. Can you find better ideas?
5. In what ways can you link the incident to concepts of status, power, and reference groups?

SUGGESTED READING

Huczynski, A. and Buchanan, D. (1991) *Organizational Behavior: an introductory text*. Part V. Management in the organization. Prentice Hall.

Brown, L. (1983) *Managing conflict at organizational interfaces*. Chapter 2: Analyzing interfaces, Chapter 3: Management strategies. Addison Wesley.

Torrington, D. and Weightman, J. (1985) *The Business of Management*. Part II Working in the organization (Organizational Politics, Winning consent without having authority). Prentice Hall.

Mintzberg, H. (1983) *Structure in Fives: Designing effective organizations*. Chapter 10 The professional bureaucracy. Prentice Hall.

Schein, E. (1980) *Organizational Psychology*. Part IV, Groups in organizations. (Structure and functioning of groups; Intergroup problems in organizations) Prentice Hall.

CASE 19

The introduction of progress teams at the ACENOR factory in Vitoria-Gasteiz, Spain

JOSÉ MARIA RODRIGUEZ

Copyright 1992 J.M. Rodriguez and IESE.

BACKGROUND

This case describes the preliminary steps leading up to the launching of the so-called 'progress teams' (PT) in one of the five factories of the ACENOR company: the factory at Vitoria-Gasteiz (see organizational chart in Figure C19.1).

ACENOR was the result of the merger of five companies in the same industry, which had historically been competitors. The factory at Vitoria-Gasteiz had undergone a significant restructuring. ACENOR had been set up to make these five companies viable. It had received substantial economic assistance from the Public Administration and from the EEC. The granting of this assistance was subject to the completion of an internal restructuring.

ACENOR belonged to an industry that was experiencing a crisis on a global scale since 1973–74, and had been undergoing restructuring internationally since 1975 and in Spain since 1980. This restructuring was being managed by the Spanish Administration and was under the control of the ECSC. The granting of the economic aid required was subject to the fulfilling of a series of conditions: (1) merger of the five companies into one; (2) specialization of the factories; (3) a reduction in joint production; (4) modernization of equipment and technology; (5) a reduction in staff; (6) financial reorganization; and (7) viable results.

In the last four years, ACENOR had made investments of more than 15 000 million pesetas. These investments had provided the group with the most technologically advanced equipment. The group had re-equipped itself technologically, incorporating new production techniques; it had created for itself an engineering society and an R&D unit. ACENOR was a cohesive group whose size was competitive with other European

Human Resources Management in Europe
Edited by Sarah Vickerstaff
Published in 1992 by Chapman & Hall, London. ISBN 0 412 45380 0

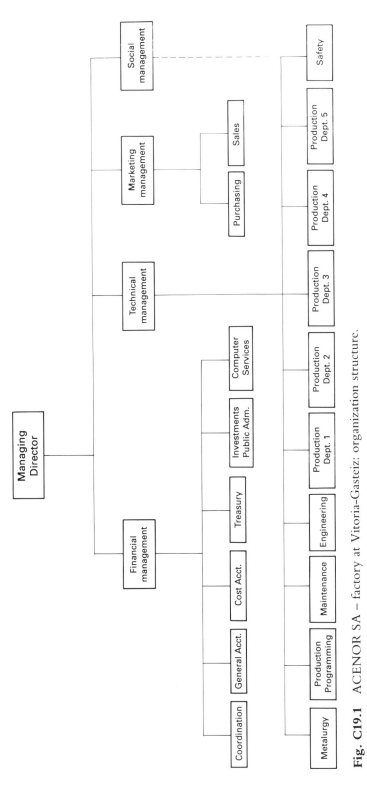

Fig. C19.1 ACENOR SA – factory at Vitoria–Gasteiz: organization structure.

producers. Its production was mainly directed towards clients with great technological demands. The quality of its production was comparable to that of its European competitors. Productivity per person had more than doubled since 1980. ACENOR exported 40% of its production, the majority of which was in Europe. However, the company's financial structure had some financial charges that had generated considerable losses in the fiscal year 1988. Currently, its greater volume of business, as well as a plan for financial reorganization, gave hope that the company would achieve positive results, as the industrial profit earned in the first quarter of 1989 indicated.

The investments made in the factory at Vitoria-Gasteiz were in the order of 3500 million pesetas. Its production equipment was comparable to that of the rest of the group. The factory at Vitoria-Gasteiz produced a range of more than a thousand products, all of which were specialty items.

The staff of the factory at Vitoria-Gasteiz had decreased from 1300 employees to 800. The average age of the employees was 43, and the average seniority was 19 years. Absenteeism (total) was 5.4%. The factory had a very rigorous security programme which had led to a very low rate of accidents. The Labour Committee was made up of representatives from four different unions, three of which were local. Hours lost due to strikes in the last year were in the order of 6000 and constituted 7% of absenteeism.

The restructuring of ACENOR, finalized by the merger of the five companies in December 1988, had turned out to be very complex and difficult in the legal, technical, economic, commercial and human aspects. This last area was difficult due to the presence of several factors: (1) clashes between inter-company cultures; (2) closing of installations; (3) product distribution; (4) centralizations; (5) reorganization; (6) retirement at the age of 52; (7) staff reductions; (8) changes in jobs; (9) uncertainty; (10) worry; and (11) tension. Great personal effort was necessary on the part of employees to adapt to the change. Thanks to this effort, the restructuring had offered positive industrial results: specialization in new products, new equipment, new technology – both acquired and internally developed – productive integral ratios, total quality, etc.

The atmosphere of the factory at Vitoria-Gasteiz was one of anxiety. At the time when the events of this case took place, the last 50 men who had to leave the factory through the system of anticipated retirement were about to leave. On the other hand, the changes that were taking place had awakened great hopes for the viability of the factory. The factory was 'boiling over' with expectation.

THE PROCESS OF CHANGE IN THE FACTORY AT VITORIA-GASTEIZ

The situation described encouraged the application of some 'special action'. On the other hand, the periodic monthly analysis of global results had led technical management to the conclusion that, despite the great personal effort on the part of all responsible, the division's level of integral quality fluctuated somewhat around an established value, valid for that moment, but possibly insufficient in the near future. This also invited the application of some sort of 'special action'. All of this led to the analysis and study of the global environment, in an effort to know what the élite companies that had achieved excellence were doing. The study ended with the elaboration of the 'Programme for the Continual Improvement of Integral Quality'.

THE PROGRAMME FOR THE CONTINUAL IMPROVEMENT OF INTEGRAL QUALITY

In 1986, technical management presented to the Management Committee of the factory the so-called 'Programme for the Continual Improvement of Integral Quality' and obtained the committee's approval. The technical director, Jose Miguel Ustaran, made a presentation of the programme to the author of this case. He began by saying that 'in order for a change to go forward successfully, three things are necessary: (1) a forceful and restless personality, (2) with influence (3) an external consultant'. The programme had an anagram that appeared in large signs posted throughout the factory and on stickers for the portfolios made especially for the programme. The anagram transmitted the idea of triumph. The following phrase appeared on the first page of the programme, which Ustaran had found in a book: 'The great realizations of the present always depend on the idealists of the past, on those who knew how to look with foresight toward tomorrow. Tomorrow should have been resolved years ago. Today we can and we must focus our attention on tomorrow'. The following presents a summary of this programme.

PROGRAMME FOR CONTINUAL IMPROVEMENT OF INTEGRAL QUALITY

Integral quality
1. Human quality
2. Quality of life of employees and quality of their social environment
3. Management quality
4. Work quality
5. Quality of equipment, technology and processes
6. Product quality
7. Quality of service
8. Quality of results
   - Human
   - Security
   - Quality
   - Productivity
   - Output
   - Consumption

- Inventory
- Sales
- Cost
- Economic

Situation-Environment
1. Accelerated change
2. Generalized crisis
3. Technological development
4. EEC (Horizon 92)
5. Global market
6. International competition
7. Industry crisis
8. Restructuring of the industry
9. Merger of ACENOR

Needs
1. Overcome the change
2. Revive hopes
3. Competivity
4. Profitability
5. Survival and progress of the company
6. Creation of social wellbeing and wealth
7. Be a leader company
8. Differentiating factor: integral quality of the company
9. Application of new management technology

Foundations of the programme for the improvement of integral quality
1. Humanity
2. Quality
3. Modernity
4. Profitability

Means: new management technology
1. Progress teams
   - Management commitee team
   - Social teams
   - Financial teams
   - Marketing teams
   - Technical teams
   - Mixed working teams, homogeneus or not, supported by group techniques, assisted by J. L. Guillén

   Advantages
   - Humanism in the company
   - Employee participation >> Motivation
   - Direct resolution of problems
   - Improvement in satisfaction, efficiency and results

2. Permanent action plans
   Concrete action plans, refering to the principal aspects of the plant, supported by modern management techniques.

Advantages
- Orderly and scientific resolution of problems
- Improvement in efficiency and results

Stages of the programme
1st stage, 1987:
- Creation of the training centre
- Preparation-Training

2nd stage, 1988–89:
- Progress teams
- Permanent action plans

3rd stage, 1990:
- Functioning of the entire programme

Progress teams phases
Phase 1, 1988. Level: Upper management to middle managers (inclusive)
Phase 2, 1989. Level: Middle managers to workers

Management team
General supervisor: Director general
Director: Technical director
Consultant: Social director
Coordinator: Director of training program
Technical secretary: Secretary of technical management

THE GENESIS OF THE PROGRESS TEAMS

The progress teams were conceived and put in place due to the initiative of two people: the technical director of the factory at Vitoria-Gasteiz, Jose Miguel Ustaran, and a management consultant, J. L. Guillén. Guillén had begun working with the company by giving a seminar on team work for the Technical Committee. Soon, in the words of Guillén,

> I discovered that there were needs and worries that could not be satisfied by the seminars on team work alone. I made Ustaran see that these seminars could be useful to managers, but that they were not going to solve the company's problems, nor were they going to contribute to achieving the goal that they had proposed: the continual improvement of integral quality. This objective required everyone's participation, giving form to the two instruments on which the programme was theoretically based: the Progress Teams and the Action Plans. So that we began to think about a way to introduce participation into the company. It took us a lot of time and effort to find the appropriate formula. We studied quality circles, but we ruled them out; quality circles only work in a labor environment of participation. In the end, we arrived at the formula of 'progress teams'. We ran into difficulties. Some managers were in favour of

the idea, others were against it. Fortunately, Ustaran had enough autonomy to promote the theme: it was 'the forceful and restless person with power'. He took a risk. The CEO gave him the go ahead.

The Technical Committee was formed in order to design the 'progress teams', made up of the technical director and of all the department managers in the factory, along with their immediate associates; in total, about 30 people. Guillén acted as moderator in the Technical Committee's meetings. Suggestions and criticisms were brought to these meetings, which helped Ustaran and Guillén to draw up a working manual for the 'progress teams'.

'It was difficult for us to find out what we were looking for', said Guillén.

> When we finished defining the progress teams, we made the decision to establish 30 teams. People from the Management Committee to middle management and foremen were included in the entirety of the progress groups. We did not include the operations people in this first phase. We realized that it was not the operations people who introduced real improvement, but the middle managers and the foremen. These improvements made up 80% of those that can be introduced in the short-term; the remaining 20% are small things that a worker can add on, but the large problems or deficiencies are not resolved by quality circles, but by those managers who know what the situation is and who know what is missing. We were looking for a vehicle that was capable of bringing together managers from different levels.

Levels and classes of progress teams

The progress teams (PTs) were inititally divided into three levels. The first level was made up of the technical manager and the department managers. The second level was made up of the department managers and their foremen. Some departments were very large, which meant that a third level had to be created to include all of the supervisors. Later a fourth level was formed, made up of the General Management Committee. It began with the progress team that was made up of the technical manager and the department managers. The members of this team had participated in the seminars on teamwork that Guillén had given, which helped them get to know him and to gain confidence in him, according to Guillén.

Two types of PTs were established. First, the PT made up of each natural work group within the company – that which was formed by the supervisor and his immediate subordinates. Secondly, teams made up of various work groups could be formed, but with a PT in the proper sense as its core. When a problem affects more than one team, a team may invite other people from outside the group. However, the team that gives the invitation must be in charge of the meeting and, to a certain degree, control the guests. The PTs basically agree with the organizational chart, although some changes have been made.

Progress teams, an instrument for participation

> Having formed the PTs [Guillén stated] it was very clear to us that they should be an instrument for participation in the company. For this reason, we established that decisions had to be made democratically, that is, by consensus, or if this was not possible, by majority vote. The team had to decide democratically the situation to address. We decided on a series of rules concerning how to select subjects. This met with a lot of resistance from many people, but we knew that if the teams did not function democratically, it would be very difficult for people to bring their ideas forward, because they would be very sensitive to the authority of their boss.

The PTs decided democratically what subject they were going to address. By general rule, the subject concerns a situation that is negatively impacting the company's efficiency. There are problems that they can solve themselves, others that require the help of people from other teams because they lack technical competence, and others that require means which they do not possess. In these cases members of other teams may be invited, who may be operational people. This is a way of introducing the operations people to participation, a way of breaking the barrier that exists within the company. 'In order to establish authentic participation within the company,' says Guillén,

> one must begin by consolidating the PTs. We have to incorporate the workers into the participation formula in a second phase, and one way of doing this is to invite them to bring their ideas to the PTs. The idea is to gradually involve them in resolving the problems of the company.

The position of the manager in progress teams

'The leading of the teams has presented a series of questions concerning the role of the manager,' says Guillén.

> To a certain degree, the manager has to return once again to a role of authority in the PT. If he does not, the meetings of these teams become simple working meetings, where the foremen or the middle managers, according to the group's level, let the boss make the decisions. In these meetings, even if the boss asks the people to participate, they do not do their utmost in the teamwork. In general, you can say that it is accepted that the manager guide the PT if he is really the group's leader. However, this situation is not easily accepted when the leader's style of action is very different from what

the PT requires. Oddly enough, the position of the manager towards his employees is not affected because another person directs the meeting. There are even teams that have introduced as a rule that the leadership of the PTs be rotational. Others have not picked up this idea because they have not reached a sufficient level of maturity. Many times, it is the group's members who reject this possibility. Recently, the leader of a PT proposed that the group's management

Progress team No:	Programme for the	ACENOR
Meeting No:	**Continual improvement of integral quality**	
Notice of the progress team meeting		

Initiator:

Attendees:

Type of meeting:

Goal of the meeting

Director of the meeting:

Agenda

1st	Internal information in both directions		20,-
2nd	Review of the agreements reached in previous meeting		10,-
3rd	Actualizing the list of problems, suggestions, etc. (previously listed)		5,-
4th	Decide issue or issues to address in this meeting		5,-
5th	Analysis, debate and decision making with respect to the issues addressed		40,-
6th	Action plans		40,-

Day:

Time:

Place:

Fig. C19.2   ACENOR SA – factory at Vitoria-Gasteiz: order of the day.

be rotational, but 3 of the 8 members of the team refused to follow this formula. It was agreed that only those who were in favour of this formula would lead the group on a rotational basis. We are convinced that the moment will come when everyone will be willing to undertake the role of group leader. What happens is that some people are afraid to direct a meeting in which their manager is participating. For other people, this is normal. We think that rotation is very positive, because if the person directing the PT meetings is always the group's manager, then spontaneous participation is not as great. Therefore, the people in the group let the boss be the one to decide what subject to address. We differentiate the PT meetings from the work meetings of each team. The work meetings are called by the manager, who established the order of the day and makes the decisions. In the PT meetings, participation is sought. Everyone contributes. Everyone is responsible. The dynamics of the PT meetings affect the dynamics of the work meetings. This means that the manager tends to open up more in the work meetings, that is, he is less authoritarian. Little by little, the manager acts in the work meetings the way he does in the PT meetings.

The working manual for the progress teams and the training process

A decisive step in launching the progress teams was writing the working manual. 'We thought', Guillén related, 'that if we didn't structure the PTs very well, we would fail in our effort to make participation extend to the grass roots of the organization. Because of this, we wrote a very complete manual'. The manual establishes that the PT meetings must take place monthly and during working hours. Since the PT members may belong to different shifts, they are paid for the hours that are not in the shift during which the meeting takes place. Meetings must last a maximum of 2 hours. The order of the day is standardized and determines the distribution of time during these 2 hours (see Figure C19.2). Meetings are not permitted to go on longer. At the end of each meeting, the director of each PT has to write up the minutes, which must be constructed according to an established model (see Figure C19.3). The minutes must be handed in to the team coordinator. The minutes must include the subject addressed, the agreements made, the action plan, the programme of action, the dates of execution and the person responsible. In each meeting a review of the decisions taken in the previous meeting is made, and the minutes must also include any revisions made. The minutes are public. The team coordinator has a file of minutes that everyone can consult. 'This' Guillén points out 'is very interesting, since in this way the members of the teams can exchange experiences'. It's like a 'data base' that is accessible to all. In order to encourage participation in PTs, in the entrance of each office there is a chart with all of the PTs, their members, their leaders, the subjects that they have studied and have

Minutes of progress team meeting

Programme for the Continual improvement of integral quality

ACENOR

Progress team No............ Meeting No............ Date:.................

Team:.................

Subject addressed	Agreement or decision	Action plan			Review of agreements	
		Activities	Date	Person responsible	Date	Observations

Other subjects addressed worth attention:

Fig. C19.3 ACENOR SA – factory at Vitoria–Gasteiz: minutes of team meeting.

	Natural team with advisor	Duration	Natural team
Session 1	<u>1st Technique</u> Develop the technique to make the current situation map 1st	2 HOURS 1 h. 30' per session with a maximum 2 sessions	<u>Make up:</u> 1°) The Lewin general for the section, for each efficiency factor 2°) The current situation map
Session 2	1st To review the work accomplished by the group (map) 2nd <u>2nd Technique</u> Problem-solving technique.	2 HOURS One session (duration 1 h. 30')	Draw up a concrete action plan for the following period
Session 3	1st To review the work accomplished by the group 2nd To consolidate the techniques of sessions 1 and 2	2 HOURS One session per month (according to rules)	Draw up an action plan for the following period
Session 4	1st To review the work accomplished by the group 2nd <u>3rd Technique</u> Presentation of ideas and recommendations	2 HOURS One session per month (according to rules)	Draw up an action plan for the following period
Session 5	2 hours with PT		General review

Fig. C19.4   ACENOR SA – factory at Vitoria-Gasteiz: progress team training programme (calendar).

resolved, the subject that is presently being addressed, the date of the last meeting and that of the next. 'This chart is a strong stimulus', Guillén emphasizes 'Nobody wants to be left out; some, very few, have complained about this, those who did not arrive at the level of the rest'.

In order to facilitate the work of the PTs, Guillén trained them in the use of three techniques: (1) the 'situation map'; (2) the selection method, analysis and problem solving in stages; (3) the presentation and sale of ideas. The goal was that each PT be capable of identifying its situation, choosing a subject within its scope and drawing up a plan of action to solve the problem. This training programme was carried out in five sessions that Guillén held with each team (see Figure C19.4). Previously, the leaders of the PTs had received training in conducting meetings, as part of the training programme that Guillén had given.

First session   In this session, Guillén trained each PT in the 'situation map' technique. This technique is based on the 'field of forces' theory and technique, elaborated by Kurt Lewin in the 1940s. In essence, the theory maintains that in every problematic situation, two types of forces operate, one that is favourable ('driving forces') and another that is restrictive ('brakes'). Based on this concept, a situation can be described graphically, noting the different types of forces on both sides of a straight line, which represents the present position of the play of forces. The 'situation map', as developed by Guillén and introduced in the PTs, incorporates a series of refinements that facilitate the analysis and resolution of problems. To draw a 'situation map', the PTs have a printed sheet that serves as a guide and allows them to represent graphically their department's situation (see Figure C19.5). The 'situation map' includes the following elements:

1. Definition of efficiency. The manual defines what must be understood by efficiency and points out a series of factors through an example. These factors are: security, quality, productivity, consumption, service, entertainment and satisfaction.
2. Classification of driving and restraining forces according to their impact: A, A lot; B, Sufficient; C, A little.
3. Classification of the situation in which each factor is found: driving forces in Normal, Good, Very Good; restraining forces in Regular, Bad, Very Bad.

The drawing of the situation map for each PT includes the following stages:

(a) Each member of the PT must make a situation map individually, by completing the corresponding printed form.
(b) The PT as a group makes a situation map, using the maps drawn up by each member as a starting point.
(c) The PT classifies driving and restraining forces according to their level of impact and identifies the situation in which each factor is found.

Guillén took charge of training the PTs in the application of this technique. He held a two-hour meeting with each PT in which he explained the technique in detail. Guillén commented on this step in the following terms:

Analysis of the situation of: ....

Date ....

Description of driving forces	Very good	Good	Average	Below average	Bad	Very bad	Description of restraining forces
A lot of impact							
Sufficient impact							
Little impact							

Fig. C19.5 ACENOR SA – factory at Vitoria–Gasteiz: departmental situation.

The force field analysis has the advantage of being very graphic. They're technicians and easily understand the concepts that are used. The situation map lets the group know where it should focus its efforts in order to increase efficiency. Obviously, each department has a different map. The map is a basic instrument. With the passing of time, it changes. It is the first analysis of the state of each department. In this manner we are able to achieve our goal that each PT have a written description of its department's situation.

Once they were shown the situation map technique, each PT had one month to make a map of their department, and could meet as many times as they needed to do this.

Second session   This session took place a month after the first. Guillén met with each PT to examine the work they had done and to give them any necessary help. The results were satisfactory and he went on to train them in the second technique: the analysis and resolution of problems in stages. The goal was to work methodically in solving the problems that had been identified in the situation map. With this goal in mind, the first step was to teach them to choose a subject with which to work concerning their situation, and to draw up a plan of action.

The situation map contained so much information that the people were overwhelmed [said Guillén], so that I had to suggest some criteria to help them choose their subjects, such as the urgency of a problem or its interest to all of the members of the group. In the end, we arrived at the conclusion that the best criteria was that the problem be in the hands of the PT and that the team not have to resort to going outside the group.

The analysis and resolution of problems technique that Guillén taught them basically consists of a series of well-defined stages. Here, the consultant showed them how to distinguish between symptom and cause. He warned them that

it is not recommendable to be exhaustive in the analysis. It is difficult to completely eliminate a restraining force. In the majority of cases it is only possible to partially improve it, enough for us to feel satisfied. There isn't time to approach and solve a problem in its entirety.

Once a subject has been chosen and a manageable and attractive cause has been identified, the next step is to formulate the alternative actions to be taken. The process is quite simple. The team meets and each member states the alternatives that they can think of. These are analysed to determine which have the most impact and are manageable for the team. Next, the action plan must be prepared. To do this, a series of questions must be answered in a specific order, without skipping any and without passing on to the next before a question is answered in its entirety. The first question to answer is 'What should be done?' For this, the team members must make a list of things that can be done. The next question

Stages		Steps to follow
1st	1st	Make a 'Lewin' general (driving and restraining forces by efficiency factors)
	2nd	Make a map of actual situation (driving and restraining forces by impact importance)
2nd	3rd	Selection of the problem or situation that the group wishes to address
	4th	Define the problem or situation
	5th	Make the problem or situation somewhat manageable
	6th	Alternatives to take
	7th	Draw up the action plan
	8th	Get the proposed plan accepted

Fig. C19.6 ACENOR SA – factory at Vitoria-Gasteiz: work processes guide for progress teams.

to answer is 'Who?' All of those people whom the team believes should contribute to resolving the problem should be pointed out. The last question to answer is 'How?' Now it is determined how each one of the previously cited people should contribute. Once these questions are resolved, the team no longer gets involved in the problem and, in order to save time, one person alone takes responsibility for putting together all of the ideas that were put forth in the meeting and for making the action plan. This does not mean that the team is being substituted but instead that it is inoperative. It has fulfilled its function, which is to supply ideas and creativity. It is possible that this person's work return later to the team in the form of a proposal to the team's leader. The second session of the progress teams ends on this point. In order to help the PTs be methodical, Guillén designed a chart that was printed on a piece of cardboard. This piece of cardboard was attached to the portfolios that each of the PTs were given (see Figure C19.6). During the time between the second and third sessions, the PTs were told to draw up a concrete action plan.

Third session   This session began with a review of the work done in the previous month. 'In this phase' commented Guillén, 'quite a few teams got stuck' and, for this reason, Guillén dedicated the second part of this session to reinforcing the techniques taught in the previous sessions. This session ended with the assignment of drawing up an action plan for the following period.

Fourth session   This session, like the previous ones, began with a revision of the work done by each PT in the previous period. Next, Guillén trained them in the technique of presentation and selling of ideas. For this he made another chart that was also printed on a piece of cardboard and attached to the portfolio (see Figure C19.7).

Fifth session   This session, which took place one month later, was dedicated to a general review of the work done by each PT.

Development of the progress teams

People have understood that the only means for improvement is participation. In the beginning, this made us very afraid. We thought that it would be a success if 50% of the progress teams worked the way we wanted them to. The surprise has been that 100% have worked. It's a great experience. Now we have one person – the coordinator of the teams – dedicated almost exclusively to following and coordinating the running of the PTs. The coordinator of the teams reports to the technical director.

Of the 30 PTs that are functioning, I would say that 20% are mature. I consider a PT to be mature when this system of work

1st **Preparation**	1. Analyse the listener	- Understanding of the listener or interlocutor. - Situating and positioning of relation to the subject. - Possible expectations, questions and objections on the part of the listener. - How to get the listener's attention.
	2. Define the objective	- Define the objective to be achieved. - Define the conclusion to be put forward. - How to explain objective and conclusions.
	3. Prepare structured documentation	- How to present the basic structure of the exposition. - Visualize a chart or table for the exposition. - What points, sub-points and facts to present. - What questions to prepare to assure understanding. - Documentation to prepare. - Documentation to hand out. - What means to use.

2nd **Exposition**	1. Create an appropriate atmosphere and get listener's	- Importance, time, place. - To make explicit the positive and the negative consequences to the receiver.
	2. Define and clarify the objective	- To expose the objective. - To forward conclusions. - To visualize the scheme. - To expose the points. - To explain every point. - To summarize each point.
	3. Structure of the exposition	- To recollect the objective. - To keep clearly a basic scheme.
	4. Review and conclusion	- To reach a conclusion.

3rd **Explanation**	1. Facilitate dialog.	- Visual contact. - Expression of support - Communicate interest and reasoning.
		Concentrate on what is said, not on who says it.
	2. Comprehension	- Make explanatory questions. - Solicit more information. - Repeat sentences.
		Everyone needs time to assimilate a new idea.
	3. Confirmation	- Repeat ideas, facts, opinions, etc. - Final review: situation, opinion, conclusions.
		Nobody knows what the other person has understood, unless that person says it.

Fig. C19.7 ACENOR SA – factory at Vitoria-Gasteiz: guide for achieving understanding in verbal communications: transmitting and making ideas understood in meetings and interviews.

has become natural, that the process of participation that we have introduced is irreversible, independently of whether the organization accepts this participation or not.

The personal development of the progress teams naturally requires the personal development of the team's leader, without forgetting that of the other members of the team. It is very difficult if a leader changes his natural conduct and behaves in a very different manner. All that we can achieve is that this person be consolidated at the point where he or she is at and that, from there, they begin to develop personally, because there are people who have gotten to this point without feeling it internally. That is, they don't do things in a spontaneous way, but instead because they realize rationally that they have to do them. In fact, nobody has been opposed to this process with which we are working, but there are people who, when they begin to perform, do so in a notably different manner from what is required by the progress teams or from what they themselves say that they possess. Their spontaneity goes in a different direction and therefore, we have to try to make this spontaneity go in the direction of the model that the process requires. For the team leader who feels this internally, the process is practically irreversible.

The teams have enough techniques to analyse their situation, to make decisions in light of this situation and to develop an action plan, as long as there is a leader capable of guiding them and of managing them correctly. Here we are running into some problems because these people are pure technicians, from the Taylor era, when technicians knew perfectly well how to do their work; they told the others what to do and they did it. Up until now this is how they operated, but presently the subject has become so complicated that the technicians themselves have realized that they are not capable of solving on their own all of the problems that arise. Even though problems arise now that are technically very complicated, this does not bother them. They are capable of solving the majority of these types of problems because they are very well prepared. What really worries the present managers are those thousands of small problems that affect efficiency, and that they can't get to for lack of time. For example, the lack of coordination with another section. This section doesn't provide us with the materials that we ask for, at the time that we ask for them. Another example: the lack of coordination in the work shifts. Information is needed about what has happened in the previous shift which, in turn, has not been informed about what has happened in earlier shifts. So, this lack of information in the previous shifts generates a series of errors that grow geometrically in a spiral of lacking information and collaboration. When we analyse the restraining forces, we see that the majority are small details that impede our normal functioning.

One way to improve participation within the team is to have its members meet periodically to analyse together their individual performance to find out in what way they are prohibiting the team from developing and from realizing its work in the most efficient manner. I have not got any of the teams to do this exercise and I have not pressured them too much to do it, even though I have worried about whether they understand the importance of it. The people know that they have to do it, but they don't dare; it's very difficult for them.

'To summarize', says Guillén,

what we have tried to achieve is that each team be capable of identifying its situation, learn to choose a subject within its scope and know how to develop an action plan to solve the problem. This they have to do on a monthly basis, so that it becomes a habit. In the beginning there were a few rejections but each day they are functioning better and there is no dissatisfaction, although sometimes they feel frustrated when they find themselves at an impass, and don't know how to proceed forward in solving a problem. Apparently, it's a lack of time in the meetings, but in the end it's a lack of method. Everyone understands that the system is very positive. There are no personal problems among the member of the PTs. The leader's style has little importance. The important thing is methodology. If the group leader doesn't respect the system's working model, the PT doesn't function. We have had to deal with very authoritarian leaders who, in the end, have admitted that they were like this and have confessed that they felt that they had to act differently. Now they have corrected this, have opened themselves up to communicating and to other ways of working, although it is very difficult for them.

OBSERVATIONS MADE BY THE AUTHOR OF THE CASE

The author of the case spent two days in the factory at Vitoria-Gasteiz and had the opportunity to attend several meetings of the PTs and to speak with some of the team leaders.

The author observed that participation on the part of the members was very high, between 80 and 100%. The four teams observed fulfilled the order of the day that had been established. In every case, the team leader began the meetings with the corresponding dossier of information. In two of the teams, the members' preparation was insufficient and the application of recommended methods left much to be desired. In one of the meetings, some friction arose but the team leader knew how to handle the situation with no problem and to reach conclusions that were satisfactory to most. In general, the atmosphere of the meetings was friendly, even openly cordial. In one of the teams, it was not the leader who conducted the meeting but one of the team's members, who carried out his task with notable efficiency; in this meeting, the leader took charge of the note taking at the blackboard. In some meetings, there was a feeling of discouragement in the air as the group confronted the difficulties that they faced in solving the problems they had undertaken. All of the teams were productive.

From interviews with various team leaders, the author extracted the following comments. Leader of team 1: 'The PT has helped us to approach problems that, without it, we would not have tackled'; 'It has increased mutual openness'; 'Before, I made the decisions. Now I share them with the group'; 'The PT has brought us closer together'. Team leader 2: 'The PT has encouraged more participation'; 'The PT helps interfunctional relationships: they no longer say "it's your problem"'; 'We can be (can't be?) disappointed if the answer from the top isn't sufficient'. Team leader 3: 'I am using the team to improve relationships, more than to obtain results'... 'before it was all orders and commands, now there has been a 180° turn'... 'the change has generated a certain distrust'... 'the turnaround has been good, but too strong'... 'they complain that we didn't listen to them before'... 'there isn't enough time'... 'the people don't respond'... 'they see that there is a desire for improvement'... 'I'm afraid I'm not a leader'... 'still, it is something that has been imposed'. Leader of team 4: 'Initially, there was scepticism, but once things got going, prioritizing the PTs and following their processes has helped them from breaking up'... 'we have chosen issues that were bothering us and we've resolved them, which has confirmed the validity of the system'.

RESULTS OF THE PROGRESS TEAMS

The result of all this work cannot be precisely calculated. 'By looking at the minutes of the meetings you can determine the effects of their plans, but there are improvements that are difficult to evaluate,' states Guillén.

We know that we have a certain number of finished plans and a plan represents a project that has been elaborated and introduced by a PT. In this first phase we have not been very demanding; we do not expect great results. We are more interested in consolidating the teams than in their efficiency. Also, I recommend that the PTs choose their subjects taking into account their possible usefulness in the development of the team itself. This is the main objective. The fruits of this is what is of most interest to the organization, which will come later on. These people are technicians, production men, and they are very aware that the final goal is improvement: an increase in efficiency. We can convert this into an irreversible process.

DISCUSSION QUESTIONS

The author of the case asked Jose Miguel Ustaran for the questions that concerned him over the development of the progress teams. The following lists the response, in his own words:

1. Will the leaders of the PTs in the future be fully convinced of the need for this programme?
2. Will the group's upper management be convinced of the importance of promoting this programme?
3. Will the PT members be willing to assume the responsibilities and the extra work that this programme demands?
4. How do we incorporate the PT issue into the list of priorities of its managers, given the existing time constraints?
5. Will they be capable of combining their day-to-day issues with plans for the future?
6. Will we be capable of changing our traditional 'Taylorism' for participation?
7. Will we be able to solve the problem of introducing the system, of establishing its techniques, and of finding the motivating factors that will encourage them?
8. What will happen if we fail in our attempt?
9. Where could the company end up if we are successful in our attempt?

SUGGESTED READING

Collard, R. and Dale, B. (1989) Quality Circles, in *Personnel Management in Britain* (ed. K. Sisson) Basil Blackwell, London, pp. 356–77.

Martinez, M. (1991) Employer identity and the politics of the labour market in Spain, in *West European Politics*, **14** pp. 41–55.

Index

References in this index are made to the theoretical introductions to each of the book's six parts, and not to the individual texts and cases. Guidance on the texts and cases can be found at the end of the relevant part introduction.